T0186112

Lecture Notes in Computer Science 13115

Founding Editors

Gerhard Goos
  Karlsruhe Institute of Technology, Karlsruhe, Germany
Juris Hartmanis
  Cornell University, Ithaca, NY, USA

Editorial Board Members

Elisa Bertino
  Purdue University, West Lafayette, IN, USA
Wen Gao
  Peking University, Beijing, China
Bernhard Steffen
  TU Dortmund University, Dortmund, Germany
Gerhard Woeginger
  RWTH Aachen, Aachen, Germany
Moti Yung
  Columbia University, New York, NY, USA

More information about this subseries at http://www.springer.com/series/7410

Nicola Tuveri · Antonis Michalas ·
Billy Bob Brumley (Eds.)

Secure IT Systems

26th Nordic Conference, NordSec 2021
Virtual Event, November 29–30, 2021
Proceedings

Editors
Nicola Tuveri 🄳
Tampere University
Tampere, Finland

Antonis Michalas 🄳
Tampere University
Tampere, Finland

Billy Bob Brumley 🄳
Tampere University
Tampere, Finland

ISSN 0302-9743 ISSN 1611-3349 (electronic)
Lecture Notes in Computer Science
ISBN 978-3-030-91624-4 ISBN 978-3-030-91625-1 (eBook)
https://doi.org/10.1007/978-3-030-91625-1

LNCS Sublibrary: SL4 – Security and Cryptology

© Springer Nature Switzerland AG 2021
This work is subject to copyright. All rights are reserved by the Publisher, whether the whole or part of the material is concerned, specifically the rights of translation, reprinting, reuse of illustrations, recitation, broadcasting, reproduction on microfilms or in any other physical way, and transmission or information storage and retrieval, electronic adaptation, computer software, or by similar or dissimilar methodology now known or hereafter developed.
The use of general descriptive names, registered names, trademarks, service marks, etc. in this publication does not imply, even in the absence of a specific statement, that such names are exempt from the relevant protective laws and regulations and therefore free for general use.
The publisher, the authors and the editors are safe to assume that the advice and information in this book are believed to be true and accurate at the date of publication. Neither the publisher nor the authors or the editors give a warranty, expressed or implied, with respect to the material contained herein or for any errors or omissions that may have been made. The publisher remains neutral with regard to jurisdictional claims in published maps and institutional affiliations.

This Springer imprint is published by the registered company Springer Nature Switzerland AG
The registered company address is: Gewerbestrasse 11, 6330 Cham, Switzerland

Preface

The NordSec conferences were started in 1996 with the aim of bringing together researchers and practitioners within computer security in the Nordic countries, thereby establishing a forum for discussions and cooperation between universities, industry, and computer societies. Over the years, NordSec has developed into an international conference that takes place in the Nordic countries on a round-robin basis. It has also become a key meeting venue for Nordic university teachers and students with an interest in security research.

These proceedings contain the papers presented at NordSec 2021: The 26th Nordic Conference on Secure IT Systems held virtually, due to COVID-19 restrictions, during November 29–30, 2021. The conference was organized by the Network and Information Security (NISEC) group at Tampere University, Finland.

All of the 29 submissions received by the extended deadline (August 31), met the requirements for peer review. Following a brief bidding process for manuscripts, the review period was set between September 8 and September 27. During this period the 45-member Program Committee produced a total of 111 reviews. The average of 3.83 reviews per manuscript achieved by this well-organized effort brought us close to our initial goal of 4 reviews per manuscript.

Based on the reviews and following a brief yet active discussion phase, we notified authors on October 1 that 11 manuscripts had been accepted for presentation at NordSec 2021, resulting in a 37.93% acceptance rate. Amongst these papers, five clear themes emerged: applied cryptography, security in Internet of Things, machine learning and security, network security, and trust.

We were honored to have two brilliant invited speakers: David Arroyo from ITEFI-CSIC, Spain, and Rafael Dowsley from Monash University, Australia.

As NordSec 2021 chairs, we extend our sincerest gratitude to everyone involved in making this year's event a success, including but not limited to the authors that submitted their hard work, the Program Committee and external reviewers, and the invited speakers.

October 2021

Billy Bob Brumley
Antonis Michalas
Nicola Tuveri

Organization

General Chair

Billy Bob Brumley   Tampere University, Finland

Program Chair

Antonis Michalas   Tampere University, Finland

Local Chair

Nicola Tuveri   Tampere University, Finland

Steering Committee

Magnus Almgren	Chalmers University of Technology, Sweden
Tuomas Aura	Aalto University, Finland
Karin Bernsmed	SINTEF ICT and Norwegian University of Science and Technology, Norway
Billy Bob Brumley	Tampere University, Finland
Sonja Buchegger	KTH Royal Institute of Technology, Sweden
Bengt Carlsson	Blekinge Institute of Technology, Sweden
Úlfar Erlingsson	Google Inc., Mountain View, USA
Simone Fischer-Huebner	Karlstad University, Sweden
Dieter Gollmann	Hamburg University of Technology, Germany
Nils Gruschka	University of Oslo, Norway
Audun Jøsang	University of Oslo, Norway
Stewart Kowalski	Norwegian University of Science and Technology, Norway
Peeter Laud	Cybernetica AS, Estonia
Helger Lipmaa	University of Tartu, Estonia
Katerina Mitrokotsa	Chalmers University of Technology, Sweden
Simin Nadjm-Tehrani	Linköping University, Sweden
Hanne Riis Nielson	Technical University of Denmark, Denmark
Juha Röning	University of Oulu, Finland
Andrei Sabelfeld	Chalmers University of Technology, Sweden

Program Committee

Magnus Almgren	Chalmers University of Technology, Sweden
Mikael Asplund	Linköping University, Sweden
Stefan Axelsson	Stockholm University, Sweden
Musard Balliu	KTH Royal Institute of Technology, Sweden
Felipe Boeira	Linköping University, Sweden
Sonja Buchegger	KTH Royal Institute of Technology, Sweden
Hai-Van Dang	Plymouth University, UK
Tassos Dimitriou	Computer Technology Institute, Greece, and Kuwait University, Kuwait
Nicola Dragoni	Technical University of Denmark, Denmark
György Dán	KTH Royal Institute of Technology, Sweden
Mathias Ekstedt	KTH Royal Institute of Technology, Sweden
Ulrik Franke	RISE, Sweden
Christian Gehrmann	Lund University, Sweden
Kristian Gjøsteen	Norwegian University of Science and Technology, Norway
Dieter Gollmann	Hamburg University of Technology, Germany
Nils Gruschka	University of Oslo, Norway
Mohammad Hamad	Technical University of Munich, Germany
Rene Rydhof Hansen	Aalborg University, Denmark
Tor Helleseth	University of Bergen, Norway
Martin Gilje Jaatun	SINTEF Digital, Norway
Meiko Jensen	Kiel University of Applied Sciences, Germany
Thomas Johansson	Lund University, Sweden
Audun Josang	University of Oslo, Norway
Ulf Kargén	Linköping University, Sweden
Mohsin Khan	University of Helsinki, Finland
Marcel Kyas	Reykjavík University, Iceland
Ville Leppänen	University of Turku, Finland
Stefan Lindskog	Karlstad University, Sweden
Olaf Maennel	Tallinn University of Technology, Estonia
Raimundas Matulevicius	University of Tartu, Estonia
Per Håkon Meland	SINTEF ICT, Norway
Simin Nadjm-Tehrani	Linköping University, Sweden
Nils Nordbotten	Thales Norway and University of Oslo, Norway
Tomas Olovsson	Chalmers University of Technology, Sweden
Nicolae Paladi	Lund University and CanaryBit AB, Sweden
Arnis Paršovs	University of Tartu, Estonia
Shahid Raza	RISE SICS, Sweden
Hans P. Reiser	University of Passau, Germany
Juha Röning	University of Oulu, Finland
Einar Snekkenes	Norwegian University of Science and Technology, Norway
Emmanouil Vasilomanolakis	Aalborg University, Denmark
Øyvind Ytrehus	University of Bergen, Norway

Additional Reviewers

David Arroyo
Mariia Bakhtina
Anton Christensen
Ignacio Delgado-Lozano
Iaroslav Gridin
Mubashar Iqbal
Johannes Köstler
Cesar Pereida García
Henrich C. Pöhls
Mari Seeba
Stefan Varga

Contents

Trust

Applied Cryptography

Communicating Through Subliminal-Free Signatures

George Teşeleanu[(✉)] [ID]

Institute of Mathematics of the Romanian Academy, Bucharest, Romania
george.teseleanu@imar.ro

Abstract. By exploiting the inherent randomness used by certain digital signature protocols, subliminal channels can subvert these protocols without degrading their security. Due to their nature, these channels cannot be easily detected by an outside observer. Therefore, they pose a severe challenge for protocol designers. More precisely, designers consider certain assumptions implicitly, but in reality these assumptions turn out to be false or cannot be enforced or verified. In this paper we exemplify exactly such a situation by presenting several subliminal channels with a small capacity in Zhang *et al.* and Dong *et al.*'s subliminal-free signature protocols.

1 Introduction

The notion of covert channels was introduced by Lampson in [8]. These channels have the capability of transporting information through system parameters apparently not intended for information transfer. In order to be efficient, covert channels should be hard to detect or control by the systems' security mechanisms.

The *prisoners' problem*, introduced by Simmons [12], captures the need of two parties to communicate secretly through normal-looking communication over an insecure channel. In the prisoners' problem *Alice* (sender) and *Bob* (receiver) are incarcerated and want to communicate confidentially and undetected by their guard *Walter* who imposes to read all their communication. Note that *Alice* and *Bob* can exchange a secret key before being incarcerated.

A special case of covert channels was introduced by Simmons [13,15–17] as a possible solution to the prisoners' problem. Subliminal channels achieve information transfer by modifying the original specifications of cryptographic primitives (for example, by modifying the way random numbers are generated). Hence, allowing *Alice* and *Bob* to communicate without being detected by *Walter*.

Within the scenario presented previously a natural question rises: how can one eliminate subliminal channels? To answer this question Simmons developed in [14] an interactive protocol between *Alice* and *Walter*. Other countermeasures against subliminal channels can be found in [1–3,5,6,10,11,21]. Unfortunately, shortly after the publication of [14], Desmedt [4] found a flaw in the protocol. When running Simmons' protocol *Alice* can stop the protocol when certain conditions are not achieved. Thus, enabling her to subliminally send a bit. This

© Springer Nature Switzerland AG 2021
N. Tuveri et al. (Eds.): NordSec 2021, LNCS 13115, pp. 3–15, 2021.
https://doi.org/10.1007/978-3-030-91625-1_1

method is called a *fail-stop* channel. To reduce the capacity of fail-stop channels, Simmons describes in [18] a cut-and-choose method. Note that fail-stop channels also exist in [6,7][1] due to their similarity to [14].

Another problem with [14] was described by Simmons himself in [16]. Simmons suggests a method in which *Walter* can corrupt the protocol in such a way that he can subliminally communicate to a third party. Such channels are called *cuckoo's channels*.

In this paper we analyse the protocols presented in [5,21]. We show that fail-stop channels exist, although the authors claim that the protocols are free of such channels. We also show that cuckoo's channels exist in both cases. Hence, we prove that their protocols are not subliminal-free. Due to their large communication overhead we suggest using other subliminal-free methods (for example, the methods proposed in [3,6,10,11][2]).

Structure of the Paper. We introduce notations and definitions in Sect. 2. In Sect. 3 we describe fail-stop and cuckoo's channels for the protocols proposed in [5,21]. We conclude in Sect. 4.

2 Preliminaries

Notations. Throughout the paper λ and κ will denote security parameters. We denote by $x\|y$ the concatenation of the strings x and y. The set $\{0,1\}^*$ denotes the set of all bit strings and the cardinality of a set S is denoted by $|S|$.

The action of selecting a random element x from a sample space X is denoted by $x \xleftarrow{\$} X$. We also denote by $x \leftarrow y$ the assignment of value y to variable x. The encryption of a message $m \in \{0,1\}$ using one-time pad is denoted by $\omega \leftarrow m \oplus b$, where b is random bit used only once.

2.1 Simmons' Signing Protocol

2.1.1 Description
In [13,15], Simmons introduced several subliminal channels that can be embedded into the DSA signature. These channels use as information carriers the ephemeral keys used by *Alice* in the signing process. A possible method for eliminating these channels was proposed by Simmons in [14]. He argued that covert communications can be stopped if the ephemeral keys where jointly generated by *Alice* and *Walter*. Thus, making the exact values indeterminate to both participants. Moreover, *Walter* must be able to check if *Alice* is honest.

We further describe the algorithms of Simmons' signing protocol. For simplicity, public parameters will further be considered implicit when describing an algorithm.

---

[1] In [6] a fail-stop channel is described, but it can be easily detected due to the protocol being implemented in devices with limited computational power.

[2] Note that in certain cases, hash channels [19,20] create the capability of subliminal communication through these proposals.

Public Parameters' Generation(κ, λ): Select a prime number $q \geq 2^\kappa$ and a prime number $p \geq 2^\lambda$ such that $q | p - 1$. Choose an element $g \in \mathbb{Z}_p$ of order q and a hash function $h : \{0, 1\}^* \to \mathbb{Z}_q^*$. Output the public parameters $pp = (p, q, g, h)$.

Signer's Key Generation(pp): Choose $x \xleftarrow{\$} \mathbb{Z}_q^*$ and compute $y \leftarrow g^x \bmod p$. Output the public key $pk = y$. The secret key is $sk = x$.

Signing Protocol(m): To sign a message $m \in \{0, 1\}^*$, the signer *Alice* and the warden *Walter* start the interactive protocol described in Fig. 1. If the protocol succeeds, then *Walter* will relay (m, r, s) to *Bob*.

Verification(m, r, s, pk): To verify the signature (r, s) of message m, compute $u_1 \leftarrow h(m)s^{-1} \bmod q$ and $u_2 \leftarrow rs^{-1} \bmod q$. Then compute $v \leftarrow (g^{u_1} y^{u_2} \bmod p) \bmod q$ and output **true** if and only if $v = r$. Otherwise, output **false**.

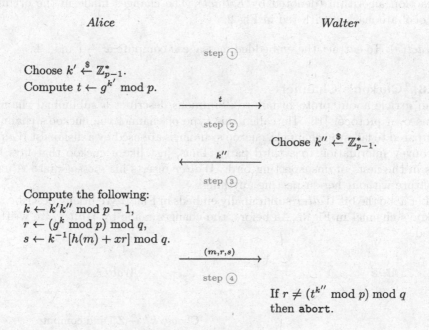

Fig. 1. Simmons' signing protocol.

2.1.2 Fail-Stop Channel

Initially introduced in [4], this mechanism allows *Alice* to subliminally communicate with *Bob* even if *Walter* imposes a protocol like the one described in Fig. 1. To communicate ω to *Bob*, *Alice* must stop the protocol if certain conditions are not achieved. If the protocol is stopped too often by *Alice*, *Walter* might become suspicious and cut off any communication between the prisoners. Thus, *Alice* can only send a few bits of data to *Bob* through this channel.

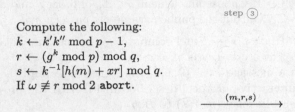

Alice   Walter

step ③

Compute the following:
$k \leftarrow k'k'' \bmod p - 1$,
$r \leftarrow (g^k \bmod p) \bmod q$,
$s \leftarrow k^{-1}[h(m) + xr] \bmod q$.
If $\omega \not\equiv r \bmod 2$ **abort**.

$\xrightarrow{\quad (m,r,s) \quad}$

Fig. 2. Desmedt's fail-stop channel. (Color figure online)

We further describe the fail-stop protocol in Fig. 2 and the corresponding extraction algorithm (denoted by *Extract*). The changes made in the original protocol are marked with red in Fig. 2.

Extract(r): To extract the embedded message ω compute $\omega \leftarrow r \bmod 2$.

2.1.3 Cuckoo's Channel

In an article about protocol failures, Simmons describes a subliminal channel in his own protocol [16]. He called this type of channel the cuckoo's channel. Compared to fail-stop channels, cuckoo's channels are used by a dishonest *Walter* to convey information to a third party. Thus, just like a cuckoo that lays his eggs in the nests of unsuspecting birds, *Walter* inserts his message into *Alice*'s signature without her suspecting anything.

Let ω be the bit *Walter* subliminally embeds in Fig. 1. We briefly describe the cuckoo's channel in Fig. 3. As before, the changes made by *Walter* are written in red.

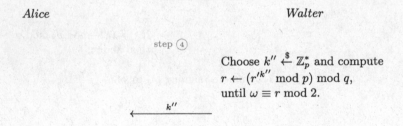

Alice   Walter

step ④

Choose $k'' \xleftarrow{\$} \mathbb{Z}_p^*$ and compute
$r \leftarrow (r'^{k''} \bmod p) \bmod q$,
until $\omega \equiv r \bmod 2$.

$\xleftarrow{\quad k'' \quad}$

Fig. 3. Simmons' cuckoo's channel. (Color figure online)

Extract(r): To extract the embedded message ω compute $\omega \leftarrow r \bmod 2$.

To achieve indistinguishablility from Simmons' protocol, *Walter* must use sufficient parallel computing power. Thus, the more power *Walter* has, the longer the conveyed message can be. Let assume that for Simmons' protocol, *Walter* uses one computing unit CU. In the case of the cuckoo's protocol presented in Fig. 3, if *Walter* uses α CU, then the probability of *Walter* transmitting his message undetected is $1 - 1/2^\alpha$. Hence, we can consider the cuckoo's channel as a noisy channel with an error probability of $1/2^\alpha$.

We further state without proof a security result from [16].

Lemma 1. *The cuckoo's channel presented in Fig. 3 preserves the distribution of r.*

3   Novel Fail-Stop and Cuckoo's Channels

By using an interactive protocol between the signer and the warden, the authors of [5,21] try to eliminate existing subliminal channels from the Schnorr signature [21] and the ECDSA signature [5]. As we will later see, the protocols presented in [5,21] do not manage to completely eliminate covert channels, although the authors claim that they are subliminal-free.

3.1   Zhang *et al.*'s Signing Protocol

3.1.1   Description

The first subliminal-free proposal that we describe was presented in [21]. According to the authors, the signer cannot control the outputs of the signature. Hence, the protocol is subliminal-free. We will see in the subsequent subsections that this is not true. Note that Zhang *et al.* assume that *Walter* is an *honest-but-curious*[3] warden that is disallowed to sign messages independently.

We further state Zhang *et al.*'s interactive protocol (Fig. 4) and the associated algorithms, as presented in [21].

Public Parameters' Generation(κ, λ): Select a prime number $q \geq 2^\kappa$ and a prime number $p \geq 2^\lambda$ such that $q|p-1$. Choose an element $g \in \mathbb{Z}_p$ of order q and two hash functions $h : \{0,1\}^* \to \mathbb{G}$ and $h' : \{0,1\}^* \times \mathbb{G} \to \mathbb{Z}_q^*$. Output the public parameters $pp = (p, q, g, h, h')$.

Warden's Key Generation(pp): Choose $t \overset{\$}{\leftarrow} \mathbb{Z}_q^*$ and compute $z \leftarrow g^t$. Output the public key $pk_w = z$. The secret key is $sk_w = t$.

Signer's Key Generation(pk_w): Choose $x \overset{\$}{\leftarrow} \mathbb{Z}_q^*$ and compute $y \leftarrow z^x$. Output the public key $pk = y$. The secret key is $sk = x$.

Signing Protocol(m): To sign a message $m \in \{0,1\}^*$, the signer *Alice* and the warden *Walter* start the interactive protocol described in Fig. 4. Note that in Step 5, Fig. 4 *Alice* uses a non-interactive zero-knowledge proof $\mathcal{P}$ to convince W that $\log_e(f) = \log_z(y)$.

Verification(m, e, s, pk): To verify the signature (e, s) of message m, compute $r \leftarrow g^s y^{-e} \bmod p$ and $u \leftarrow h'(m\|r)$. Output true if and only if $u = e$. Else output false.

---

[3] According to [9,21], an *honest-but-curious* adversary is a legitimate participant in a communication protocol who will not deviate from the defined protocol but will attempt to learn all possible information from legitimately received messages.

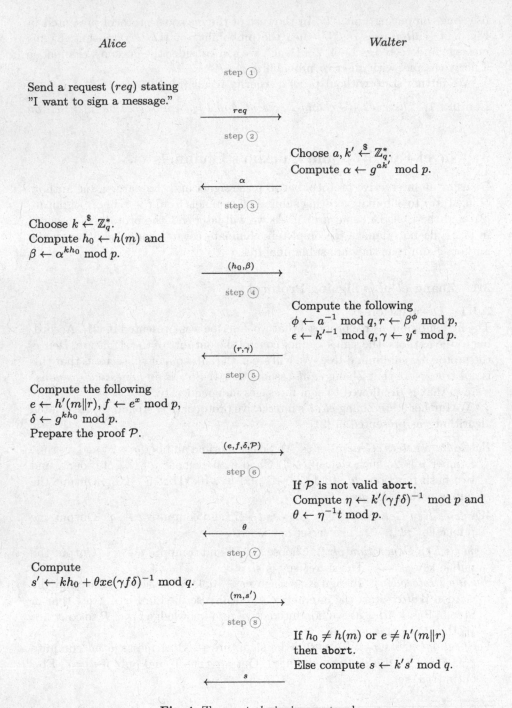

Alice   Walter

step ①

Send a request (req) stating
"I want to sign a message."
                        $\xrightarrow{\quad req \quad}$

step ②

                                          Choose $a, k' \xleftarrow{\$} \mathbb{Z}_q^*$.
                                          Compute $\alpha \leftarrow g^{ak'} \bmod p$.
                        $\xleftarrow{\quad \alpha \quad}$

step ③

Choose $k \xleftarrow{\$} \mathbb{Z}_q^*$.
Compute $h_0 \leftarrow h(m)$ and
$\beta \leftarrow \alpha^{kh_0} \bmod p$.
                        $\xrightarrow{\quad (h_0,\beta) \quad}$

step ④

                                          Compute the following
                                          $\phi \leftarrow a^{-1} \bmod q, r \leftarrow \beta^\phi \bmod p,$
                                          $\epsilon \leftarrow k'^{-1} \bmod q, \gamma \leftarrow y^\epsilon \bmod p.$
                        $\xleftarrow{\quad (r,\gamma) \quad}$

step ⑤

Compute the following
$e \leftarrow h'(m\|r), f \leftarrow e^x \bmod p,$
$\delta \leftarrow g^{kh_0} \bmod p.$
Prepare the proof $\mathcal{P}$.
                        $\xrightarrow{\quad (e,f,\delta,\mathcal{P}) \quad}$

step ⑥

                                          If $\mathcal{P}$ is not valid **abort**.
                                          Compute $\eta \leftarrow k'(\gamma f\delta)^{-1} \bmod p$ and
                                          $\theta \leftarrow \eta^{-1} t \bmod p.$
                        $\xleftarrow{\quad \theta \quad}$

step ⑦

Compute
$s' \leftarrow kh_0 + \theta xe(\gamma f\delta)^{-1} \bmod q.$
                        $\xrightarrow{\quad (m,s') \quad}$

step ⑧

                                          If $h_0 \neq h(m)$ or $e \neq h'(m\|r)$
                                          then **abort**.
                                          Else compute $s \leftarrow k's' \bmod q.$
                        $\xleftarrow{\quad s \quad}$

Fig. 4. Zhang *et al.* signing protocol.

3.1.2 Fail-Stop Channel

To bypass the protections set in place by Zhang *et al.* we use a fail-stop channel. Although *Alice* cannot control e, r and s, she can control if the protocol is successful or not. Hence, since the final value of r is not modified by *Walter* after Step 4, Fig. 4 she can use it to carry out her message.

We further describe our proposed fail-stop protocol (Fig. 5) and its corresponding extraction algorithm. The changes made in the original protocol are marked with red in Fig. 5.

Alice   *Walter*

step ⑤

If $\omega \not\equiv r \bmod 2$ **abort**.
Compute the following
$e \leftarrow h(m\|r), f \leftarrow e^x \bmod p$,
$\delta \leftarrow g^{kh_0} \bmod p$.
Prepare the proof $\mathcal{P}$.

$$\xrightarrow{\quad (e, f, \delta, \mathcal{P}) \quad}$$

Fig. 5. A fail-stop channel embedded into Zhang *et al.*'s protocol. (Color figure online)

Extract(e, s, pk): To extract the embedded message ω compute $r \leftarrow g^s y^{-e} \bmod p$ and $\omega \leftarrow r \bmod 2$.

3.1.3 Cuckoo's Channel

According to [21], *Walter* will not deviate from the signing protocol. Thus, in Step 4, Fig. 4 *Walter* has to supply *Alice* with (r, γ), θ and s of a given distribution. Keeping this restriction in mind, we have developed a cuckoo's channel in Zhang *et al.*'s protocol.

We briefly describe our proposed cuckoo's channel in Fig. 6. As before, the changes made by *Walter* are written in red.

Extract(e, s, pk): To extract the embedded message ω compute $r \leftarrow g^s y^{-e}$ and $\omega \leftarrow r \bmod 2$.

Correctness. The correctness of the *Verification* algorithm follows from the equality

$$
\begin{aligned}
s \equiv k''s' &\equiv k''[kh_0 + \theta x e(\gamma f \delta)^{-1}] \\
&\equiv kk''h_0 + k''(\eta^{-1}t)xe(\gamma f \delta)^{-1} \\
&\equiv kk''h_0 + k''[k''^{-1}(\gamma f \delta)t]xe(\gamma f \delta)^{-1} \\
&\equiv kk''h_0 + txe \bmod q,
\end{aligned}
$$

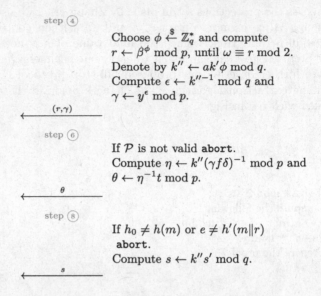

Alice   *Walter*

step ④

Choose $\phi \xleftarrow{\$} \mathbb{Z}_q^*$ and compute
$r \leftarrow \beta^\phi \bmod p$, until $\omega \equiv r \bmod 2$.
Denote by $k'' \leftarrow ak'\phi \bmod q$.
Compute $\epsilon \leftarrow k''^{-1} \bmod q$ and
$\gamma \leftarrow y^\epsilon \bmod p$.

$\xleftarrow{\quad (r,\gamma) \quad}$

step ⑥

If $\mathcal{P}$ is not valid **abort**.
Compute $\eta \leftarrow k''(\gamma f\delta)^{-1} \bmod p$ and
$\theta \leftarrow \eta^{-1} t \bmod p$.

$\xleftarrow{\quad \theta \quad}$

step ⑧

If $h_0 \neq h(m)$ or $e \neq h'(m\|r)$
abort.
Compute $s \leftarrow k''s' \bmod q$.

$\xleftarrow{\quad s \quad}$

Fig. 6. A cuckoo's channel embedded into Zhang *et al.*'s protocol. (Color figure online)

which leads to

$$r \equiv g^s y^{-e} \equiv g^{kk''h_0} g^{txe} y^{-e} \equiv g^{kk''h_0} \equiv g^{k(ak'\phi)h_0} \equiv \alpha^{k\phi h_0} \equiv \beta^\phi \bmod p.$$

The following lemma proves that no matter how much computing power *Alice* has, she will not be able to detect *Walter*'s cuckoo's channel and she will not be able to accuse *Walter* of being dishonest. Therefore, from the point of view of *Alice*, *Walter* is honest-but-curious, even though he is not.

Lemma 2. *The cuckoo's channel preserves the distributions of (r, γ), θ and s.*

Proof. In Zhang *et al.*'s protocol we have

$$r \equiv g^{kk'h_0} \bmod p, \ \epsilon \equiv k'^{-1} \bmod q, \ \eta \equiv k'(\gamma f\delta)^{-1} \bmod p \text{ and } s \equiv k's' \bmod q,$$

while in the cuckoo's version we have

$$r \equiv g^{kk''h_0} \bmod p, \ \epsilon \equiv k''^{-1} \bmod q, \ \eta \equiv k''(\gamma f\delta)^{-1} \bmod p \text{ and } s \equiv k''s' \bmod q.$$

Since $\phi \in \mathbb{Z}_q^*$ is chosen at random in the cuckoo's version, then $k'' \equiv ak'\phi \bmod q$ is also a random element from $\mathbb{Z}_q^*$. Therefore, k'' has the same distribution as k' value from Zhang *et al.*'s protocol. Thus, the distributions of (r, γ), θ and s are preserved. $\qquad\square$

3.2 Dong *et al.*'s Signing Protocol

3.2.1 Description

The authors of [5] use a similar approach to Zhang *et al.*'s for eliminating subliminal channels. Note that in this case, the authors do not impose that *Walter* is
honest-but-curious. Fortunately for us, we were able to devise a fail-stop channel
and a cuckoo's channel.

   Before stating our results, we first describe Dong *et al.*'s protocol (Fig. 7) and
the associated algorithms, as presented in [5].

Public Parameters' Generation(λ): Select an elliptic curve $E(\mathbb{Z}_p)$ defined over
   $\mathbb{Z}_p$, where p is prime. Generate a prime number $q \geq 2^\lambda$, such that q divides
   $|E(\mathbb{Z}_p)|$. Generate a point $P \in E(\mathbb{Z}_p)$ of order q and select a hash function
   $h : \{0,1\}^* \to \mathbb{Z}_q^*$. Output the public parameters $pp = (q, P, E(\mathbb{Z}_p), h)$.

Signer's Key Generation(pp): Choose $d \xleftarrow{\$} \mathbb{Z}_q^*$ and compute $Q \leftarrow dP$. Output the
   public key $pk = Q$. The secret key is $sk = d$.

Warden's Key Generation(pk): Choose $t \xleftarrow{\$} \mathbb{Z}_q^*$ and compute $T \leftarrow tQ = (x_t, y_t)$.
   Let $h_t = h(x_t \| y_t)$. Output the public key $pk_w = h_t$. The secret key is $sk_w = t$.

Signing Protocol(m): To sign a message $m \in \{0,1\}^*$, the signer *Alice* and the
   warden *Walter* start the interactive protocol described in Fig. 7. Note that in
   Step 6, Fig. 7 *Walter* uses the *Verification* algorithm to check the validity of
   (r, s, T).

Verification(m, r, s, T, pk_w): To verify the signature (r, s, T) of message m, com-
   pute $u_1 \leftarrow h(m)s^{-1} \bmod q$, $u_2 \leftarrow rs^{-1} \bmod q$ and $h_t^* = h(x_t \| y_t)$. Then com-
   pute $u_1 P + u_2 T = (x_1, y_1)$ and $v \leftarrow x_1 \bmod q$. Output `true` if and only if
   $v = r$ and $h_t^* = h_t$. Otherwise, output `false`.

3.2.2 Fail-Stop Channel
The authors of [5] claim that they eliminate fail-
stop channels. Their main argument is that *Alice* does not know any information
about (r, s) before *Walter* finishes the signature and thus she cannot use r as a
carrier. Contrary to their statement, we managed to find such a channel.

   We further describe our proposed channel (Fig. 8) and its corresponding
extraction algorithm. The changes made to the original protocol are written
in red in Fig. 8.

Extract(r, T): To extract the embedded message ω compute $rT = (x_s, y_s)$ and
   $\omega \leftarrow x_s \bmod 2$.

Correctness. The correctness of the *Extract* algorithm follows from the following
equality

$$\theta^{-1}Q = rtQ = rT.$$

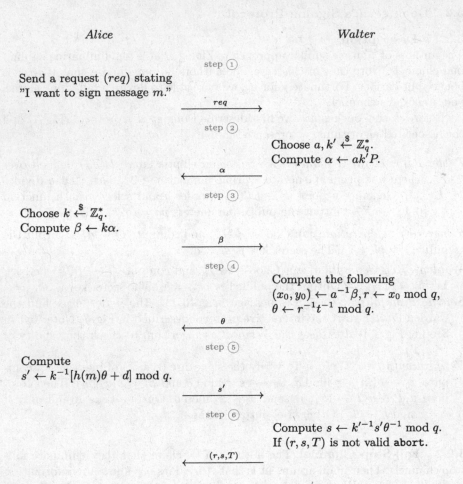

Fig. 7. Dong *et al.* signing protocol.

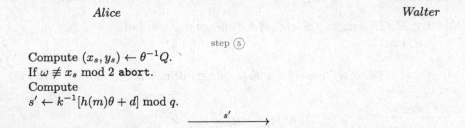

Fig. 8. A fail-stop channel embedded into Dong *et al.*'s protocol. (Color figure online)

3.2.3 Cuckoo's Channel

Using a technique similar to the Zhang *et al.* cuckoo's channel, we further present in Fig. 9 a cuckoo's channel that can be inserted into the Dong *et al.*'s protocol. As before, the changes made by *Walter* are written in red.

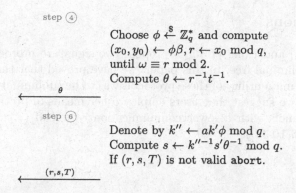

Fig. 9. A cuckoo's channel embedded into Dong *et al.*'s protocol. (Color figure online)

Extract(r): To extract the embedded message compute $\omega \leftarrow r \bmod 2$.

Correctness. The check the correctness of the *Verification* algorithm we first compute

$$s \equiv k''^{-1}s'\theta^{-1} \equiv k''^{-1}k^{-1}[h(m)\theta + d]\theta^{-1}$$
$$\equiv k^{-1}k''^{-1}[h(m) + d\theta^{-1}]$$
$$\equiv k^{-1}k''^{-1}[h(m) + drt] \bmod q,$$

which leads to

$$u_1 P + u_2 T = s^{-1}[h(m)P + rT] = s^{-1}[h(m) + rtd]P$$
$$= kk''P = k(ak'\phi)P = k\phi\alpha = \phi\beta.$$

In order to be secure, we need to prove that our proposal cannot be detected by *Alice* no matter how much computing power she has at her disposal. This is proven in the following lemma.

Lemma 3. *The cuckoo's channel preserves the distributions of θ and (r, s).*

Proof. In Dong *et al.*'s protocol we have

$$(x_0, y_0) \leftarrow kk'P, \quad \text{and} \quad s \leftarrow k'^{-1}s'\theta^{-1} \bmod q,$$

while in the cuckoo's version we have

$$(x_0, y_0) \leftarrow kk''P, \quad \text{and} \quad s \leftarrow k''^{-1}s'\theta^{-1} \bmod q.$$

Since $\phi \in \mathbb{Z}_q^*$ is chosen at random in the cuckoo's version, then $k'' \equiv ak'\phi \bmod q$ is also a random element from $\mathbb{Z}_q^*$. Therefore, k'' has the same distribution as k' value from Dong et $al.$'s protocol. Thus, the distributions of θ and (r, s) are preserved.   □

4   Conclusions

Zhang et $al.$ [21] and Dong et $al.$ [5] propose two signature protocols that they claim to be subliminal-free. In this paper, we have proved that their claims are false. Since, the main utility of these protocols was to be subliminal-free and they failed to be so, we suggest that users employ other means of protection against subliminal channels with a lower communication overhead ($e.g.$ the methods proposed in [3,6,10,11]).

References

1. Ateniese, G., Magri, B., Venturi, D.: Subversion-resilient signature schemes. In: ACM-CCS 2015, pp. 364–375. ACM (2015)
2. Bohli, J.-M., González Vasco, M.I., Steinwandt, R.: A subliminal-free variant of ECDSA. In: Camenisch, J.L., Collberg, C.S., Johnson, N.F., Şallee, P. (eds.) IH 2006. LNCS, vol. 4437, pp. 375–387. Springer, Heidelberg (2007). https://doi.org/10.1007/978-3-540-74124-4_25
3. Choi, J.Y., Golle, P., Jakobsson, M.: Tamper-evident digital signature protecting certification authorities against malware. In: DASC 2006, pp. 37–44. IEEE (2006)
4. Desmedt, Y.: Simmons' protocol is not free of subliminal channels. In: Ninth IEEE Computer Security Foundations Workshop, pp. 170–175. IEEE (1996)
5. Dong, Q., Xiao, G.: A subliminal-free variant of ECDSA using interactive protocol. In: ICEEE 2010, pp. 1–3. IEEE (2010)
6. Hanzlik, L., Kluczniak, K., Kutyłowski, M.: Controlled randomness – a defense against backdoors in cryptographic devices. In: Phan, R.C.-W., Yung, M. (eds.) Mycrypt 2016. LNCS, vol. 10311, pp. 215–232. Springer, Cham (2017). https://doi.org/10.1007/978-3-319-61273-7_11
7. Horster, P., Michels, M., Petersen, H.: Subliminal Channels in Digital Logarithm Based Signature Schemes and How to Avoid Them. Technical Report TR-94-13 (1994)
8. Lampson, B.W.: A Note on the Confinement Problem. Commun. ACM **16**(10), 613–615 (1973)
9. Paverd, A.J., Martin, A., Brown, I.: Modelling and Automatically Analysing Privacy Properties for Honest-but-Curious Adversaries. Technical report (2014)
10. Russell, A., Tang, Q., Yung, M., Zhou, H.-S.: Cliptography: clipping the power of kleptographic attacks. In: Cheon, J.H., Takagi, T. (eds.) ASIACRYPT 2016. LNCS, vol. 10032, pp. 34–64. Springer, Heidelberg (2016). https://doi.org/10.1007/978-3-662-53890-6_2
11. Russell, A., Tang, Q., Yung, M., Zhou, H.S.: Generic semantic security against a kleptographic adversary. In: ACM-CCS 2017, pp. 907–922. ACM (2017)
12. Simmons, G.J.: The prisoners' problem and the subliminal channel. In: CRYPTO 1983, pp. 51–67. Plenum Press, New York (1983)

13. Simmons, G.J.: The subliminal channel and digital signatures. In: Beth, T., Cot, N., Ingemarsson, I. (eds.) EUROCRYPT 1984. LNCS, vol. 209, pp. 364–378. Springer, Heidelberg (1985). https://doi.org/10.1007/3-540-39757-4_25
14. Simmons, G.J.: An introductions to the mathematics of trust in security protocols. In: CSFW 1993, pp. 121–127. IEEE (1993)
15. Simmons, G.J.: Subliminal communication is easy using the DSA. In: Helleseth, T. (ed.) EUROCRYPT 1993. LNCS, vol. 765, pp. 218–232. Springer, Heidelberg (1994). https://doi.org/10.1007/3-540-48285-7_18
16. Simmons, G.J.: Cryptanalysis and protocol failures. Commun. ACM **37**(11), 56–65 (1994)
17. Simmons, G.J.: Subliminal channels; past and present. Eur. Trans. Telecommun. **5**(4), 459–474 (1994)
18. Simmons, G.J.: Results concerning the bandwidth of subliminal channels. IEEE J. Sel. Areas Commun. **16**(4), 463–473 (1998)
19. Teşeleanu, G.: Subliminal hash channels. In: Gueye, C.T., Persichetti, E., Cayrel, P.-L., Buchmann, J. (eds.) A2C 2019. CCIS, vol. 1133, pp. 149–165. Springer, Cham (2019). https://doi.org/10.1007/978-3-030-36237-9_9
20. Chuan-Kun, W.: Hash channels. Comput. Secur. **24**(8), 653–661 (2005)
21. Zhang, Y., Li, H., Li, X., Zhu, H.: Provably secure and subliminal-free variant of schnorr signature. In: Mustofa, K., Neuhold, E.J., Tjoa, A.M., Weippl, E., You, I. (eds.) ICT-EurAsia 2013. LNCS, vol. 7804, pp. 383–391. Springer, Heidelberg (2013). https://doi.org/10.1007/978-3-642-36818-9_42

Size, Speed, and Security: An Ed25519 Case Study

Cesar Pereida García[1]([⊠])(iD) and Sampo Sovio[2](iD)

[1] Tampere University, Tampere, Finland
cesar.pereidagarcia@tuni.fi
[2] Huawei Technologies Oy, Helsinki, Finland
sampo.sovio@huawei.com

Abstract. Ed25519 has significant performance benefits compared to ECDSA using Weierstrass curves such as NIST P-256, therefore it is considered a state-of-the-art digital signature algorithm, specially for low performance IoT devices. However, such devices often have very limited resources and thus, implementations for these devices need to be as small and as performant as possible while being secure. In this paper we describe a scenario in which an obvious strategy to aggressively optimize an Ed25519 implementation for code size leads to a small memory footprint that is functionally correct but vulnerable to side-channel attacks. This strategy serves as an example of aggressive optimizations that might be considered by cryptography engineers, developers, and practitioners unfamiliar with the power of Side-Channel Analysis (SCA). As a solution to the flawed implementation example, we use a computer-aided cryptography tool generating formally verified finite field arithmetic to generate two secure Ed25519 implementations fulfilling different size requirements. After benchmarking and comparing these implementations to other widely used implementations our results show that computer-aided cryptography is capable of generating competitive code in terms of security, speed, and size.

Keywords: Applied cryptography · Public key cryptography · EdDSA · Ed25519 · Side-channel analysis · SCA · Computer-aided cryptography

1 Introduction

The growing number of IoT devices around us is ever increasing, and thus the need to secure these devices and their communication is of utmost importance. Moreover, due to their nature, the attack surface of IoT devices is higher compared to commodity PCs and servers, as attackers are able to get physical access to them, thus exposing them to both physical and remote attacks, resulting

C. P. García—This research was done while the author was an intern at Huawei Technologies Oy.

© Springer Nature Switzerland AG 2021
N. Tuveri et al. (Eds.): NordSec 2021, LNCS 13115, pp. 16–30, 2021.
https://doi.org/10.1007/978-3-030-91625-1_2

in new threat scenarios. Cryptography engineers face multiple challenges when securing these devices as cryptography implementations must be not only secure but also competitive in terms of speed and size since these are constrained devices with limited power, memory, and processing resources.

EdDSA, and more specifically Ed25519 [7], is a popular algorithm choice for digital signatures in the IoT world as it is small, fast, and it does not require fresh randomness per signature thus reducing the risk of using a faulty random number generator (RNG). EdDSA instead computes a deterministic nonce as a function of the hashed message and the private key, and in general, it provides a more robust security against several attacks when compared to ECDSA. During the development of Ed25519, choices were made to decrease the chances of implementation flaws and unintentional information leakage. However, these secure choices need to be clearly understood by cryptography engineers, as a small deviation from the original specification can lead back to insecure implementations.

Cryptography engineers must follow general recommendations and coding best practices when implementing algorithms that receive confidential information as input values. These recommendations are mostly to protect against Side-Channel Analysis (SCA), and failing to follow any of the best practices can have devastating effects on the practical security of any implementation. Some of these best practices include: (i) using algorithms that execute in constant-time, i.e., the runtime of the algorithm is independent from the input secret value; (ii) avoiding branching based on secret values; (iii) avoiding table-lookups indexed by secret values; (iv) avoiding looping through a piece of code with a bound dictated by a secret value. Generally speaking, cryptography engineers must be aware that any line of code they write dealing with secret values, must not leak any information through either execution time, EM emanations, power consumption, microarchitecture components, temperature, or any other so-called side-channel, thus all of them must be considered for IoT security.

In this work we present a case study on how aggressive optimizations aiming for a small memory footprint can lead to SCA vulnerabilities on an otherwise secure Ed25519 implementation. We describe the rationale for the aggressive optimizations from the point of view of a cryptography engineer without SCA expertise, trying to meet the requirements, and then we briefly analyse why the approach is insecure against an adversary with SCA expertise. As a countermeasure, we replace the flawed implementation with a secure one generated with the help of ECCKiila [5], a computer-aided cryptography tool. We compare the performance of the computer-aided Ed25519 against other well established implementations on Intel and ARM architectures.

In summary, Sect. 2 gives an overview of background information and related work. Section 3 describes the example of a flawed implementation due to aggressive optimizations and its implications, we give a brief side-channel analysis. Section 4 describes two implementations generated with the help of ECCKiila and provides a performance comparison against other well established Ed25519 implementations. We conclude in Sect. 5.

2 Background

2.1 EdDSA

The Edwards-curve Digital Signature Algorithm (EdDSA) is an elliptic curve variant of the Schnorr signature system [27], thus it is a deterministic digital signature scheme constructed over twisted Edwards curves. Despite being a relatively new cryptographic primitive, EdDSA has gained traction over the last five years on both, the research community, and industry, due to being fast, secure, and hard to implement wrong—at least compared to ECDSA. Notably, EdDSA does not require fresh randomness for each signature generated—therefore it is more resilient against side-channel analysis (SCA)—and no special cases for the point at infinity need to be handled due to exception free formulas for point addition. EdDSA is generally defined by eleven parameters. An odd prime p defining the Galois field $GF(p)$, two elements $a, d \in GF(p)$ defining the twisted Edwards curve.

$$E : ax^2 + y^2 = 1 + dx^2 y^2 \tag{1}$$

An element $B \in E$ different from the neutral element. An integer c and an odd prime ℓ such that $\#E = 2^c \ell$. An integer b defining the size of the EdDSA public keys and EdDSA signatures in bits, an integer n defining the scalar size, an encoding of the elements in $GF(p)$, a hash function H and an optional "prehash" function PH. Choosing parameter is outside of the scope of our work, but we refer the reader to Bernstein et al. [7], RFC 8032 [19] and FIPS 186-5 [1].

Generally speaking, EdDSA is composed by three algorithms, namely, key generation, signature generation, and signature verification. Each of these algorithms is composed by several specific algorithms, which when converted to code, dictate the security properties of the whole EdDSA scheme.

2.2 Ed25519

Originally described by Bernstein et al. [7], Ed25519 is EdDSA instantiated with a twisted Edwards curve that is birationally equivalent to Curve25519 [6]. Ed25519 is allegedly the most widely used instance of EdDSA, and it is instantiated with the parameters present in Table 1.

Key Generation. Given a random and uniformly chosen private key k, the user hashes it using the chosen hash function H such that $H(k) = (h_0, h_1, ..., h_{2s-1}) = (a, b)$ where a is a private scalar value, b is an auxiliary key, and then computes the public key $A = [a]B$.

Signature Generation. Given the private scalar a, the auxiliary key b, and a hash function H, the signature (R, S) on the message M is created by

$$\begin{aligned} r &= H(b, M) & R &= [r]B \\ h &= H(R, A, M) & S &= (r + ha) \bmod \ell \end{aligned} \tag{2}$$

Signature Verification. Given the base point B, the public key A, and the signature tuple (R, S), on the message M, the EdDSA signature is valid if $h = H(R, A, M)$ satisfies the equation

Table 1. Ed25519 domain parameters.

Description	Symbol	Value
Power for $GF(p)$	p	$2^{255} - 19$
Element in $GF(p)$	a	-1
Nonsquare in $GF(p)$	d	$-121665/121666$
Base point	B	(x, y) from [7]
Order of base point	ℓ	$2^{252} + 27742317777372353535851937790883648493$
Key length	s	256
$log_2(cofactor)$	c	3
Scalar size	n	254
Hash function	H	SHA-512
Prehash function	PH	None

$$8SB = 8R + 8hA \tag{3}$$

Security. The mathematical security of EdDSA (and Ed25519) is similar to that of other ECC primitives, namely, it relies on the hardness of the *Elliptic Curve Discrete Logarithm Problem (ECDLP)*, i.e., given a known base B and an elliptic curve element $[r]B$, it is infeasible to compute the integer r. Additionally, during EdDSA construction several choices were made to avoid common flaws and vulnerabilities affecting the well established ECDSA. Some of these choices include: (i) the usage of a deterministic ephemeral nonce instead of a random nonce per signature, avoiding potential issues with a faulty RNG; (ii) the usage of twisted Edwards curves providing complete addition law and thus avoiding special cases that can be exploited; (iii) provide an open and freely available reference implementation that is secure in the mathematical model and also against SCA.

2.3 Ed25519 Implementations

In 2011, together with the original mathematical and technical description of the new Ed25519, Bernstein et al. [7] released multiple implementations of their new digital signature algorithm to the public domain through the eBACS project [8]. The objective was to promote the widespread adoption of the new primitive by providing implementations suitable for different architectures and systems with different requirements. The original release included a portable, slow but secure implementation written in C language named `ref`, a portable and faster implementation with competitive performance also written in C language named `ref10`, and two additional `x86_64`-specific, fast and highly optimized implementations written in *assembly* language named `amd64-64-24k` and `amd64-51-30k` using radix 2^{64} and 2^{51} for field element representation, respectively. Shortly after, the so-called `donna`[1] implementation was released which included high performance, portable 32-bit and 64-bit implementations for Ed25519.

---

[1] https://github.com/floodyberry/ed25519-donna.

Built on top of the reference implementation, Bernstein et al. [9] released NaCl as an easy-to-use high-speed software library offering several state-of-the-art implementations for several types of cryptographic primitives such as encryption, decryption, and signing. Similarly, libsodium[2] was born as a fork of NaCl to expand on the original API while supporting a variety of compilers and operating systems, becoming the de-facto library for Ed25519 at that time.

In 2015, BoringSSL added support[3] for Ed25519 to its codebase. Different to previous implementations, instead of using custom finite field arithmetic code, BoringSSL adopted formally verified finite field arithmetic generated with `fiat-crypto`[4] [15].

In 2017 `monocypher`[5] was released, including its own implementation of Ed25519 influenced by the `ref10` implementation. This specific implementation targets devices with limited resources, and it offers a compact and portable implementation compatible with `libsodium`.

In 2018 Tuveri and Brumley [28] added unofficial support for Ed25519 in OpenSSL through their `libsuola` ENGINE, by leveraging Ed25519 computations to the libsodium library. Official support was later added to the code base during the same year with the release of the newer version OpenSSL 1.1.1[6].

At the time of writing, most of the widely used general-purpose TLS and cryptography libraries support Ed25519. One notable exception is the `mbedTLS` library which is currently under development with an unspecified release date[7]. It is worth noting that despite the variety of implementations, most of them use code from the original reference implementations. This ultimately confirms that the original goal of widespread adoption of Ed25519 was achieved by providing robust reference implementations for other projects[8].

2.4   Related Work

Although EdDSA is a secure signature algorithm, it is susceptible to attacks derived from implementation flaws and SCA. Despite making secure design choices to minimize the probability of bad implementations, EdDSA still requires specialized knowledge and attention to detail during implementation, to avoid leaking confidential information that renders the primitive insecure.

Samwel et al. [26] demonstrate that failing to protect the auxiliary key b for any given signature can potentially lead to full key recovery, allowing an attacker to forge signatures. More specifically, the authors apply Differential Power Analysis (DPA) on the underline SHA-512 function of the WolfSSL library to recover the auxiliary key b during the computation of the ephemeral nonce

---

[2] https://github.com/jedisct1/libsodium.
[3] https://boringssl.googlesource.com/boringssl/+/4fb0dc4b.
[4] https://github.com/mit-plv/fiat-crypto.
[5] https://monocypher.org/.
[6] https://www.openssl.org/blog/blog/2018/09/11/release111/.
[7] https://github.com/ARMmbed/mbedtls/pull/3245.
[8] https://ianix.com/pub/ed25519-deployment.html.

r, which allows them to ultimately forge signatures for any message of their choosing.

Romailler and Pelissier [24] propose the first differential fault attack (DFA) on Ed25519 against an 8-bit Arduino nano device. The authors introduce a fault to the output of the hash function, however this value is not public, thus they need to bruteforce the value in order to exploit it to forge signatures.

Following the same attack principle, Samwel and Batina [25] introduce a fault during the computation of R, resulting in R' and therefore in a faulty hash computation h'. Using a single pair of correct and faulty signatures, the authors are able to recover the private scalar a solving a simple system of equations and consequentially, forge signatures for any given message.

Similarly, Ambrose et al. [3] study the effects of DFA on deterministic digital signature schemes, including EdDSA. In their work, the authors propose several attacks against EdDSA using DFA and describe the place and the type of fault that is needed allowing them to recover enough confidential information to forge signatures. Moreover, the authors discuss practical countermeasures against DFA, and possible changes to EdDSA to protect against this type of attacks.

On the software side, Poddebniak et al. [23] demonstrate a practical cross-VM fault attack against EdDSA by using the Rowhammer technique from a malicious VM to introduce faults to the target VM running `Minisign`. The authors successfully recover the private scalar a that allows them to forge signatures.

Exploiting the hardware translation lookaside buffers (TLBs), Gras et al. [17] recover the full keys for an insecure Ed25519 implementation on `libgcrypt` `v1.6.3`. Finally, Gras et al. [16] show a system that synthesizes new (port) contention-based side-channels. The authors demonstrate the working system on both, secure and insecure implementations of Ed25519 on `libgcrypt`.

3   When Optimization Goes Wrong

In this section we focus on how a relatively small change to the reference implementation trying to reduce the memory footprint, leads to a functionally correct but insecure implementation of Ed25519. The implementation that we describe in here is a custom implementation, thus this is not a real implementation affecting any system nor an open source cryptography library. However, we believe that this flawed implementation is a representative of aggressive optimizations that might be considered by cryptography engineers and practitioners in order to achieve specific memory requirements.

Implementation Description. In the original work, Bernstein et al. [7] describe two different algorithms for scalar multiplication to be used during Ed25519: a fixed-point scalar multiplication for key and signature generation, and a double-scalar multiplication for signature verification. Additionally, each scalar multiplication algorithm requires a recoded scalar value in a suitable form for the chosen scalar multiplication algorithm, thus this involves additional recoding algorithms which also affect the overall implementation size.

For fixed-point scalar multiplication, the original implementation follows a standard technique first discussed by Pippenger [22]. The technique consists of computing the scalar multiplication as a sum of precomputed values with the addition of supporting negative coefficients. This algorithm by itself does not prevent nor protect against SCA, but instead allows to load all the precomputed values into memory and then compute the correct value by using arithmetic operations that do not branch or otherwise reveal the secret value through the index accessed. After an analysis, the authors decide that a balance on performance versus memory size is reached by storing 256 curve points consuming a total of 30 kilobytes of RAM. In fact, the authors mention is possible to reduce the table size by half at the expense of 8 additional elliptic curve doubles. While this change already potentially reduces the size of the table by half, it might not be enough for a constrained device, and more aggressive optimizations for code size might be considered.

For the double-scalar algorithm the original implementation uses standard techniques similar to the windowed Non-Adjacent Form (wNAF) scalar multiplication [21] which allows them to compute the result for both scalar values in a single call, instead of performing a more costly fixed-point and variable-point scalar multiplications. This algorithm achieves a fast result at a low memory cost, as it does not require a precomputed table. However the algorithm execution is highly dependent on its inputs, thus it is specially suitable during signature verification where all the input values are public.

Considering these two algorithms to achieve the same result, namely a scalar multiplication, an appealing approach to reduce code size is not only to use the algorithm with the smallest memory footprint but also the most flexible algorithm that can be adapted for multiple use cases. Therefore, the double-scalar multiplication algorithm is a good candidate that can be adapted for usage in key generation, signature generation, and signature verification.

Our custom implementation continues with this idea, by simply adding conditional branches at the top of the double-scalar multiplication algorithm, we are able to cover all use cases for Ed25519: if the input value to the function containing the variable-point is empty then the algorithm is equivalent to a fixed-point scalar multiplication; if the input value to the function containing the fixed-point is empty then the algorithm is equivalent to a variable-point scalar multiplication; otherwise it is the standard double-scalar multiplication. By following this approach the implementation saves more than 30 KB of code since it does not require a 30 KB precomputed table, and it only uses a single algorithm for fixed-point, variable-point, and double-point scalar multiplication—and consequently only one algorithm for scalar recoding.

SCA Analysis. We now give a brief analysis from a SCA perspective to demonstrate the vulnerabilities enabled by the previous modifications to the original implementation.

Recall that prior to the scalar multiplication computation, the integer representing the scalar value must be recoded into a different form. The algorithm used for recoding, as any other algorithm dealing with secret information, must behave in a constant-time manner, i.e., no correlation must be observable between the input value and the execution of the algorithm in order to prevent SCA leakage. The reference implementation achieves this by cleverly using arithmetic and bitwise operations to recode the scalar as digits in the range $[-8, 7]$. These arithmetic and bitwise operations do not branch nor loop based on the scalar value, thus they are secure against SCA. However, one problem arises when using the double-scalar multiplication as a fixed-point scalar multiplication, as the recoding algorithm used for the latter is different than in the former. The recoding algorithm for double-scalar multiplication is based on the work by Avanzi [4], a left-to-right recoding variant commonly used during wNAF scalar multiplication. This variant in particular branches out according to individual bits of the scalar value, therefore its usage is only suitable when the scalar is a public value and does not need SCA protection, however this is not the case when using it for fixed-point scalar multiplications as in our vulnerable implementation. Despite being known to leak information, recoding algorithms were mostly ignored on SCA research as attacking them requires techniques with fine granularity allowing to capture leakage at a single-branch level. It was until recently, when Hassan et al. [18] demonstrated that it is possible to recover the scalar value by performing a microarchitecture attack on the wNAF recoding algorithm used in Mozilla's NSS during `secp384r1` ECDSA computation.

A second, and more well known, SCA vulnerability in our example implementation is the double-scalar multiplication algorithm itself. Even if a SCA secure recoding algorithm is in use, the scalar multiplication algorithm itself is vulnerable against a SCA attacker, since its execution is highly dependent on the wNAF representation of the scalar value. While the double-scalar multiplication algorithm has not been exploited in the past, it follows the same execution flow of the wNAF scalar multiplication algorithm, which has been repeatedly shown to be vulnerable [2,12,29]. On a high level, this scalar multiplication algorithm performs an elliptic curve point double for each recoded scalar digit, and an elliptic curve point addition only when the recoded scalar digit is non-zero, thus the general idea is that a SCA attacker is able to recognize the zero and non-zero digits of the recoded scalar value, as well as being able to identify which was the value of the digit since it is the index of the multiplier accessed from the precomputed table during the elliptic curve point addition, giving enough information to ultimately recover the private key.

Scalar multiplications are a basic operation for digital signature algorithms, thus an attacker with SCA capabilities would have opportunity to recover a secret key not only during key generation but also during signature generation. We reckon that specifically for Ed25519, an attacker would require (near) perfect traces as no practical lattice attacks have been demonstrated against it but we speculate is only a matter of time before it is possible.

4   Computer-Aided Ed25519

It is easy to see from the analysis presented in Sect. 3 that an easy fix to the SCA flaws presented is to either use a well established cryptography library providing an Ed25519 implementation, revert back to the reference implementation best suited to our needs, or implement constant-time versions of those algorithms leaking sensitive information. However, we decided to explore a different approach. We decided to make use of a cryptography tool to generate "new" Ed25519 implementations, and then we compared them to other available implementations. This approach serves two purposes, it allows us: (i) to analyze the easiness of producing and implementing different SCA-secure Ed25519 implementations with the added benefit of (partial) formal verification; (ii) and to compare the performance among computer-aided and widely used implementations.

For the computer-aided Ed25519 implementations, we used the ECCKiila[9] cryptography tool created by Belyavsky et al. [5]. The tool uses the fiat-crypto project to generate formally verified Galois Field (GF) arithmetic [15] for many ECC curves including Ed25519, and on top of this layer it generates complete EC arithmetic. Everything generated as portable code for 32-bit and 64-bit architectures, therefore useful for several use cases.

New Implementations. Harnessing the power of ECCKiila, we created two portable and SCA-secure Ed25519 implementations with different memory size requirements targeting different architectures: (i) a full-fledge portable implementation with a 30 KB precomputed table filling up an average L1 memory cache which we call ecckiila-precomp; and a lighter 32-bit implementation with a small 2.5 KB precomputed table suitable for smaller devices which we call ecckiila-no-precomp. The ecckiila-precomp implementation uses a constant-time fixed-point scalar multiplication based on the *comb* method [14, 9.3.3] and regular-NAF scalar recoding [20], while ecckiila-no-precomp uses a constant-time variable-point scalar multiplication and regular-NAF scalar recoding. Both implementations use the variable-time double-point scalar multiplication based on textbook wNAF [4] and Shamir's trick [14, 9.1.5].

Once we generated all the EC arithmetic using the tool, we were left with the task of adding EdDSA specific algorithms and creating the upper API layer. For the missing Ed25519 specific algorithms—i.e., point decompression, multiply and add, and modular reduction by the order of the base point—we ported them from the ref10 implementation and adapted them accordingly. Then we implemented the public API layer on top them, resulting in a working implementation.

4.1   Benchmarking

After generating two computer-aided Ed25519 implementations, we decided to benchmark their performance and compare them against our aggressively optimized implementation from Sect. 3 (called overoptimized) and against other widely used implementations. For benchmarking we used the SUPERCOP[10] framework developed as part of the EBACS [8] project. SUPERCOP is a well established and well known cryptography benchmarking framework containing several different implementations for all types of cryptographic primitives,

---

[9] https://gitlab.com/nisec/ecckiila/.
[10] https://bench.cr.yp.to/supercop.html.

including hash functions, stream ciphers, block ciphers, key exchange, digital signatures, etc. Moreover, SUPERCOP runs on several architectures, allowing us to expand our comparison of implementations to include Intel and ARM architectures for 32 and 64 bits.

SUPERCOP already ships with the original reference implementations in its code, and in addition we included and adapted donna, monocypher, ecckiila-no-precomp and ecckiila-precomp to its required API in order to benchmark their performance. It is worth mentioning that adapting these implementations to SUPERCOP's required API does not affect their performance, but the reported values in this work might differ from each project self-reported values. This is due to each implementation using different RNG and hash function implementations—i.e., for our benchmarks all of the Ed25519 implementations use SUPERCOP's own RNG and hash functions.

Intel Setup. For both 64-bit and 32-bit benchmarks our setup consists of an Intel Xeon E5-1650 v2 Ivy Bridge EP at 3.50 GHz running Ubuntu 18.04 LTS "Bionic Beaver". We disabled TurboBoost and set the frequency scaling governor to performance.

ARM Setup. For both 64-bit and 32-bit benchmarks our setup consists of a Raspberry Pi 3B equipped with a quad-core 1.2 GHz Broadcom BCM2837 64-bit CPU and 1 GB RAM, running Ubuntu 18.04 LTS "Bionic Beaver". The 64-bit aarch64 has Linux kernel version 5.4.0-1026-raspi, and the 32-bit armv7l has Linux kernel version 5.4.0-1015-raspi. We disabled frequency scaling via software.

SUPERCOP Setup. SUPERCOP and all the implementations were compiled with stock gcc version 7.5.0, and using the -O3 optimization level. The reported values are in thousands of clock cycles and they correspond to the median value of many measurements (as defined by SUPERCOP) for an operation on a 59-byte message.

Results. Table 2 and Table 3 show the results of our benchmarks for Intel and ARM architectures, respectively. Without surprise, donna is the most performant among all the implementations on both architectures, and it specially excels on the Intel architecture, where it is twice as fast as ref10. Another observation is that monocypher shows good results for being an implementation with a smaller memory footprint targeting IoT devices.

Our results confirm that optimizing for memory size not only has detrimental results for security, but also for speed, as observed in the overoptimized results where we observe a decreased performance by 2.5× at the cost of saving slightly more than 30 KB of memory used for precomputed tables during scalar multiplication.

For our two computer-aided implementations the results show, on the one hand, that ecckiila-no-precomp achieves similar size and performance results as overoptimized on the Intel 32-bit architecture, with the added benefit of being secure against SCA. On the other hand, we were positively surprised to

Table 2. Comparison of timings on Intel architecture. □ is the baseline. ▲ means a speedup (better) w.r.t. baseline. ▽ means a slowdown (worst) w.r.t. baseline. Timings are given in clock cycles (thousands).

Architecture	Implementation	Sign	Verify	KeyGen
x86_64	ref10	140 (□ base)	455 (□ base)	135 (□ base)
	ref	1560 (▽11.1x)	5218 (▽11.4x)	1531 (▽11.3x)
	amd64-64-24k	64 (▲2.18x)	225 (▲2.02x)	60 (▲2.25x)
	amd64-51-30k	66 (▲2.12x)	210 (▲2.16x)	62 (▲2.17x)
	donna	64 (▲2.18x)	217 (▲2.09x)	59 (▲2.28x)
	monocypher	230 (▽1.64x)	525 (▽1.15x)	210 (▽1.55x)
	overoptimized	264 (▽1.88x)	455 (▽1.00x)	227 (▽1.68x)
	ecckiila-precomp	101 (▲1.38x)	280 (▲1.62x)	96 (▲1.4x)
x86	ref10	399 (□ base)	1155 (□ base)	374 (□ base)
	ref	4137 (▽10.3x)	14105 (▽12.2x)	4086 (▽10.9x)
	amd64-64-24k	–	–	–
	amd64-51-30k	–	–	–
	donna	310 (▲1.28x)	962 (▲1.20x)	291 (▲1.28x)
	monocypher	533 (▽1.33x)	1347 (▽1.16x)	471 (▽1.25x)
	overoptimized	958 (▽2.40x)	1155 (▽1.00x)	914 (▽2.44x)
	ecckiila-no-precomp	1133 (▽2.83x)	1231 (▽1.06x)	1075 (▽2.87x)
	ecckiila-precomp	427 (▽1.07x)	1228 (▽1.06x)	368 (▲1.01x)

Table 3. Comparison of timings on ARM architecture. □ is the baseline. ▲ means a speedup (better) w.r.t. baseline. ▽ means a slowdown (worst) w.r.t. baseline. Timings are given in clock cycles (thousands).

Architecture	Implementation	Sign	Verify	KeyGen
aarch64	ref10	245 (□ base)	688 (□ base)	238 (□ base)
	ref	2924 (▽11.9x)	9579 (▽13.9x)	2425 (▽10.1x)
	amd64-64-24k	–	–	–
	amd64-51-30k	–	–	–
	donna	196 (▲1.25x)	638 (▲1.07x)	162 (▲1.46x)
	monocypher	422 (▽1.72x)	812 (▽1.18x)	366 (▽1.53x)
	overoptimized	726 (▽2.96x)	688 (▽1.00x)	635 (▽2.66x)
	ecckiila-precomp	270 (▽1.10x)	808 (▽1.17x)	261 (▽1.09x)
armv71	ref10	597 (□ base)	1755 (□ base)	582 (□ base)
	ref	9933 (▽16.6x)	28642 (▽16.3x)	8442 (▽14.5x)
	amd64-64-24k	–	–	–
	amd64-51-30k	–	–	–
	donna	508 (▲1.17x)	1508 (▲1.16x)	495 (▲1.17x)
	monocypher	983 (▽1.64x)	2505 (▽1.42x)	987 (▽1.69x)
	overoptimized	1622 (▽2.71x)	1800 (▽1.02x)	1534 (▽2.63x)
	ecckiila-no-precomp	2134 (▽3.57x)	2237 (▽1.27x)	2050 (▽3.52x)
	ecckiila-precomp	815 (▽1.36x)	2213 (▽1.26x)	732 (▽1.25x)

observe that `ecckiila-precomp` outperforms `ref10` on the Intel 64-bit architecture and has very similar results on the Intel 32-bit architecture.

On ARM architecture both `ecckiila-no-precomp` and `ecckiila-precomp` clearly lag behind when compared to their Intel counterpart. We speculate that these underperforming results on ARM are due to internal parameters in the ECCKiila tool used during code generation. These parameters try to calculate the correct size of the precomputed tables, however these parameters were not fine-tuned for our ARM benchmark devices. Our devices were incapable of internally generating the precomputed tables due to intensive computation by `fiat-crypto`, thus we generated them externally. We believe the ARM results could improve by correctly tweaking these parameters. In light of our results, it is interesting to observe that `ECCKiila` generates competitive portable ECC code that can potentially outperform handwritten, highly optimized code.

Finally, one more thing to consider for Ed25519 is that widely used implementations such as `ref10` and `donna` were originally published almost a decade ago, so these implementations do not consider new research results [10, 11, 13, 30] that further improve the security and performance of Ed25519.

5   Conclusion

Our toy example demonstrates, yet again, that implementing one's own cryptography is a complex task with a small margin for error, specially when strict requirements must be met. Aggressive optimizations can easily lead to a situation where both security and speed are greatly reduced at the cost of size as observed from our experiments, so we hope this serves as a lesson of a strategy to avoid. If implementation size is the main concern, a possible strategy to adopt is to use a SCA-secure variable-point scalar multiplication algorithm for key generation, signature generation, and signature verification. This reduces substantially the speed of all the operations but is secure and saves memory by avoiding precomputation tables, and additional recoding and scalar multiplication algorithms.

More generally, we recommend cryptography engineers, developers, and practitioners to avoid the usage of variable time algorithms on confidential inputs; the mix usage of SCA-secure and SCA-vulnerable algorithms, and we recommend to consider SCA good practices and recommendations if implementing cryptography is a must.

Additionally, our results show that computer-aided cryptographic tools have reached a maturity level where they can compete against code written by cryptography researchers with advanced skills on software and hardware engineering, as reflected on their adoption in BoringSSL and NSS cryptographic libraries [18]. Therefore, we highly recommend adopting them as part of the development process.

Acknowledgments. The authors would like to thank Philip Ginzboorg for the comments during the development of this research.

The first author thanks the Nokia Foundation for the generous support through a Nokia Scholarship.

This project received funding from the European Research Council (ERC) under the European Union's Horizon 2020 research and innovation programme (grant agreement No 804476).

References

1. Digital signature standard (DSS): FIPS-PUB 186-5. National Institute of Standards and Technology, October 2019. https://doi.org/10.6028/NIST.FIPS.186-5-draft
2. Allan, T., Brumley, B.B., Falkner, K.E., van de Pol, J., Yarom, Y.: Amplifying side channels through performance degradation. In: Schwab, S., Robertson, W.K., Balzarotti, D. (eds.) Proceedings of the 32nd Annual Conference on Computer Security Applications, ACSAC 2016, Los Angeles, CA, USA, 5–9 December 2016, pp. 422–435. ACM (2016). http://dl.acm.org/citation.cfm?id=2991084
3. Ambrose, C., Bos, J.W., Fay, B., Joye, M., Lochter, M., Murray, B.: Differential attacks on deterministic signatures. In: Smart, N.P. (ed.) CT-RSA 2018. LNCS, vol. 10808, pp. 339–353. Springer, Cham (2018). https://doi.org/10.1007/978-3-319-76953-0_18
4. Avanzi, R.M.: A note on the signed sliding window integer recoding and a left-to-right analogue. In: Handschuh, H., Hasan, M.A. (eds.) SAC 2004. LNCS, vol. 3357, pp. 130–143. Springer, Heidelberg (2004). https://doi.org/10.1007/978-3-540-30564-4_9
5. Belyavsky, D., Brumley, B.B., Chi-Domínguez, J., Rivera-Zamarripa, L., Ustinov, I.: Set it and forget it! turnkey ECC for instant integration. In: ACSAC 2020: Annual Computer Security Applications Conference, Virtual Event/Austin, TX, USA, 7–11 December 2020, pp. 760–771. ACM (2020), https://doi.org/10.1145/3427228.3427291
6. Bernstein, D.J.: Curve25519: new Diffie-Hellman speed records. In: Yung, M., Dodis, Y., Kiayias, A., Malkin, T. (eds.) PKC 2006. LNCS, vol. 3958, pp. 207–228. Springer, Heidelberg (2006). https://doi.org/10.1007/11745853_14
7. Bernstein, D.J., Duif, N., Lange, T., Schwabe, P., Yang, B.: High-speed high-security signatures. J. Cryptogr. Eng. 2(2), 77–89 (2012). https://doi.org/10.1007/s13389-012-0027-1
8. Bernstein, D.J., Lange, T.: eBACS: ECRYPT Benchmarking of Cryptographic Systems, September 2020. https://bench.cr.yp.to
9. Bernstein, D.J., Lange, T., Schwabe, P.: The security impact of a new cryptographic library. In: Hevia, A., Neven, G. (eds.) LATINCRYPT 2012. LNCS, vol. 7533, pp. 159–176. Springer, Heidelberg (2012). https://doi.org/10.1007/978-3-642-33481-8_9
10. Bernstein, D.J., Yang, B.: Fast constant-time gcd computation and modular inversion. IACR Trans. Cryptogr. Hardw. Embed. Syst. **2019**(3), 340–398 (2019). https://doi.org/10.13154/tches.v2019.i3.340-398
11. Brendel, J., Cremers, C., Jackson, D., Zhao, M.: The provable security of ed25519: theory and practice. IACR Cryptol. ePrint Arch. 2020, 823 (2020). https://eprint.iacr.org/2020/823
12. Brumley, B.B., Hakala, R.M.: Cache-timing template attacks. In: Matsui, M. (ed.) ASIACRYPT 2009. LNCS, vol. 5912, pp. 667–684. Springer, Heidelberg (2009). https://doi.org/10.1007/978-3-642-10366-7_39
13. Chalkias, K., Garillot, F., Nikolaenko, V.: Taming the many EdDSAs. In: van der Merwe, T., Mitchell, C., Mehrnezhad, M. (eds.) SSR 2020. LNCS, vol. 12529, pp. 67–90. Springer, Cham (2020). https://doi.org/10.1007/978-3-030-64357-7_4
14. Cohen, H., et al. (eds.): Handbook of Elliptic and Hyperelliptic Curve Cryptography. Chapman and Hall/CRC, Boca Raton (2005). https://doi.org/10.1201/9781420034981

15. Erbsen, A., Philipoom, J., Gross, J., Sloan, R., Chlipala, A.: Simple high-level code for cryptographic arithmetic - with proofs, without compromises. In: 2019 IEEE Symposium on Security and Privacy, SP 2019, San Francisco, CA, USA, 19–23 May 2019, pp. 1202–1219. IEEE (2019). https://doi.org/10.1109/SP.2019.00005
16. Gras, B., Giuffrida, C., Kurth, M., Bos, H., Razavi, K.: Absynthe: automatic blackbox side-channel synthesis on commodity microarchitectures. In: 27th Annual Network and Distributed System Security Symposium, NDSS 2020, San Diego, California, USA, 23–26 February 2020. The Internet Society (2020). https://www.ndss-symposium.org/ndss-paper/absynthe-automatic-blackbox-side-channel-synthesis-on-commodity-microarchitectures/
17. Gras, B., Razavi, K., Bos, H., Giuffrida, C.: Translation leak-aside buffer: defeating cache side-channel protections with TLB attacks. In: Enck, W., Felt, A.P. (eds.) 27th USENIX Security Symposium, USENIX Security 2018, Baltimore, MD, USA, 15–17 August 2018, pp. 955–972. USENIX Association (2018). https://www.usenix.org/conference/usenixsecurity18/presentation/gras
18. ul Hassan, S., et al.: Side-channel analysis of Mozilla's NSS. In: Ligatti, J., Ou, X., Katz, J., Vigna, G. (eds.) CCS 2020: 2020 ACM SIGSAC Conference on Computer and Communications Security, Virtual Event, USA, 9–13 November 2020, pp. 1887–1902. ACM (2020). https://doi.org/10.1145/3372297.3421761
19. Josefsson, S., Liusvaara, I.: Edwards-curve digital signature algorithm (EdDSA). In: RFC 8032, pp. 1–60 (2017). https://doi.org/10.17487/RFC8032
20. Joye, M., Tunstall, M.: Exponent recoding and regular exponentiation algorithms. In: Preneel, B. (ed.) AFRICACRYPT 2009. LNCS, vol. 5580, pp. 334–349. Springer, Heidelberg (2009). https://doi.org/10.1007/978-3-642-02384-2_21
21. Möller, B.: Algorithms for multi-exponentiation. In: Vaudenay, S., Youssef, A.M. (eds.) SAC 2001. LNCS, vol. 2259, pp. 165–180. Springer, Heidelberg (2001). https://doi.org/10.1007/3-540-45537-X_13
22. Pippenger, N.: On the evaluation of powers and related problems (preliminary version). In: 17th Annual Symposium on Foundations of Computer Science, Houston, TX, USA, 25–27 October 1976. pp. 258–263. IEEE Computer Society (1976). https://doi.org/10.1109/SFCS.1976.21
23. Poddebniak, D., Somorovsky, J., Schinzel, S., Lochter, M., Rösler, P.: Attacking deterministic signature schemes using fault attacks. In: 2018 IEEE European Symposium on Security and Privacy, EuroS&P 2018, London, UK, 24–26 April 2018. pp. 338–352. IEEE (2018). https://doi.org/10.1109/EuroSP.2018.00031
24. Romailler, Y., Pelissier, S.: Practical fault attack against the ed25519 and eddsa signature schemes. In: 2017 Workshop on Fault Diagnosis and Tolerance in Cryptography, FDTC 2017, Taipei, Taiwan, 25 September 2017, pp. 17–24. IEEE Computer Society (2017). https://doi.org/10.1109/FDTC.2017.12
25. Samwel, N., Batina, L.: Practical fault injection on deterministic signatures: the case of EdDSA. In: Joux, A., Nitaj, A., Rachidi, T. (eds.) AFRICACRYPT 2018. LNCS, vol. 10831, pp. 306–321. Springer, Cham (2018). https://doi.org/10.1007/978-3-319-89339-6_17
26. Samwel, N., Batina, L., Bertoni, G., Daemen, J., Susella, R.: Breaking Ed25519 in WolfSSL. In: Smart, N.P. (ed.) CT-RSA 2018. LNCS, vol. 10808, pp. 1–20. Springer, Cham (2018). https://doi.org/10.1007/978-3-319-76953-0_1
27. Schnorr, C.P.: Efficient identification and signatures for smart cards. In: Brassard, G. (ed.) CRYPTO 1989. LNCS, vol. 435, pp. 239–252. Springer, New York (1990). https://doi.org/10.1007/0-387-34805-0_22

28. Tuveri, N., Brumley, B.B.: Start your ENGINEs: dynamically loadable contemporary crypto. In: 2019 IEEE Cybersecurity Development, SecDev 2019, Tysons Corner, VA, USA, 23–25September 2019, pp. 4–19. IEEE (2019). https://doi.org/10.1109/SecDev.2019.00014

29. Tuveri, N., ul Hassan, S., Pereida García, C., Brumley, B.B.: Side-channel analysis of SM2: a late-stage featurization case study. In: Proceedings of the 34th Annual Computer Security Applications Conference, ACSAC 2018, San Juan, PR, USA, 03–07 December 2018, pp. 147–160. ACM (2018), https://doi.org/10.1145/3274694.3274725

30. de Valence, H., Grigg, J., Tankersley, G., Valsorda, F., Lovecruft, I.: The ristretto255 group. Tech. Rep, IETF CFRG Internet Draft (2019)

Arrows in a Quiver: A Secure Certificateless Group Key Distribution Protocol for Drones

Eugene Frimpong$^{(\boxtimes)}$ (ID), Reyhaneh Rabbaninejad (ID), and Antonis Michalas (ID)

Tampere University, 33720 Tampere, Finland
{eugene.frimpong,reyhaneh.rabbaninejad,antonios.michalas}@tuni.fi
https://research.tuni.fi/nisec/

Abstract. Drone-based applications continue to garner a lot of attention due to their significant potential in both commercial and non-commercial use. Owing to this increasing popularity, researchers have begun to pay attention to the communication security requirements involved in deploying drone-based applications and services on a large scale, with particular emphasis on group communication. The majority of existing works in this field focus on the use of symmetric key cryptographic schemes or group key agreement schemes. However, in this paper, we propose a pairing-free certificateless group authenticated key distribution protocol for drone-based applications which takes into consideration drones with varying computational resources. The proposed scheme ensures key freshness, group key secrecy, forward secrecy, and backward secrecy while ensuring that the scheme is lightweight enough to be implemented on very resource-constrained drones or smart devices. We extensively prove the security of our scheme and demonstrate its real-world applicability by evaluating its performance on three different kinds of drone boards (UP Xtreme i7 board, SamL11-Xpro board, and a Zolertia Re-mote Revb board).

Keywords: Certificateless public key cryptography · Group key distribution · Drones

1 Introduction

Unmanned Aerial Vehicles (UAV) are gaining popularity in the Industries, Academia, and peoples' personal lives at a rapid and accelerating pace. Big organizations, like Uber and Amazon, are constantly hinting at offering drone-based services such as package and food delivery [1]. Additionally, drones have been used for other consumer-related activities such as aerial photography, landscape surveying, and in some cases, delivering medical supplies to remote places. These

This research has received funding from the Technology Innovation Institute (TII), Abu Dhabi for the project ARROWSMITH: Living (Securely) on the Edge.

© Springer Nature Switzerland AG 2021
N. Tuveri et al. (Eds.): NordSec 2021, LNCS 13115, pp. 31–48, 2021.
https://doi.org/10.1007/978-3-030-91625-1_3

devices come equipped with various capabilities and features – from high definition cameras to temperature sensors. Although drones are expected to offer numerous benefits to consumers and companies, the proliferating adoption of drone-based services presents a myriad of security concerns and requirements, chief among them being secure communication [2,3]. Secure communication in drones centres around securing the communication channel between drones and their command centre, between individual drones, or groups of drones.

In this paper, we propose a pairing-free certificateless authenticated group key distribution protocol for drone-based applications. Early group key management schemes predominantly focused on symmetric-key based approaches where symmetric session keys were pre-installed on devices. However, this approach proved not be scalable for Wireless Sensor Networks (WSNs), a classification that applies to drones [4]. Subsequently, improvements to Elliptic Curve Cryptographic (ECC) primitives have led to an increased adoption of Public Key Cryptographic (PKC) schemes for resource-constrained environments [5]. Unfortunately, ECC schemes with certificates and pairing-based operations, incur additional certificate and computational overhead. To mitigate the limitations related to certificate overhead, many Certificateless Group Key Agreement (CL-GKA) schemes [6–8] have been proposed. However, these schemes are based on Group Key Agreement (GKA) protocols (all group members collaboratively calculate the group session key without depending on a trusted party), as compared to the Group Key Distribution (GKD) model we follow. There have been many arguments for GKA over GKD, such as the security of GKD protocols being broken when the group manager is compromised as well as its inappropriateness for distributed environments where a trusted authority or central authority is unavailable [9].

Contrary to these points, we argue that, for a drone-based application such as a Smart City consisting of different drones with varying computational resources and smart devices with equally varying resources, a GKA approach is inefficient. To support our argument, we consider a case study involving a drone team leader who receives mission plans and tasks from a central point and a group of edge drones deployed to accomplish the tasks allocated by the drone team leader. For our case study, the edge drones are assumed to have limited computational resources, with the team leader, on the other hand having considerably high ones. In such a case, a GKA approach is inefficient and is not scalable as the number of edge drones increases. This is due to the fact that in order to compute a session key, all devices are required to be online – which also introduces an additional communication overhead. Our protocol provides an efficient group authenticated key distribution protocol suitable for the case study described. Additionally, it can also be extended for environments consisting of resource-constrained smart devices deployed to sense and generate data.

Contributions: The contributions for this paper are summarized below:

C1. We propose a pairing-free certificateless group authenticated key distribution protocol for multi-drone applications and environments. The security of existing identity-based public key solutions is impacted by the use of a

fully trusted KGC (i.e., Key Escrow problem). In our proposed scheme, the
KGC is not fully trusted.

C2. We provide a comprehensive security analysis to prove the security of the
proposed protocol.

C3. Finally, we implement and evaluate the performance of the proposed protocol on three different device platforms to demonstrate its benefits and
applicability.

2 Related Work

One of the early key distribution schemes was introduced by Tian et al. [10].
They presented a scheme based on Identity-based cryptography (ID-PKC) and
bilinear pairings. Traditional ID-PKC suffer from the key escrow problem while
the computational costs required for pairing operations are considerably higher
than standard ECC operations such as EC point multiplications on resource-
constrained devices. Kumar et al. [11] also proposed an efficient centralized group
key distribution protocol based on the RSA public key cryptosystem, with particular emphasis on reducing the computation costs and storage complexity at
the Key Server (KS). The scheme offers both *forward* and *backward secrecy* -
an essential requirement [9,12] for any secure group key distribution protocol.
A few notable drawbacks with this scheme are the same key escrow problem,
certificate management overhead, and the computational complexity of the RSA
scheme on resource-constrained devices and environments [13]. As a result of the
key escrow and certificate management overhead, several certificateless public
key cryptography schemes have been proposed [6–8,14–16], both for one-to-one
communication and group-based communication instances.

In [6], authors propose a certificateless GKA scheme for unmanned aerial
vehicles. Similar to majority of key agreement protocols [17–21], this protocol
requires that each user contributes to the generation of the group key by way
of a series of key establishment requests. At the end of the final round of the
protocol, each user generates a similar session key. This work along with other
certificateless schemes such as [14] and [7] ensure mutual key agreement, key
escrow elimination, joint key control and key freshness. However, this scheme
incurs relatively high computational burden at each user based on the pairing-
based computations and does not consider a dynamic group where members of
the group can join or leave a group. Similar certificateless key agreement schemes
such as [16] and [15] also do not consider group environments.

More recently, a blockchain-based mutual healing group key distribution
scheme was proposed in [22]. In this work, the Ground control Station (GCS)
for the drones builds a private blockchain where the distributed group keys generated by the GCS as well as a list of membership certificates are recorded. The
GCS acts as the KS for this scheme and uses the blockchain to record transactions. Transactions, in the context of this scheme, are instances when members
leave or join the group. Although authors prove that the proposed scheme is resistant to various attacks as compared to other mutual healing schemes [10,23,24],

it poses significant computational overhead resulting from constant interaction with the blockchain.

To design an efficient and resource friendly protocol, AinQ, our pairing-free certificateless key distribution protocol, uses a Key Generation Center (KGC) to distribute partial private and public keypairs to all users. Our scheme utilizes a hybrid encryption for multiple users and combines a data encapsulation and a key encapsulation mechanism to distribute the group session key. Additionally, the computational burden rests primarily on the team leader. As such, AinQ can be extended to an IoT environment with significantly resource-constrained devices.

3 System Model

Our setup consists of four entities: *(i)* Key Generation Center, *(ii)* Cloud Service Provider (CSP), *(iii)* Edge Drones, and *(iv)* Team Leaders.

1. **KGC**: This is a semi-trusted entity responsible for generating and setting the system parameters for the complete run of the protocol. The KGC generates partial private and public key pairs for each registered drone during the protocol initialization phase.
2. **CSP**: We assume the existence of a CSP, an abstract external platform that consists of cloud hosts operating virtual machines that communicate through a network. The CSP will be the final destination of messages aggregated by the set of drones within our environment. Specific capabilities and features of the CSP are beyond the focus of this paper and as such are not discussed in detail. Our proposed scheme is independent of the underlying cloud platform.
3. **Edge Drones**: Let $\mathcal{D} = \{d_1, \ldots, d_n\}$ be the set of all edge drones in our environment. Each drone is equipped with a number of sensors to monitor and report on sensed events. Each d_i accepts mission tasks and securely stores and updates mission data so that no adversary can learn anything.
4. **Team Leaders**: Let $\mathcal{Q} = \{q_1, \ldots, q_m\}$ be the set of drones elected as Team Leaders in our protocol. Each drone team leader maintains a group list which contains the group members and their respective public keys. This group list is updated when a drone joins or leaves the group. Each team leader accepts missions from the CSP and assigns individual tasks to members of its group. Note that a team leader is assumed to be a more powerful drone with far more computational resources compared to a regular edge drone.

4 Arrows in a Quiver (AinQ)

In this section, we present AinQ, which constitutes the core of our contribution. AinQ's description is divided into two parts:

1. The construction of a scheme containing algorithms for individual and group key generation, key retrieval and re-keying.
2. A protocol showing how our scheme can be effectively used to allow drones to form groups and securely agree on secret keys that will allow them to securely exchange information over an encrypted channel.

4.1   AinQ Scheme

For the purposes of AinQ, we extend the functionalities of eCLSC-TKEM [16] with the **GenGroupKey,KeyRetrieval**, and **Re − Key** algorithms to support group key distribution (using a form of Multiple-Recipient/Multiple-Message Public Key Encryption (MR-MM-PKE) [25]). In total, our scheme consists of the following seven probabilistic algorithms.

Setup: This algorithm is run by the KGC to generate the system parameters for the scheme and a master secret key. The algorithm takes as input a security parameter $\lambda \in \mathbb{Z}^+$, and outputs the system parameters Ω, and the KGC's master secret key msk. Given λ, KGC executes the following steps:

Step 1. Chooses a λ-bit prime q and a point P on the curve G_q.
Step 2. Chooses msk as $x \in \mathbb{Z}^*$.
Step 3. Computes the corresponding public key as $P_{pub} = xP$.
Step 4. Chooses the following cryptographic hash functions where n is the key length of the symmetric key encryption scheme:

- $H_0 : \{0,1\}^* \times G_q^2 \times \{0,1\}^* \to \mathbb{Z}_q^*$*,
- $H_1 : G_q^3 \times \{0,1\}^* \times G_q \to \{0,1\}^n$,

Step 5. Publishes the system parameters $\Omega = \{G_q, P_{pub}, P, H_0, H_1\}$.

GenSecretValue: Each edge drone $d_i \in \mathcal{D}$ and team leader run this algorithm to generate a secret value and a public key. The algorithm takes as input the system parameters Ω generated in the Setup algorithm, the drone identity d_i, and outputs a secret value x_i along with a corresponding public key P_i. Given Ω, d_i executes the following steps:

Step 1. Chooses a secret value $x_i \in \mathbb{Z}^*$,
Step 2. Computes the corresponding public key as $P_i = x_i P$.

GenPartialKey: The KGC runs this algorithm to generate a partial key for all registered drones. It takes as input the drone's identity d_i, its public key P_i, and the master secret key x. On a successful run, GenPartialKey outputs the partial private and public keys for d_i. Given P_i, the KGC executes the following steps:

Step 1. Chooses $r_i \in \mathbb{Z}^*$
Step 2. $R_i = r_i \cdot P$
Step 3. $s_i = r_i + x H_0(d_i, R_i, P_i) \mod q$

FullKeyGen: Each registered drone runs this algorithm to generate it's full private key sk$_i$ and public key pk$_i$. The algorithm takes as input the drone's secret value x_i, partial secret key s_i, public key P_i and partial public key R_i. On successful run, it returns the drone's full private and public key pair.

GenGroupKey: This algorithm is run by a designated team leader $q_k \in \mathcal{Q}$ to generate a symmetric group session key K$_g$ for the group. Given a group list $GL = \{d_1, \ldots, d_h\}$ containing a list of valid group members and their respective public keys pk$_i$, $i \in \{1, \ldots, h\}$, q_k generates a list of ciphertexts C_i, $i \in \{1, \ldots, h\}$. The algorithm takes as input the group list GL and the valid time period t_g. Given GL, q_k executes the following steps:

Step 1. Chooses $K_g \in \mathbb{Z}^*$ and $l_k \in \mathbb{Z}^*$ at random.
Step 2. Computes $V = l_k \cdot P$.
Step 3. Parses pk_i as (R_i, P_i) for all $d_i \in GL$.
Step 4. For each pk_i:

- $Y_i = R_i + H_0(d_i, R_i, P_i) \cdot P_{pub} + P_i$.
- $T_i = l_k \cdot Y_i$.
- $C_i = K_g \oplus H_1(V, T_i, q_k, pk_k, d_i, pk_i, t_g)$.

Step 5. Outputs $(V, C_1, C_2, \ldots, C_h, t_g)$.

KeyRetrieval: This is the key retrieval algorithm run by each drone $d_i \in GL$ to obtain the group key K_g generated by q_k in GenGroupKey. Given the broadcast message containing the list of ciphertexts $(V, C_1, C_2, \ldots, C_h)$, and the respective private key and public key of the recipient drone, d_i retrieves the group key K_g. We denote this by: $K_g \leftarrow$ KeyRetrieval$(V, C_1, C_2, \ldots, C_h, sk_i, pk_i)$. Given $(V, C_1, C_2, \ldots, C_h)$, each $d_i \in GL$ executes the following steps:

- **Step 1.** Computes $T_i = (s_i + x_i) \cdot V$

$$(s_i + x_i) \cdot l_k \cdot P = l_k \cdot Y_i$$

- **Step 2.** $K_g = C_i \oplus H_1(V, T_i, q_k, pk_k, d_i, pk_i, t_g)$.

Re − Key: This algorithm is run by the team leader q_k whenever a new drone joins the group, an existing member leaves, or the an existing group key expires and a new one has to be issued. Given an updated group list $GL = \{d_1, \ldots, d_h\}$ containing an up-to-date information on group members, q_k generates a new group key K_g'. We denote this by: $(V, C_1', C_2', \ldots, C_h') \leftarrow$ ReKey(GL). Given the updated GL, q_k executes the following steps:

Step 1. Chooses a new group key $K_g' \in \mathbb{Z}^*$
Step 2. If d_i is a new member:

- Parse pk_i as (R_i, P_i) for $d_i \in GL$.
- $Y_i = R_i + H_0(d_i, R_i, P_i,) \cdot P_{pub} + P_i$.
- $T_i = l_k \cdot Y_i$.

Step 3. $C_i' = K_g' \oplus H_1(V, T_i, q_k, pk_k, d_i, pk_i, t_g')$
Step 4. Outputs $(V, C_1', C_2', \ldots, C_h')$.

4.2 AinQ Protocol

The proposed protocol is divided into 3 phases; (i) Setup and Initialization, (ii) Key Generation and Retrieval, and (iii) Group Re-keying. To provide a detailed and comprehensive description of each phase, we consider a drone-based scenario consisting of an elected drone group leader and a number of edge drones in its group. In our assumed scenario, the elected drone team leader q_k wishes to distribute a group key K_g to all edge drones belonging to GL in the presence of a KGC. Furthermore, we assume that all drones have a maximum flight time of t_g and are stored in a secure location when not on a mission.

AinQ - Setup and Initialization. The KGC runs the Setup algorithm at the beginning of the protocol to generate a master secret key and system parameters. The algorithm returns the system parameters, Ω, and the master secret key x. These system parameters are public and accessible to each registered entity partaking in the protocol. Each registered drone runs the GenSecretValue algorithm to generate a secret value and a corresponding public key. On successful run of this algorithm, the drones send their identity and public key to the KGC in order to receive partial private and public keys valid for the length of their flight. The KGC runs the GenPartialKey algorithm and returns to each drone the partial private and public key pair. All communication in this phase of the protocol occurs before the drones leave for a mission and is assumed to be over a secure channel.

Upon receiving the partial private/public keypair, each drone runs the GenPrivKey and GenPubKey to generate a full public/private key pair. We assume that each drone makes its public key available to all other drones.

AinQ - Key Generation and Retrieval. In this phase of AinQ, the team leader q_k first generates a random number r_1, and runs the GenGroupKey algorithm to generate the symmetric group key K_g and the list of ciphertexts $(C_1, C_2, \ldots, C_h)$. K_g that will be used to secure all ensuing communication between the group members as well as with the team leader.

On successful run of the GenGroupKey algorithm, the team leader sends the following broadcast message to drones in the network: $m_1 = \langle r_1, V, C_1, C_2, \ldots, C_h, q_k, t_g, \sigma_{q_k} \rangle$ where $\sigma_{q_k} = sig_{sk_k}(r_1||V||K_g)$. Upon receiving m_1, each registered drone executes the KeyRetrieval algorithm to retrieve the group key K_g. The freshness and integrity of m_1 is verified using the team leader's public key and the generated group key. The protocol is aborted if the signature verification process fails. Figure 1 provides an illustration of this phase.

AinQ - Group Re-Key. The team leader q_k runs the Re$-$Key algorithm in this phase to generate a new group key K_g' whenever a new drone joins its group or an existing drone leaves the group. The re-keying process ensures that AinQ is both forward and backward private. When a drone leaves or joins a group, the leader updates the group list GL', generates a new random number r_2, and broadcasts a new message m_2 to the network. $m_2 = \langle r_2, V, C_1', C_2', \ldots, C_h', q_k, t_g', \sigma_{q_k}' \rangle$ where $\sigma_{q_k}' = sig_{sk_k}(r_2||V||K_g')$.

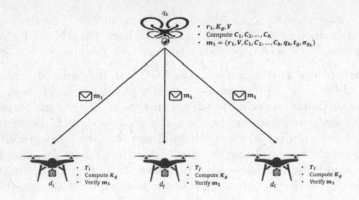

Fig. 1. Key Generation and Retrieval Phase

5   Security Analysis

In this section, we proceed to prove the security of our construction in the presence of a malicious adversary $\mathcal{A}$, who can be an outside adversary– which covers a variety from a passive eavesdropper who just listens to the network to a malicious entity who has captured some drones–, or inside adversaries including a corrupt KGC and a revoked user. We begin by describing the main security properties that a group key distribution scheme should satisfy (5) and follow this up with the necessary security definitions that we consider for our threat model (5).

Security Requirements: Consider a group where edge drones dynamically join or leave. Furthermore, let $\mathcal{K} = \{K_g^0, \ldots, K_g^s\}$ be the set of sequential group keys generated during s successive sessions. Below we provide a list of the main security properties that a GKD scheme should satisfy.

1. *Key Freshness:* A GKD scheme has this property if it guarantees a key to be new, thus preventing the reuse an old key by an adversary.
2. *Group Key Secrecy:* A GKD scheme must guarantee that a session key is only known to legitimate drones. This means that extracting a session key $K_g^i \in \mathcal{K}, i \in [0, s]$ is computationally infeasible for an adversary.
3. *Forward Secrecy:* Assume an adversary possesses a consecutive subset of session keys (e.g., $\{K_g^0, K_g^1, \ldots, K_g^i\}$). This property guarantees that he can learn nothing about a future session key K_g^j, for all $i < j$. Therefore, a revoked drone cannot discover future session keys.
4. *Backward Secrecy:* Assume an adversary possesses a consecutive subset of session keys (e.g., $\{K_g^i, K_g^{i+1}, \ldots, K_g^j\}$). This property guarantees that he can learn nothing about a past session key K_g^l, for all $l < i < j$. Therefore, a newly joined drone cannot discover previous session keys.

Security Model: We now formally define indistinguishability against adaptive chosen ciphertext attack (IND-CCA2) through the following game between an adversary $\mathcal{A}$ (this can be an outside adversary, a corrupt KGC, or a revoked user) and a challenger $\mathcal{B}$.

Ainq-IND-CCA2 Game

- Challenger $\mathcal{B}$ runs the Setup algorithm to generate msk, the corresponding public key P_{pub}, and system parameters Ω. $\mathcal{B}$ then forwards Ω and P_{pub} to $\mathcal{A}$ and keeps msk confidential. In case $\mathcal{A}$ is a corrupt KGC, msk is also sent to $\mathcal{A}$.
- Adversary $\mathcal{A}$ can make the following queries to the challenger. In case $\mathcal{A}$ is a revoked user, the run time of the operations executed by $\mathcal{B}$ is less than the challenge time period.
    1. *GenSecretValue* Query. Adversary $\mathcal{A}$ queries the secret value and the corresponding public key of a specified drone. $\mathcal{B}$ runs the GenSecretValue algorithm and forwards the output to $\mathcal{A}$. Note that we exclude a corrupt KGC from these queries.
    2. *GenPartialKey* Query. To respond to a query on the partial private and public keypair of a specified drone from $\mathcal{A}$, $\mathcal{B}$ runs the GenPartialKey algorithm with msk and the drone's public key as inputs, and forwards the output to $\mathcal{A}$.
    3. *GenGroupKey* Query. Adversary $\mathcal{A}$ sends a query to $\mathcal{O}_{GenGroupKey}$ oracle by giving as input the group list GL, identity q_k of the team leader, and the valid time period t_g. Using the key for group of drones GL generated by team leader q_k for time period t_g. $\mathcal{B}$ runs GenGroupKey algorithm and forwards the output to $\mathcal{A}$.
    4. *KeyRetrieval* Query. Adversary $\mathcal{A}$ queries $\mathcal{O}_{KeyRetrieval}$ oracle to extract a group key from the broadcast message. $\mathcal{B}$ runs KeyRetrieval algorithm and forwards the output to $\mathcal{A}$. Note that we exclude a corrupt KGC from these queries.
    5. $Re - Key$ Query. Adversary $\mathcal{A}$ sends a query to $\mathcal{O}_{Re-Key}$ oracle by giving as input an updated group list GL, the team leader's identity q_k, and the valid time period t_g. $\mathcal{B}$ runs $Re - Key$ algorithm and forwards the output to $\mathcal{A}$.
- At the end of query phase, $\mathcal{A}$ submits challenge inputs including group list GL^*, team leader identity q_k^*, and a valid time period t_g^*, and two session keys K_g^0, K_g^1. $\mathcal{A}$ may not have made $FullKeyGen$ queries on any of the identities in GL^* and q_k^* by querying both $\mathcal{O}_{GenSecretValue}$ and $\mathcal{O}_{GenPartialKey}$ oracles. Also, $\mathcal{A}$ may not have made $KeyRetrieval$ query on tuple (GL^*, q_k^*, t_g^*) in the query phase. In case $\mathcal{A}$ is a revoked user, the condition $t_g^* > t_R$ must also hold, where t_R is the revocation time. That is, in the challenge time period, $\mathcal{A}$ has no access to new information. $\mathcal{B}$ picks a random $b \in \{0,1\}$ and runs $(V^*, C_1^*, C_2^*, \ldots, C_h^*) \leftarrow$ GenGroupKey$(GL^*, q_k^*, t_g^*, K_g^b)$, where $C_i^* = K_g^b \oplus H_1(V^*, T_i, q_k^*, pk_k^*, d_i^*, pk_i^*, t_g^*)$. Finally, $\mathcal{B}$ sends $(V^*, C_1^*, C_2^*, \ldots, C_h^*)$ as challenge to $\mathcal{A}$.
- Excluding the case where $\mathcal{A}$ is a revoked user, $\mathcal{A}$ can continue the query phase by adaptively making a polynomially bounded number of queries. $\mathcal{A}$

may not make $FullKeyGen$ queries on any identities in GL^* and q_k^* by querying both $\mathcal{O}_{GenSecretValue}$ and $\mathcal{O}_{GenPartialKey}$ oracles. Also, $\mathcal{A}$ may not make $KeyRetrieval$ query on same group list GL^*, team leader identity q_k^*, and time period t_g^*. Finally, $\mathcal{A}$ outputs a bit b' and wins the game if $b' = b$.

Definition. AinQ is IND-CCA2 secure if any probabilistic polynomial-time adversary $\mathcal{A}$ has at most negligible advantage in the above security game. $\mathcal{A}$'s advantage is defined as below:

$$Adv^{IND-CCA2}(\mathcal{A}) = |Pr[b' = b] - \frac{1}{2}|. \qquad (1)$$

5.1   Security Proof

Below, we provide the formal security proof for AinQ which relies on the hardness of decisional Diffie-Hellman problem.

Definition: Decisional Diffie-Hellman (DDH) Assumption. Given a prime q and a generator P on the curve G_q, for randomly and independently chosen $a, b \in \mathbb{Z}_q$, the value abP is indistinguishable from a random element in G_q. Formally, for each probabilistic polynomial-time adversary $\mathcal{A}$ which is given $(D_1 = aP, D_2 = bP)$ and a candidate solution D_3, $\mathcal{A}$'s advantage to distinguish whether $D_3 = abP$ or whether D_3 was chosen at random from G_q is negligible. In other words, for any probabilistic polynomial-time algorithm $\mathcal{A}$, we have:

$$|Pr[\mathcal{A}_{DDH}(G_q, P, aP, bP, cP) = 1]$$
$$- Pr[\mathcal{A}_{DDH}(G_q, P, aP, bP, abP) = 1]| \leq \mathsf{negl}(\lambda),$$

where $a, b, c \in \mathbb{Z}_q$ are chosen at random.

Theorem 1. AinQ is IND-CCA2 secure under DDH assumption in the random oracle model.

Proof. As noted in the security model, we consider three types of adversaries: an outside adversary – which covers a variety from a passive eavesdropper who just listens to the network to a malicious entity who has captured some drones–, and inside adversaries including malicious KGC and a revoked user. Here we formally prove AinQ security against an outside adversary. Security proofs against malicious KGC and revoked user follow same arguments as proof below, which are omitted due to the space limitation.

–Security Against Outside Adversary: Extracting a session key is computationally infeasible for an outside adversary. To show this, we prove that if an outside adversary $\mathcal{A}$ has a non-negligible advantage in IND-CCA2 game, then there exists an algorithm $\mathcal{B}$ that solves the DDH problem with overwhelming probability.

Setup. Given a DDH challenge $(D_1 = aP, D_2 = bP, D_3)$, $\mathcal{B}$ sets the public key $P_{pub} = D_1$ and forwards it to $\mathcal{A}$. Here, the virtual master secret key msk is equal to $x = a$.

GenSecretValue Query. To answer a query on secret value of drone d_i submitted by $\mathcal{A}$, $\mathcal{B}$ chooses random $x_i \in \mathbb{Z}^*$ and sets the corresponding public key as $P_i = x_i P$. Then, $\mathcal{B}$ sends (x_i, P_i) to $\mathcal{A}$ and also saves the pair (x_i, P_i) into a table T_{d_i}.

GenPartialKey Query. To answer a query on the partial key of a drone d_i submitted by $\mathcal{A}$, since $\mathcal{B}$ does not possess msk, he generates $s_i = r_i + x H_0(d_i, R_i, P_i)$ mod q by controlling the output of H_0 as follows. $\mathcal{B}$ chooses random $s_i \in \mathbb{Z}^*$ as the queried partial key. $\mathcal{B}$ also selects random $c_i \in \mathbb{Z}^*$ as the output of $H_0(d_i, R_i, P_i)$ and computes $R_i = s_i P - c_i D_1$. Finally, $\mathcal{B}$ checks if $(\{d_i, R_i, P_i\}, .)$ is an entry in table T_{H_0}; if it is so, the random c_i assigned to $H_0(d_i, R_i, P_i)$ is not correct and the game aborts. Otherwise, $\mathcal{B}$ saves $(\{d_i, R_i, P_i\}, c_i)$ in table T_{H_0} and outputs the queried partial key as (s_i, R_i) which is also recorded in table T_{d_i}.

Hash Query. To answer H query on input a_i, $\mathcal{B}$ first checks previously queried values in table T_H. If there is the same entry in T_H, he outputs the corresponding value. Otherwise, he outputs a random value $c_i \in \mathbb{Z}^*$ and saves (a_i, c_i) in T_H.

GenGroupKey Query. Adversary $\mathcal{A}$ sends GL, q_k, t_g to query $\mathcal{O}_{GenGroupKey}$ oracle. To answer this query, $\mathcal{B}$ chooses $\mathsf{K_g} \in \mathbb{Z}^*$ and $l'_k \in \mathbb{Z}^*$ at random, and computes $V = l'_k \cdot D_2$. Next, $\mathcal{B}$ extracts $\mathsf{pk_i} = (R_i, P_i)$ from table T_{d_i}, for all $d_i \in GL$. Note that if table T_{d_i} for a drone $d_i \in GL$ was empty, $\mathcal{B}$ generates the corresponding values by calling $\mathcal{O}_{GenSecretValue}$ and $\mathcal{O}_{GenPartialKey}$ oracles. For all $\mathsf{pk_i}$, $\mathcal{B}$ computes $T_i = l'_k s_i \cdot D_2 + l'_k c_i \cdot D_3 + l'_k x_i \cdot D_2$ and $C_i = K_g \oplus H_1(V, T_i, q_k, pk_k, d_i, pk_i, t_g)$. Finally, $\mathcal{B}$ outputs $(V, C_1, C_2, \ldots, C_h, t_g)$ as response to the query.

KeyRetrieval Query. Adversary $\mathcal{A}$ queries $\mathcal{B}$ to extract group key from a broadcast message $(V, C_1, C_2, \ldots, C_h, t_g)$. $\mathcal{B}$ extracts $\mathsf{sk_i} = (s_i, x_i)$ from table T_{d_i}, for one d_i in group list GL corresponding to the broadcast message. $\mathcal{B}$ then computes $T_i = (s_i + x_i) \cdot V$ and $K_g = C_i \oplus H_1(V, T_i, q_k, pk_k, d_i, pk_i, t_g)$ to retrieve the session key and forwards K_g to $\mathcal{A}$.

Re-Key Query. Adversary $\mathcal{A}$ sends an updated group list GL, team leader q_k, and valid time period t_g to query $\mathcal{O}_{Re-Key}$ oracle. To answer this query, $\mathcal{B}$ performs same process as he did in GenGroupKey Query except that the T_i values for old drones can be reused from previous runs. Finally, the output is forwarded to $\mathcal{A}$.

Challenge. At the end of query phase, $\mathcal{A}$ submits challenge inputs including group list GL^*, team leader identity q_k^*, and a valid time period t_g^*, and two session keys K_g^0, K_g^1. If the conditions described in Ainq-IND-CCA2 game hold, $\mathcal{B}$ (1) picks a random $b \in \{0, 1\}$ (2) runs GenGroupKey Query on input $(K_g^b, GL^*, q_k^*, t_g^*)$ to generate $(V^*, C_1^*, C_2^*, \ldots, C_h^*)$ (3) sends it as challenge to $\mathcal{A}$.

Response. $\mathcal{A}$ can run another query phase by adaptively making a polynomially bounded number of queries which must meet the conditions described in Ainq-IND-CCA2 game. Finally, (1) $\mathcal{A}$ outputs a bit b' (2) $\mathcal{B}$ responds to the DDH challenge by outputtig 1 if $b' = b$, and 0 otherwise.

Analysis. Th probability of aborting in the above game, is equal to the probability of collision in H_0 which is at most $q_H/2^\lambda$, where q_H is the total number of queries to H_0. So, the probability that $\mathcal{A}$ wins the game is $\epsilon(\lambda)(1 - q_H/2^\lambda)$. Regarding $\mathcal{B}$'s response, two cases can be considered:

Case 1. The DDH challenge given to $\mathcal{B}$ is generated by randomly choosing $a, b, c \in \mathbb{Z}_q$, and setting $D_1 := aP$, $D_2 := bP$, and $D_3 := cP$. In this case, D_3 is a random element in G_q and thus $T_i^* = l'^*_k s_i \cdot D_2 + l'^*_k c_i \cdot D_3 + l'^*_k x_i \cdot D_2$ is uniformly distributed in G_q. Therefore, the view of $\mathcal{A}$ on the challenge ciphertext $C_i^* = K_g^b \oplus H_1(V^*, T_i^*, q_k^*, pk_k^*, d_i, pk_i, t_g^*)$, is distributed exactly as $\mathcal{A}$'s view in one-time pad (OTP). Since $\mathcal{B}$ outputs 1 exactly when the output b' of $\mathcal{A}$ is equal to b, we have that:

$$Pr[\mathcal{B}_{DDH}(G_q, P, aP, bP, cP) = 1]$$
$$= (1 - q_H/2^\lambda) \cdot Pr[\mathcal{A}_{OTP}(b = b')]$$
$$= \frac{1}{2} \cdot (1 - q_H/2^\lambda).$$

Case 2. The DDH challenge given to $\mathcal{B}$ is generated by randomly choosing $a, b \in \mathbb{Z}_q$, and setting $D_1 := aP$, $D_2 := bP$, and $D_3 := abP$. In this case, the view of $\mathcal{A}$ on the challenge ciphertext $C_i^* = K_g^b \oplus H_1(V^*, T_i^*, q_k^*, pk_k^*, d_i, pk_i, t_g^*)$ is distributed exactly as $\mathcal{A}$'s view in AinQ. Since $\mathcal{B}$ outputs 1 exactly when the output b' of $\mathcal{A}$ is equal to b, we have that:

$$Pr[\mathcal{B}_{DDH}(G_q, P, aP, bP, abP) = 1]$$
$$= (1 - q_H/2^\lambda) \cdot Pr[\mathcal{A}_{AinQ}(b = b')]$$
$$= (\frac{1}{2} + \epsilon(\lambda)) \cdot (1 - q_H/2^\lambda).$$

Therefore, $\mathcal{B}$'s advantage in solving the DDH challenge is:

$$|Pr[\mathcal{B}_{DDH}(G_q, P, aP, bP, cP) = 1]$$
$$- Pr[\mathcal{B}_{DDH}(G_q, P, aP, bP, abP) = 1]|$$
$$= |\frac{1}{2} - (\frac{1}{2} + \epsilon(\lambda))| \cdot (1 - q_H/2^\lambda)$$

which implies that if $\epsilon(\lambda)$ is non-negligible, then the probability of solving DDH problem $\epsilon(\lambda) \cdot (1 - q_H/2^\lambda)$ is non-negligible too, completing the proof. $\square$

Discussion. Now we consider how security requirements are satisfied by AinQ. (1) *key Freshness:* this requirement is trivially satisfied since each new session key is chosen uniformly at random from the key space making the event of repetitious session keys unlikely to happen. (2) *Group Key Secrecy:* this is a trivial inference of Theorem 1. (3) *Forward Secrecy:* whenever a revocation happens, the team leader executes $\mathsf{Re - Key}$ algorithm to refresh session key and distributes it through the network. Since the refreshed session key K_g^j is chosen independent from all previous session keys $\{K_g^0, K_g^1, \ldots, K_g^i\}$ known to the leaving drone, revoked drone's view is exactly same as the view of an outside adversary. There-fore, a former drone cannot discover subsequent session keys. This can be also deduced from Theorem 1. (4) *Backward Secrecy:* whenever a new drone joins the group, the team leader executes Re − Key algorithm to refresh session key randomly and distributes it through the network. Since all the new session keys $\{K_g^i, K_g^{i+1}, ..., K_g^j\}$ known to the new drone are chosen independent from a pre-vious session key K_g^l, for all $l < i < j$, new drone's view with respect to the prior session keys is exactly same as the view of an outside adversary. Therefore, based on Theorem 1, a new drone can learn about previous session keys only with negligible advantage.

6   Experiments

In this section, we evaluate the performance of the AinQ's core functions and their impact on our target devices. For the purposes of this experiment, we implemented the protocol on devices that are considered to be commercially available. Our testbed was made up of the following boards:

- **Team Leader**: An UP Xtreme board equipped with an Intel Core i7-8665UE SoC, 16 GB RAM, 64 GB storage capacity and an Intel UHD Graphics 620 graphics card[1]. We installed Ubuntu 20.04 on this board and utilized the MIRACL cryptographic library [26] to implement the proposed protocol.
- **Edge Drones**: To provide a comprehensive evaluation on resource-constrai-ned devices, we considered two boards for this role. The Zolertia Re-Mote Revb board which comes equipped with a 32 MHz ARM Cortex-M3 SoC with 512 KB flash, and 32 KB RAM[2], and the SAML11 Xplained Pro board with a 32 MHz ARM Cortex-M23 SoC, 64 KB flash, and 16KB SRAM[3]. Implementations for both boards were built on top of the RIOT [27] OS using the C25519 cryptographic library[4] for RIOT.

6.1   Performance of Core Cryptographic Functions

In this phase of our experiments, we evaluated the performance of the proposed cryptographic functions by measuring their execution times. For each specific entity, we focused on the functions it executes directly. For example, when evalu-ating the performance on the resource-constrained edge drone, we focused exclu-sively on the GenSecretValue, and KeyRetrieval functions. For the team leader, we focused on the GenSecretValue, GenGroupKey, and Re − Key functions.

---

[1] https://up-board.org/up-xtreme/.
[2] https://github.com/Zolertia/Resources/wiki/RE-Mote.
[3] https://www.microchip.com/Developmenttools/ProductDetails/DM320205.
[4] https://www.dlbeer.co.nz/oss/c25519.html.

Edge Drone. During the course of these experiments, we observed that the performance of the proposed functions on the resource-constrained edge drones depended heavily on the number of EC point multiplications performed by the device. Based on the specifications of the chosen target devices, we noticed a considerable difference in the execution times. The SAML11-xpro executed an EC multiplication in approximately 4.782 s while the Zolertia Re-mote board used approximately 2.598 s. Subsequently, the SAML11-xpro executed the GenSecretValue in approximately 5.343 s and the KeyRetrieval function in approximately 4.783 s. The Zolertia Re-mote board on the other hand, executed the GenSecretValue in approximately 2.943 s and the KeyRetrieval function in approximately 2.613 s.

Table 1. Edge drone performance

	EM	SAML11-Xpro Time (sec)	Zolertia Re-mote Time (sec)
EC Multiplication	0	4.782	2.598
GenSecretValue	1	5.343	2.943
KeyRetrieval	1	4.783	2.613

Table 1 provides an overview of the results of the experiments conducted on the edge drone. Each experiment was conducted 50 times with the average time recorded. From the results, we observe that the Zolertia Re-mote is almost twice as efficient as the SAML11 Xplained pro. The difference in the performance results was to be expected based on the resources available to each of the boards.

Team Leader. The overall performance of our proposed protocol at the team leader is determined by the execution of the GenGroupKey and Re − Key functions. To this end, we measure the execution time of the GenGroupKey function for a varying number of edge drones, ranging from 1 to 2,000. When the number of edge drones was 1, GenGroupKey took approximately 0.66 ms to execute whereas when the number of edge drones was 2,000, it executed in approximately 0.72 s. We observed that as the number of edge drones in the group increased, the execution time increased in an efficient manner due to the re-use of the same V parameter for all drones. To be more precise, multiplying 0.66 ms by 2,000 drones resulted in approximately 1.32 s. Consequently, we conclude that the GenGroupKey algorithm achieved an execution time which was about 50% more efficient than the expected performance.

As stated in Subsect. 4.1, the Re − Key function is executed when an edge drone joins the group, leaves the group or the current group key expires. To this end, we measured the execution of the Re − Key function by performing two sets of experiments. The first set focused on renewing an expired key. Similar to the experiments for the GenGroupKey function, we executed the function for a range of 1 to 2,000 edge drones. For the instance of only 1 drone, the function execution

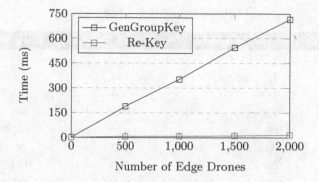

Fig. 2. Performance of the team leader

time was approximately 0.03 ms, while when the number of drones in the group was 2,000, the execution time was approximately 15.28 ms. Figure 2 shows the overall execution times of both the GenGroupKey and Re − Key functions when the number of edge drones ranged from 1 to 2,000.

As a next step, we evaluated the performance of the Re − Key function when new edge drones join a group. To do this, we measured the execution of the Re − Key function when a varying number of new edge drones joined a group while maintaining a varying number of existing group members. When a new drone joins group containing 1 member, the Re − Key function takes approximately 0.47 ms to execute while when 1,000 users join a group which has 1,000 existing members, Re − Key function takes approximately 389.88 ms. Table 2 illustrates the results from these sets of experiments. It is worth mentioning that we exclude evaluations when a drone leaves a group as this is similar to a simple group key re-keying operation.

Comparison with Similar Works: One of our intentions during the experiments, was to compare our scheme with other similar works. We firmly believe that this would make our experimental evaluation more comprehensive. However, this proved to be difficult as similar works based on GKD techniques have not make their code publicly available and therefore we were unable to reproduce their results. However, since we believe that comparison with similar works can give valuable insights about the performance of our work, we attempted to compare our scheme to that presented in [6]. It is worth noting that the scheme in [6] is a certificateless GKA scheme (CL-GAKA) whereas AinQ is certificateless GKD scheme. As such, a comparison was *not* straightforward. For example, we compared the performance of the group key generation by the team leader in AinQ to the group key agreement by x number of users in CL-GAKA. For the purposes of this comparison, we implemented the CL-GAKA scheme on our UP Xtreme board using the PBC library[5]. The implementation was executed over a loopback interface (i.e. the same node emulates all clients considered

---

[5] https://crypto.stanford.edu/pbc/.

Table 2. Group re-key function

Existing Group Members	New Group Members	Time (ms)
1	1	0.47
1	100	32.48
1	500	185.79
1	1000	352.34
100	1	0.98
100	100	35.61
100	500	174.21
100	1000	355.44
500	1	0.59
500	100	39.89
500	500	183.71
500	1000	391.56
1000	1	8.40
1000	100	51.69
1000	500	209.42
1000	1000	389.88

during our experiments), with all measurements recorded over 50 iterations. We measured the performance of CL-GAKA's key agreement phase for three users, excluding the communication overhead, and observed an average time of 24.3 ms. Additionally, we measured a user's performance when executing the computations needed to contribute to the key agreement phase and observed an average time of 5.5 ms. On the other hand, the group key generation phase of AinQ takes approximately 1.22 ms for three users while each user takes an average of 0.22 ms to retrieve a received group key (summing up the group key retrieval time for three users equates to approximately 0.66 ms). These results prove that the key distribution and pairing-free cryptographic approach employed by AinQ make it considerably more efficient than the pairing-based key agreement approach used by CL-GAKA. We acknowledge that the number of users considered for our implementation of CL-GAKA could have been more. However, practically implementing a GKA scheme with a large numbers of users was not a straightforward task; hence, supporting our argument that a GKD scheme is more scalable than a GKA scheme.

Open Science and Reproducible Research: To support open science and reproducible research, our source code for the experiments is publicly available on Github[6].

---

[6] https://github.com/iammrgenie/AinQ.

7   Conclusion

In this paper, a secure pairing-free certificateless group authenticated key distribution protocol is presented. The proposed scheme, AinQ, meets the requirements for a secure group key distribution protocol and considers multiple drones with varying resource constraints. AinQ has been proven efficient for a group with up to 2,000 edge drones when considering a team leader with high computational resources. Our experimental testbed also assessed the performance of AinQ on the Zolertia Re-mote Revb and SamL11-xpro boards, which have minimal resources, with results showing that the scheme can be extended to IoT devices with significant resource constraints. We hope to use AinQ as a foundational scheme to build more secure drone-based applications that can be applied to multiple domains in future works. Additionally, we plan to investigate how to accommodate edge drones off-line during the initial group key broadcast phase using either self-healing, mutual healing, or any lightweight technique that would compliment AinQ efficiently.

References

1. Kugler, L.: Real-world applications for drones. Commun. ACM **62**(11), 19–21 (2019)
2. Altawy, R., Youssef, A.M.: Security, privacy, and safety aspects of civilian drones. ACM Trans. Cyber-Phys. Syst. **1**(2), 1–25 (2017)
3. Akram, R.N., et al.: Security, privacy and safety evaluation of dynamic and static fleets of drones. In: 2017 IEEE/AIAA 36th Digital Avionics Systems Conference (DASC) (2017)
4. Frimpong, E., Bakas, A., Dang, H.-V., Michalas, A.: Do not tell me what i cannot do! (the constrained device shouted under the cover of the fog): implementing symmetric searchable encryption on constrained devices. In: Proceedings of the 5th International Conference on Internet of Things, Big Data and Security (2020)
5. Frimpong, E., Michalas, A.: IoT-CryptoDiet: implementing a lightweight cryptographic library based on ECDH and ECDSA for the development of secure and privacy-preserving protocols in Contiki-NG. In: Proceedings of the 5th International Conference on Internet of Things, Big Data and Security (2020)
6. Semal, B., Markantonakis, K., Akram, R.N.: A certificateless group authenticated key agreement protocol for secure communication in untrusted UAV networks. In: 2018 IEEE/AIAA 37th Digital Avionics Systems Conference (DASC) (2018)
7. Sun, H., Wen, Q., Zhang, H., Jin, Z.: A novel pairing-free certificateless authenticated key agreement protocol with provable security. Front. Comput. Sci. **7**(4), 544–557 (2013)
8. Yang, G., Tan, C.-H.: Strongly secure certificateless key exchange without pairing. In: Proceedings of the 6th ACM Symposium on Information, Computer and Communications Security - ASIACCS 2011 (2011)
9. Xiong, H., Yan, W., Zhenyu, L.: A survey of group key agreement protocols with constant rounds. ACM Comput. Surv. **52**(3), 1–32 (2019)
10. Tian, B., Han, S., Jiankun, H., Dillon, T.: A mutual-healing key distribution scheme in wireless sensor networks. J. Netw. Comput. Appl. **34**(1), 80–88 (2011)

11. Kumar, V., Kumar, R., Pandey, S.K.: A computationally efficient centralized group key distribution protocol for secure multicast communications based upon RSA public key cryptosystem. J. King Saud Univ. Comput. Inf. Sci. **32**(9), 1081–1094 (2020)
12. Katz, J., Yung, M.: Scalable protocols for authenticated group key exchange. In: Boneh, D. (ed.) CRYPTO 2003. LNCS, vol. 2729, pp. 110–125. Springer, Heidelberg (2003). https://doi.org/10.1007/978-3-540-45146-4_7
13. Al-Riyami, S.S., Paterson, K.G.: Certificateless public key cryptography. In: Advances in Cryptology - ASIACRYPT 2003, pp. 452–473 (2003)
14. Lee, E.-J., Lee, S.-E., Yoo, K.-Y.: A certificateless authenticated group key agreement protocol providing forward secrecy. In: 2008 International Symposium on Ubiquitous Multimedia Computing (2008)
15. Tedeschi, P., Sciancalepore, S., Eliyan, A., Di Pietro, R.: LiKe: lightweight certificateless key agreement for secure IoT communications. IEEE Internet Things J. **7**(1), 621–638 (2020)
16. Won, J., Seo, S.-H., Bertino, E.: A secure communication protocol for drones and smart objects. In: Proceedings of the 10th ACM Symposium on Information, Computer and Communications Security (2015)
17. Boyd, C., Nieto, J.M.: Round-optimal contributory conference key agreement. In: Public Key Cryptography - PKC 2003, pp. 161–174 (2002)
18. Bresson, E., Catalano, D.: Constant round authenticated group key agreement via distributed computation. In: Public Key Cryptography - PKC 2004, pp. 115–129 (2004)
19. Dutta, R., Barua, R.: Constant round dynamic group key agreement. In: Zhou, J., Lopez, J., Deng, R.H., Bao, F. (eds.) ISC 2005. LNCS, vol. 3650, pp. 74–88. Springer, Heidelberg (2005). https://doi.org/10.1007/11556992_6
20. Nam, J., Lee, J., Kim, S., Won, D.: DDH-based group key agreement in a mobile environment. J. Syst. Softw. **78**(1), 73–83 (2005)
21. Rafaeli, S., Hutchison, D.: A survey of key management for secure group communication. ACM Comput. Surv. **35**(3), 309–329 (2003)
22. Li, X., Wang, Y., Vijayakumar, P., He, D., Kumar, N., Ma, J.: Blockchain-based mutual-healing group key distribution scheme in unmanned aerial vehicles ad-hoc network. IEEE Trans. Veh. Technol. **68**(11), 11309–11322 (2019)
23. Agrawal, S., Das, M.L.: Mutual healing enabled group-key distribution protocol in wireless sensor networks. Comput. Commun. **112**, 131–140 (2017)
24. Agrawal, S., Patel, J., Das, M.L.: Pairing based mutual healing in wireless sensor networks. In: 2016 8th International Conference on Communication Systems and Networks (COMSNETS) (2016)
25. Kurosawa, K.: Multi-recipient public-key encryption with shortened ciphertext. In: Naccache, D., Paillier, P. (eds.) PKC 2002. LNCS, vol. 2274, pp. 48–63. Springer, Heidelberg (2002). https://doi.org/10.1007/3-540-45664-3_4
26. Scott, M., McCusker, K., Budroni, A.: The MIRACL core library. https://github.com/miracl/core
27. Baccelli, E., Hahm, O., Gunes, M., Wahlisch, M., Schmidt, T.: RIOT OS: towards an OS for the internet of things. In: 2013 IEEE Conference on Computer Communications Workshops (INFOCOM WKSHPS) (2013)

Security in Internet of Things

X-Pro: Distributed XDP Proxies Against Botnets of Things

Syafiq Al Atiiq[(⊠)] and Christian Gehrmann

Department of Electrical and Information Technology, Lund University,
Lund, Sweden
{syafiq_al.atiiq,christian.gehrmann}@eit.lth.se

Abstract. The steadily increasing Internet of Things (IoT) devices are vulnerable to be used as bots to launch distributed-denial-of-service (DDoS) attacks. In this paper, we present X-Pro, a distributed XDP proxy to counteract DDoS attacks. We propose a source-based defense mechanism where proxies located between the IoT devices and the victim performs flow policing on all IoT traffic from a single administrative domain. The proposed proxy architecture can be integrated in widely used IoT frameworks as well as telecommunication networks. The proxies are working synchronously to block bogus messages and to detect traffic levels above predefined thresholds. Our implementation leverages eXpress Data Path (XDP), a programmable packet processing in the Linux kernel, as the main engine in the proxy. We evaluate X-Pro from several standpoints and conclude that our solution offers efficient DoS traffic blocking for both low-rate or massive attacks. Depending on the device side implementation selection, the computational overhead is cheap at the cost of some bandwidth loss.

Keywords: Proxy · Denial of Service · Security

1 Introduction

Denial of Service Attacks (DoS) has harmed the internet since the early 1980s. DoS prevents legitimate users from reaching their services and still constitute a major problem. In September 2016, a tremendous Distributed DoS (DDoS) attack was launched against several high-profile websites: OVH [1], Dyn [2], and Krebs on Security [3]. Surprisingly, the source came from a vast amount of embedded devices turned into bots. A master process controls these bots, which is later known as the Mirai botnets [4]. Mirai scanned the internet and infected embedded devices running with insecure default password.

Based on the attack strategy, an adversary can design the botnets to be launched, either as a periodically low-rate [5–7], or a massive [8] DDoS attack. The low-rate DDoS behaves identically to the regular traffic pattern, making

Work supported by framework grant RIT17-0032 from the Swedish Foundation for Strategic Research and the EU H2020 project CloudiFacturing under grant 768892.

© Springer Nature Switzerland AG 2021
N. Tuveri et al. (Eds.): NordSec 2021, LNCS 13115, pp. 51–71, 2021.
https://doi.org/10.1007/978-3-030-91625-1_4

it difficult to detect by firewalls, routers, and switches. Furthermore, in an IoT setting, low-rate DDoS is not only a threat against the target nodes; as IoT devices often are battery-driven and resource-constrained, such attacks can severely harm the device itself.

Traditionally, DoS is handled at the victim-end or core-end, applying network-level detection and filtering [9]. However, as the type of DoS threats are very diverse, so are the suggested countermeasures. The majority of the works focus on the detection and blocking of harmful traffic [10]. Three main detection approaches occur in the literature: Signature-Based Approach (SBA), Anomaly Based Approach (ABA), and Entropy-Based Approach (EBA). SBA and ABA share many characteristics with traditional intrusion detection systems, while EBA is a pure traffic analysis approach [11].

We have observed that this traditional way of handling DDoS does not consider the new IoT communication patterns. Especially, the following aspects are fundamentally different from an IoT perspective:

- IoT devices typically do not primarily communicate with general internet services but are directed towards a specific backend.
- Botnet threats on IoT entities are undesirable from a resource perspective, and this gives a large incentive for IoT device owners to implement DDoS countermeasures at the *source* not just on the network level.

Inspired by earlier successful of source-end approaches such as D-WARD [12], we reconsider the DDoS problem from an IoT application perspective. We argue that DDoS blocking and detection can efficiently be applied by strong policing on IoT *flow* level and that such policing preferably takes place at the IoT backend. As we show in our paper, X-Pro can be easily integrated into an existing IoT backend as well as into already deployed telecommunication network. To show that this is indeed an efficient approach, we have designed a DDoS filtering architecture based on simple flow counts where packet count and policing take place on ordinary backend servers. This is very similar to an EBA detection mechanism, but we argue that we can filter using absolute flow thresholds in a strong and controlled IoT environment. To be able to get a fast packet processing in the kernel context, we utilize XDP [13]. X-Pro can be combined with traditional DoS detection mechanisms using, for instance, SBA or ABA. However, to secure basic functionality and IoT availability, the first step is to filter using flow thresholds. In this paper, we show how to use our architecture with such flow threshold values and policing. We call our solution X-Pro, coordinated XDP proxies running together as distributed systems to detect and filter out attack messages. Our solution can be combined with more advanced detection mechanisms, which will be left for future work. Our main purpose is to show that our approach is efficient in terms of overload blocking and that it can be implemented in existing IoT backends and devices with a reasonable performance overhead. In summary, the paper presents the following contributions:

- We provide a new framework (namely X-Pro) to counteract an attack towards a victim from the context of the IoT unit as the adversary.

- We suggest novel algorithms for packet filtering within a proxy and packet data synchronization between proxies.
- We provide an implementation and performance evaluation of the proxy using XDP, a novel programmable packet processing hook in the Linux kernel.
- We present IoT side realization and show the packet handling overhead.

The rest of the paper is organized as follows. We discuss related works and backgrounds in Sects. 2 and 3. We provide the solution in Sect. 4. Section 5 presents the implementation, while in Sect. 6, we provide the performance evaluation. Section 7 draws our conclusions and anticipates future works.

2   Related Work

First, we distinguish between high and low-rate DDoS. We start by discussing the former and then continue with the latter. DDoS can be performed by flooding the victim with massive and bogus messages to consume bandwidth or resources. Such mechanism, behavior, mitigation strategies, and the detailed taxonomy are defined in [8]. The author distinguishes the DDoS mitigation strategy into two categories, namely: (i.) *collaborative*, where multiple nodes are cooperating to mitigate DDoS, and (ii.) *non-cooperative*, in which no collaboration between network elements occurred.

Examples of *collaborative* strategies: FireCol [14], CoFence [15], and CoDef [16]. FireCol observes the occurrence of DDoS attacks at the Internet Service Provider (ISP) level, in which the ISPs form a subscription mechanism between each other. If FireCol detects an attack within an ISP, it informs the occurrence to the upstream ISPs, which consecutively perform a similar mitigation process. To detect such an attack, one of the most widely used method is Kullback-Leibler divergence and Shannon's entropy, where malicious traffic is detected based on IP address or packet size distribution statistics [17,18]. Our investigations use simple packet frequency thresholds for DDoS detection, and we also adopt a detection window approach. However, we do not focus on advanced detection rules but use firm and a priori thresholds. This is motivated by the fact that the main research goal in this paper *is not* to evaluate detection principles but rather to introduce a new proxy model for DDoS prevention, an efficient filter based on XDP and corresponding packet distribution data sharing principle between the proxies. Our approach can be extended to handle traditional, statistical detection methods based on the frequency counts provided by our solution.

Non-cooperative strategies include dynamic resource scaling [19], scaling via low-cost untrusted CDN (Content Delivery Network) [20], and harnessing DPI (Deep Packet Inspection) in SDN (Software Defined Networks) [21]. The dynamic resource scaling offers a resource allocation strategy based on the queueing theory when idle VMs (Virtual Machine) are utilized once DDoS occurred. However, as the VM is not free, the occurrence of DDoS might emerge to become an Economic-DoS [22], where the adversary shifts the target to the economic aspect of the victim. In this case, the resources in the intermediate nodes are occupied as the attack reaches the network between adversaries and victims.

Both *collaborative* and *non-cooperative* mitigation approaches mentioned are for high-rate DDoS. We argue that the occurrence of high-rate DDoS should be solved along with the low-rate DDoS at the same time. Examples of low-rate DDoS are shrew-attack [5], LoRDAS [6], and reduction-of-quality (ROQ) [7]. Shrew-attack abuses the weakness of TCP's retransmission timeout (RTO) procedure. A legitimate TCP flow is being attacked by regularly dispatching a high-rate bogus message simultaneously of the RTO. This way, once a sender restores from timeout, they will instantly receive a subsequent attack and probably go back to the timeout phase again. Low-rate DDoS are usually detected by employing a frequency domain analysis, i.e., Discrete-Fourier-Transform in one of the component in the system. Example of such mechanism is described in [23]. To this point, X-Pro does not utilize or employ such analysis or any related statistical method to perform DDoS occurrence detection. But rather, we provide the data to be used by the system designer to employ such a method. It is possible to use an advanced method, i.e., machine learning working together alongside X-Pro, to perform more sophisticated analysis to set the X-Pro filtering thresholds. Extending X-Pro in this regard is for future work.

We utilize XDP extensively in this work. XDP has been around for a couple of years and has been used by some companies and open source projects to perform high-speed packet processing. Cloudflare [24] publicly announce that XDP is used in their DDoS mitigation pipeline. Suricata, an open-source Intrusion Detection System (IDS) provides XDP plugin [25] to their IDS. Also, Facebook has been extensively harnessing XDP as they claim that every packet reaching their network is being processing by XDP enabled application [26].

3   XDP and BPF Maps

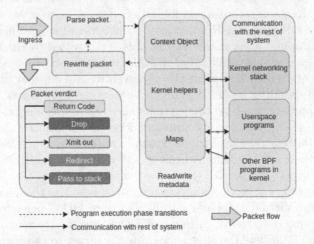

Fig. 1. Execution flow of a typical XDP program, as described in [13]

XDP [13] is a novel programmable packet processing hook living inside the kernel-space. In XDP, the underlying operating system accommodates a safe execution environment to run an eBPF[1] program. This execution happens within the device driver context. XDP has been part of the mainland Linux kernel since 4.8 [28]. XDP provides a safe, fast, and customizable packet processing integrated with the kernel networking stack. An execution flow of a typical XDP program can be seen in Fig. 1. The logic of the eBPF program running inside the XDP hook is written in a high-level language, i.e., C, and compiled into bytecode. The kernel has the job of safeguarding the eBPF program by verifying it. This verification happens during the load time of the program.

Within the XDP execution environment, eBPF programs are executed in return to an event, i.e., when the packet arrives. The eBPF program does not have access to persistent memory within the boundary of its program context. Instead, the kernel provides the eBPF program a similar feature with access to a so-called *BPF maps* [13]. It is a generic data structure to store many different data types. Similar to a database, the format of BPF maps are key/value stores defined before loading an eBPF program to an interface. An eBPF code can refer to BPF maps within its codebase, just like referring to a memory. Figure 1 shows the relationship between BPF maps with other entities in the system.

4   The X-Pro Solution

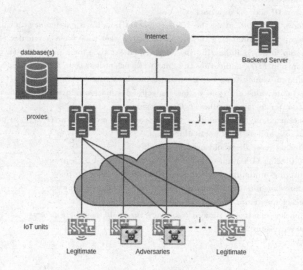

Fig. 2. Overall X-Pro architecture

---

[1] eBPF [27] refers to extended-BPF, the newer version of original BPF (Berkeley Packet Filter).

In this section, we present X-Pro, a distributed XDP-based proxy to counteract DDoS. Under the assumption that an adversary can infect IoT units but not prevent packets from flowing over the proxies (see also our discussion regarding device-side implementation in Sect. 4.5), X-Pro prevents servers from being overwhelmed by DDoS by blocking the unwanted traffic with distributed proxies. When a filtering decision is taken, the system also automatically detects a potential DDoS attempt. To handle distributed DoS, information about traffic condition is shared between the proxies via a centralized database node. For the rest of the paper, we follow notations from Table 1.

4.1 Overall Architecture and Solution

Table 1. Notations

U	Set of IoT units in the system
$u \in U$	An IoT unit
P	Set of proxies in the system
$p \in P$	Proxy
i	A unique index given to an IoT unit
u_i	An IoT unit with index i
j	A proxy unique network address associated with a proxy
p_j	A proxy with address j
M_{DB}	A centralized database
L_{DB}	A local database at p_j
D_{addr}	Destination IP address of a packet
ts_1'	Time stamp in p_j indicating the "oldest" packet time for a particular (i, D_{addr})
ts_2'	Time stamp in p_j indicating the "most recent" packet time for a particular (i, D_{addr})
ts_1	Time stamp in M_{DB} indicating the "oldest" packet time for a particular (i, D_{addr})
ts_2	Time stamp in M_{DB} indicating the "most recent" packet time for a particular (i, D_{addr})
ts_1*	The minimum value of ts_1 in p_j for a specific destination address among U
ts_2*	The maximum value of ts_2 in p_j for a specific destination address among U
c	Packet counter for a particular (i, D_{addr}) pair
dc	Delta packet counter (internally within a proxy) for a particular (i, D_{addr}) pair
$c*$	The sum of c and dc for a particular D_{addr}
T_{T1}	First filtering reset threshold used by a proxy
T_{T2}	Second Filtering minimum measure time threshold used by a proxy
T_{T3}	Third filtering minimum measure time threshold used by a proxy
T_{T4}	Fourth filtering minimum measure time threshold used by a proxy
T_{F1}	First packet maximum allowed frequency threshold used by a proxy
T_{F2}	Second packet maximum allowed frequency threshold used by a proxy
r	Frequency division factor

The X-Pro overall architecture can be seen in Fig. 2. The first part is a set of proxy $P \ni p_1, ..., p_n$ interconnected through internal network. To have a broader view of the system at a particular time, each proxy node shares logging and load information between each other, leveraging a centralized database M_{DB}. The synched information is described in more detail in Sect. 4.3. The next part in the system is IoT units ($U \ni u_1, ..., u_n$). Each unit must have the connectivity to at least one available proxy within $p_1, ..., p_n$. It is possible to have multiple connections from a single u_i towards multiple p_j. We allow the adversaries to control IoT units U, meaning that a message proxy p_j receives from an IoT unit might be bogus.

One can apply X-Pro into an existing IoT backend, such as Thingsboard [29] and Mainflux [30]. In Thingsboard, there is a transport layer where the job is to receive messages from the devices, then parse the messages, which are then forwarded to one of the queues. X-Pro acts as a complement of Thingsboard transport with an additional feature of DDoS mitigation. As we show later in Sect. 4.5, X-Pro requires an IoT device to set up an IP tunnel to the proxy. This fits naturally in the connection between the device and the Thingsboard transport. An advantage of this approach is the device does not have to resolve the domain of the Thingsboard transport as everything happens in the IP layer. However, as we require all the traffic from the device to pass the proxy, there is an additional mechanism to forward the packet outside the Thingsboard core if devices want to send the packet outside the X-Pro network. Hence, X-Pro can live to coexist without having to break the existing implementation.

Another option is to put X-Pro into an existing telecom infrastructure. The 5G network allows us to have multi-access edge computing (MEC) [31] close to the radio base station. As the purpose of MEC is to get an application closer to the user, we can utilize distributed MEC to be attached with X-Pro software in its network interface. This will make sure that the changes in the network operator side will be as minimum as possible. Even if, for example, 5G network deployment is still far away plan for some network operator, we can deploy X-Pro (within MEC) in the existing 4G network [32]. One possibility is to make X-Pro acts as a user plane packet inspection in the S1U interface between SGW (Serving Gateway) and eNodeB.

4.2 Filtering Design

We use a filtering approach where each packet arrived at a particular proxy, is analyzed, and potentially blocked[2]. Such mechanism is performed as early as possible, i.e., in the XDP hook. The blocking decision is based on a set of threshold parameters (see also the notation in Table 1). These can be *tuned* to get the right trade-off between security and false blocking decisions. We discuss and review different threshold parameter selections, performance, and DoS packet endpoint reaching rates in Sect. 6.

---

[2] Blocking automatically also implies a potential attack detection. Our solution can be adapted such that we use lower threshold values for detection than blocking decisions. For simplicity, we only consider a single blocking threshold.

The filtering is done using a time window, defined by two-time values, ts_1 and ts_2 for each target address for any ongoing traffic flow at any p_j. Each p_j is assumed to keep corresponding time values and packet counts. The current *local* view of the time window is denoted by ts'_1 and ts'_2. The packet frequency for each target destination is calculated regularly and compared with the frequency thresholds T_{F1} and T_{F2}. The first frequency threshold T_{F1} indicates the maximum allowed packet rate from one particular IoT unit to one *specific* endpoint. The second threshold T_{F2} indicates the *accumulated* maximum allowed packet rate (from all connected IoT units) towards one specific endpoint. In a corner case, it might be possible for the legitimate u_i to be falsely blocked by p_j due to a circumstance when a single victim is being attacked with a low-rate traffic from many compromised u_i. This will make the accumulated traffic become higher than T_{F2}. To accommodate this case, we provide a non-policed flow to be attached to a specific source (i.e. legitimate u_i). However, as it is now being done manually, the proposal for performing this task automatically is left for future work. For simplicity, we only consider a system-wide and *common* threshold values, T_{F1} and T_{F2}. However, the very same principle can be applied to a system where *individual* threshold values are given to specific destination addresses or destination address ranges. The latter would be the case envisioned for most applications, but our simplification will not make any major difference when evaluating the effectiveness of our approach. The complete filtering algorithm (Algorithm 2) is shown in Appendix B.

4.3   Synchronization Design

To have the same visibility on each proxy, one needs to have a synchronization function between them. This section explains in more detail such procedures. For every time period t, each proxy p_j performs the synchronization procedure with the centralized database, M_{DB}. p_j iterates through every (i, D_{addr}) received from M_{DB}, and for each pair of (i, D_{addr}), p_j looks up at the corresponding values in the local database, L_{DB}. If a newer data is available, each entity (either p_j or M_{DB}) will update each other. The rule of thumb here is that a newer data will always replace an older one. The synchronization between p_j and M_{DB} are assumed to be over a secure end-to-end communication channel. We consider $p \in P$ are trustworthy, hence a direct attack on them are out of scope of this paper. We have come up with a synchronization procedure that tries to cover the most important aspects for keeping consistent time window and counts among the proxies; see the Algorithm 1 in Appendix A. The way M_{DB} implemented is agnostic to any particular technology. We assume that M_{DB} is robust, reliable, and impossible to be killed no matter how high the DDoS attack is. To achieve that, it is possible to design M_{DB} as a distributed system as described in [33, 34]. However, the design of such system is out of scope of this paper.

The main challenge with the synchronization lies in the counts and count window in L_{DB} might be different from M_{DB} since the last synchronization. Hence, the synchronization must be able to cope with these changes. The algorithm handles this by comparing the local time window ts_1' and ts_2' with the corresponding ones loaded from M_{DB}, ts_1 and ts_2. Furthermore, to stop the count window growing to infinity, we must reduce the size if the time window is getting too large. Such identification happens locally, and the rest of the proxies must adjust their values accordingly at their next synchronization. Besides, if no record for a particular address occurs for a while, our filtering algorithm resets the count (this is indicated through a `mark` parameter). Such reset should be propagated to the rest of the proxies *only* if they have not received a similar destination packet for a time exceeding a predefined threshold. These aspects, as well as making sure that the counts and the window are consistent, are the primary purpose of our synchronization design which has been verified through the experiments. The different time thresholds can be tuned to get the suitable trade-off between filtering efficiency and synchronization overhead.

4.4 Proxy Design Based on XDP

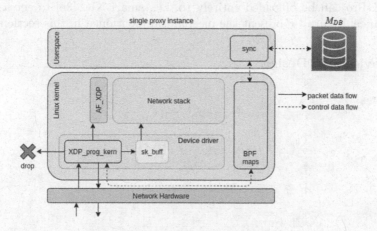

Fig. 3. A proxy instance

As mentioned in Sect. 3, XDP can process the packet at the earliest possible hook. An advantage of this feature is the associated device driver, which handles the packet, does not need to allocate the memory if it turns out that the incoming packet is not legitimate. This, in return, would require a lot less resource on the proxy if the attack turns out to be massive. We intend to exploit this feature as the underlying mechanism as defined in more detail in this chapter.

As described in Sect. 4.3, the information ts_1, ts_2, c for each incoming packet needs to be shared among P. It is natural to pass this information to p_j's userspace first, then perform the synchronization with M_{DB} from there. The sync function should be executed between the local database, L_{DB}, which is represented by BPF maps, and the centralized M_{DB}. It is fairly trivial to integrate such mechanism using API provided by M_{DB} as well as local API of BPF maps [35]. For any new information ts_1, ts_2, c recorded from the XDP program, the data is stored in L_{DB}. If newer data is found, the old data is replaced.

Once the local BPF maps are filled with the needed information, the next job is to propagate this to all other proxies in P, via M_{DB}, as well as retrieving data from M_{DB} that is not available locally. Note that all the synchronized information is only statistics of the packet, not the packet itself. Meaning that, only small amount of transactions between p_j and M_{DB} is needed. This mechanism allows us to pass the information between proxies without sending the invalid packet to the userspace. Hence, reducing the resource utilization in the userspace. Therefore, the proxy can allocate the resource to a more essential task, i.e., packet filtering in the kernel. Our rationale is that the fewer tasks performed in the userspace, the more resource can be utilized by the XDP to block the invalid messages; hence we get more packet filtering capacity in the kernel. Furthermore, as our codebase does not require access to a specific kernel helper, X-Pro can be offloaded entirely to, i.e., smart-NIC [36] to get a better performance. Figure 3 represent the mechanism mentioned in this section.

4.5   Device Side Design

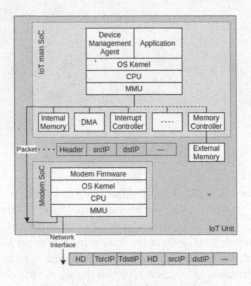

Fig. 4. An IoT implementation

The X-Pro design requires all traffic from the IoT units are routed through the proxy. An attacker aware of this principle can circumvent this mechanism by avoiding the whole proxy network, and fulfill the DoS target. Therefore, it is a mandatory design requirement for the IoT device to prevent its IP traffic control part from being infected by a malicious software. A legacy IoT device can connect to p_j as long as it has a way to separate the main and network MCU securely, i.e. through secure virtualization. Several different techniques are possible. In this section, we discuss a possible design where the modem SoC is separated from the main SoC, allowing secure proxy packet encapsulation.

The job of the modem SoC is to perform proxy management and provides a standard network interface from the operating system within an IoT device. Figure 4 shows the connection between the main SoC and the modem SoC within the IoT unit u_i. The modem SoC keeps track of available proxies P in the system. It is possible to change the current destination proxy, p_j, if, for example, the one currently used is overloaded or unavailable. Information about load and availability is obtained through a probing mechanism. Two different solutions are possible:

- The modem SoC connected to an arbitrary proxy p and received the load information of all the proxies within P. The received information is then used to decide which p_j has the minimum load among the proxies, P.
- The modem SoC measures multiple p_j within P at once by sending a ping request and calculate the lowest response time among the measured proxies.

As shown in Fig. 4, the modem SoC embed an additional header as a tunnel header. It tunnels all outbound traffic to the selected proxy from the previous mechanism. The tunnel itself can be implemented as a raw IP tunnel, HTTP, or even CoAP [37] where the source IP packet is encapsulated. This way, X-Pro would not prevent an IP level (or even HTTP) end-to-end security, such as IPSec. Unlike the outbound connections, the inbound traffic is treated entirely transparent and does not affect the modem or the whole IoT unit in any way.

5   Implementation

This section will describe the technical implementation of proxies, the centralized database, and the device packet handling in more detail. The code is available as open-source[3].

5.1   Proxy

The proxy implementation consists of two different parts, that is kernel space and userspace. The kernel space implementation mostly deals with the filtering mechanism for each incoming packet, whereas the userspace implementation deals with the synchronization between proxies. Within the kernel space, the

---

[3] https://github.com/syafiq/xpro.

Algorithm 2 is implemented as an eBPF program [38], written in C. The eBPF program is attached to one of the interfaces in the proxy, p_j.

Each proxy p_j synchronizes the local BPF map to M_{DB} for every pre-defined period t. The synchronization utilizes BPF helpers [39], i.e. bpf_map_lookup_elem and bpf_map_get_next_key. These functions is periodically called to iterate through the BPF maps and update the M_{DB}. To read/write through the M_{DB}, we harness hiredis [40], a redis client written as a C library.

5.2   Centralized Database

The database M_{DB} is a single Redis instance running inside a virtual machine. M_{DB} must have connectivity to all the proxies in the system.

5.3   IoT Units

We have developed the proof of concept for the IoT units using a low-cost platform ESP32 [41] and FiPy [42]. The aim is to provide a real-world example of performing procedures explained in Sect. 4.5. The process should be transparent to the applications running in the main SoC, and both processes should be completely separated from each other. It means the application should not handle the proxy selections and packet encapsulation mechanism, but rather the modem SoC does. This gives a solid separation between the systems and strong protection against software attacks of the main system. In our proof of concept, the ESP32 acts as the modem SoC, whereas FiPy acts as the main SoC. Both boards are connected through the UART pinouts. In our PoC, the ESP32 board runs on a native operating system from espressif, esp-idf [41]. We modify the firmware such that any outgoing packet is always encapsulated, with one of the proxy p being the new destination IP. As mentioned earlier, the old destination IP is preserved, along with the payload from the application in the main SoC.

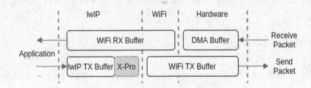

Fig. 5. TCP/IP stack modification in ESP32

As UART speed is fairly slow compared to, i.e., wireless connection, we decided to build a second prototype in which the encapsulation process happens in the TCP/IP stack. We modify the lightweight TCP/IP stack from the ESP32 firmware at the last point of IP encapsulation (within the lwIP TX buffer) before the packet is moved into the WiFi TX buffer. Figure 5 shows where exactly our modification happen within the ESP32 TCP/IP stack. From a security point of view, this would require either of the two following options:

- The logic from Sect. 4.5 is implemented in a hardware (i.e., VHDL), such that adversaries cannot tamper or modify the encapsulation process.
- The TCP/IP stack lives in a trusted environment (i.e., ARM TrustZone [43, 44]) such that the isolation is built-in into the main CPU and SoC.

In our proof of concept, we have *not* made a full implementation of any of these two options. However, the overhead with a pure hardware solution would undoubtedly be less than our chosen proof of concept implementation. The Trust-Zone option or any other virtualization options like using a thin I/O hypervisor [45] is left for future work.

6   Experimental Evaluation

Next, we evaluate the design and realization through a proof of concept. We have made a full implementation of the design on the proxy and the device side as described in Sect. 5. The proxies and the centralized database are implemented as a virtual machine in Fedora 30 operating system, running kernel version 5.6. All of the VMs of the proxies and centralized database are running with one vCPU and 1024 MB of memory. We simulate the IoT units (infected and non-infected with botnets) with a Linux machine, running PKTGEN [46] software from the Linux kernel tree, with adjustable intensity. PKTGEN sends CoAP messages, in which the size of each packet is 64 bytes. Message rates can easily be set through the *ratep* value in the PKTGEN configuration file.

Our evaluation goal is to measure how effective the suggested solution in terms of packet blocking for both single high-rate attack and low-rate attacks using fixed attack thresholds. We also measure the pure overhead at the device side for our two different implementation options (see also Sect. 5.3). As some IoT units might be expected to send relatively high amount of traffic, typically directed to a particular server node, we would like to measure how well our DoS blocking principle works in a situation where we have a mixture of such high rate, valid traffic, and DoS traffic. We use a simple approach where some IoT units are allowed to send traffic at their maximum capacity without being blocked while the rest are subject for the filtering with thresholds. In a more realistic setting, the flows that should be policed or not can be set in a more fine grained way and vary over time. However, to simplify our measurement, we only use two static categories of devices, i.e. units with non policed traffic and devices with policed flows. A more advanced principle that label flows in a more intelligent way using for instance, machine learning, is left for future work [47,48].

6.1   Single-Proxy

In this scenario, a single proxy instance p_j sits between IoT units and the victim. An infected unit becomes an adversary and an unit without policed traffic (without upper-threshold) that is assumed to be not infected by the botnets. Both the units, either the infected or the non blocked one, are sending packets towards the victim with various intensity, ranging from 50000–400000 packets per second. These values are picked merely based on the capability of our test hardware[4]. While performing packet forwarding to the backend server (or victim), p_j drops incoming messages if it senses a DoS attack. This mechanism is based on the algorithm we mention in Sect. 4.4. Even though it does not seem to make sense that a single IoT unit can generate such magnitude of the attack, we argue this measurement is still crucial for the following reason. We can test the limit on how high proxy p_j can cope with a DoS attack within the context of provided hardware, i.e., one vCPU and 1 GB RAM.

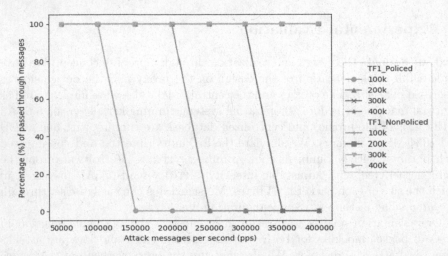

Fig. 6. % of passed through messages on a single proxy varies to the attack intensity

Figure 6 shows the percentages of packets being passed to the backend server by p_j varies to the attack intensity in packets per second (PPS). As the intensity of the incoming packet exceeds the value of TF_1, more than 99% of the packets are efficiently dropped if the source comes from the infected IoT units. When this happens, only less than 1% of the bogus messages are forwarded as p_j needs some time to calculate the frequency before deciding what action needs to be performed for the subsequent packet. For example, when $TF_1 = 300k$ and attack messages $= 400k$, only 0.3% of total messages are forwarded to the final destination, while the rest are dropped. However, no messages from IoT units marked to not be subject to blocking are dropped by p_j.

---

[4] To put into perspective, the whole New York area has been deployed with 15000 security cameras by NYPD [49]. So, depends on what application is used and how many sensors needed, we think that 50000–400000 make sense.

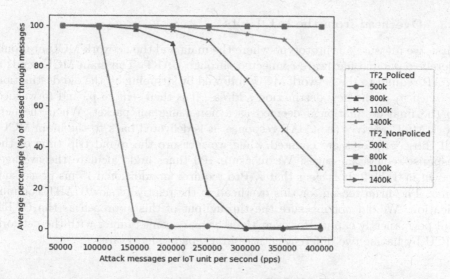

Fig. 7. Average % of passed through messages on the multiple proxies P varies to the attack intensity

6.2 Multiple-Proxy Working Together

In this scenario, a set of proxies $p_j \in P$, where $j = 1, 2, 3, 4$ sits between multiple IoT units. Also, a set of IoT units $u_i \in U$ where $i = 1, 2, ..., 8$ are connected to the set of proxies P. Each p_j is connected to two IoT units $u_{i_{odd}}$ and $u_{i_{even}}$, where $u_{i_{odd}} = 2j - 1$ and $u_{i_{even}} = 2j$. It means, for example, p_1 is connected to u_1 and u_2, p_2 is connected to u_3 and u_4, and so on. In this experiment, we have set $u_{i_{odd}}$ to acts as an infected IoT unit, while $u_{i_{even}}$ are not subject to traffic policing, i.e. they are allowed to send traffic at their maximum capacity. Each unit sends packets to the victim with various intensity, ranging from 50000–400000 PPS, and p_j performs a synchronization towards M_{DB} for every 4 s. Note that these values are determined heuristically, in which the equation and/or derivation of such values are out of the scope of this paper.

We perform this measurement to show how X-Pro handles a situation where multiple adversaries are trying to launch an attack under the radar, i.e., sending attack messages just below TF_1 with the hope that attack packets can slip through p_j. As we can see later, this is not the case as p_j has been implemented with the procedure mentioned in Sect. 4.4. Figure 7 shows the average percentages of packets being passed by p_j varies to the packets intensity per second from each u_i. In the infected IoT units $u_{i_{odd}}$, we can clearly see that all $p_j \in P$ start to drop incoming packet from $u_{i_{odd}}$ when 4× incoming packets is greater than TF_2. This is expected, as we have four units of devices turned into botnets.

Among the units $u_{i_{even}}$, all packets are forwarded to the backend server as the incoming packets from these sources are not counted to get the frequency value. We can see from Fig. 7, that the average percentages for $u_{i_{even}}$ are 100%.

6.3 Overhead from the IoT Units

First, we measure our prototype where the main and the network MCU are completely separated hardware connected through UART. The main MCU sends a CoAP request to the network MCU, followed by stripping off the old destination IP with p_j as the new destination address. It is then sent to p_j and forwarded to the final destination if deemed as a non-malignant packet. When the network MCU receives the CoAP response, it is delivered back to the main MCU. All those processes are counted while we measure the round trip time of the response-request messages. We measure 100 times and calculate the average, shown in Table 2. It is clear that X-Pro requires an additional 15 ms processing time. The main reason for this overhead is the relatively slow UART communication. We did not measure the throughput of this approach as the UART will permanently cap it. However, the adversary can't tamper with the network MCU by having two different entities in a separate hardware.

Table 2. Overhead of the IoT device

	Separated main MCU and network MCU	lwIP logic of encapsulation	
	Average RTT (ms)	Average RTT (ms)	Average throughput (Mbits/s)
X-Pro	50.55	37.67	25.86
vanilla	35.96	36.78	30.37

Second, to get a clear picture of how much overhead is added when we have such an encapsulation process, we decided to implement our solution in a fully softwarized manner. However, this is with the assumption that already mentioned in Sect. 5.3. We can see from Table 2 that our solution only adds about 1 ms of the total round trip time. However, the throughput is a bit decreased by around 5 Mbits/s. The reason is there is additional overhead to process each packet due to the IP tunnel, i.e., encapsulating a new header such that the new destination IP is one of the proxy $p_j \in P$. This gives an extra 32-bits (the size of an IPv4) for each packet because the real destination should be preserved while the new destination is installed.

All the IoT unit overheads and extra implementation penalties can be avoided in the network situations where layer two mechanisms allow network enforced routing through proxies. It is possible to mix such configuration with IoT IP tunneling configurations for some IoT units in the system. It is also possible to dynamically switch on and off the proxy forwarding function in the IoT units. When a DDoS attack is not expected, the protection mechanism is switched off, avoiding the bandwidth loss penalty for a certain amount of time.

To complement the example that has been provided in Sect. 4.1, we measure the average round trip time (RTT) from the IoT device to the Thingsboard backend. The IoT device sends a CoAP message with the method POST and subsequently expecting an acknowledgment message. We measure the RTT as the time difference when the IoT device sends the CoAP message and receives the respective acknowledgment. The CoAP POST message is repeated 100 times, and the average value is calculated, as shown in Table 3. We can see that X-Pro adds 2 ms overhead, a small fraction of the total average time.

Table 3. Thingsboard with and without X-Pro

	Average RTT (ms)
Thingsboard + X-Pro	82.93
Thingsboard	80.98

7   Conclusion and Future Work

This paper has presented X-Pro, a distributed XDP proxies against botnets of things. The design of distributed proxies is armed with a centralized database, allowing the proxies to inform each other about the latest event in the networks. Through this collaboration, it is possible to defend the victim amid the situations when the adversaries are trying to send, (i.) a massive and well-coordinated attack towards the victim through a single proxy, (ii.) periodically low-rate bogus messages spanned to multiple proxies in which the intention is to fly under the radar. We have proven that this is indeed the case in practice through our experimental evaluations. The obtained results show that our solution allows strong protection of overload to both of the IoT backend and external attack targets. X-Pro requires the IoT units to be modified in regards to the network interface modem. As the adversary cannot tamper with the modification, they cannot re-route the destination of an outgoing packet, which always be forwarded to one of X-Pro's proxies.

Our paper shows that X-Pro is possible to realize with low overhead in typical IoT scenarios and that it can be used to give protection from all kinds of packet overload attacks. In future work, we will extend the solution with more advanced DDoS detection mechanisms (i.e., machine learning), which will allow automatic DDoS infection detection combined with efficient blocking.

Appendix A   Proxy Synchronization Protocol

Algorithm 1. Proxy Synchronization Protocol

1: p_j looks all the pair (i, D_{addr}), for $u_i \in U$
2: **for each** (i, D_{addr}) in M_{DB} **do**
3:     **if** $L_{DB} \ni i, D_{addr}$ **then**
4:         **if** $(mark' = 1)$ **then**
5:             $< mark' = 0 >$
6:             **if** $(ts'_1 - ts_1 > T_{T1})$ **then**
7:                 $< dc' = 0 >$
8:                 $< ts_1 = ts'_1, ts_2 = ts'_2, c = c' >$
9:             **end if**
10:         **else if** $(mark' \neq 1)$ **or** $(mark' = 1 \; \& \; ts'_1 - ts_1 < T_{T1})$ **then**
11:             **if** $ts'_2 < ts_2$ **then**
12:                 $< ts'_2 = ts_2 >$
13:             **else**
14:                 **if** $ts'_2 - ts_1 > T_{T4}$ **then**
15:                     $< ts'_1 = ts'_2 - (ts'_2 - ts_1)/r >$
16:                     $< c = \lfloor c/r \rfloor, ts_1 = ts'_1, ts_2 = ts'_2 >$
17:                 **end if**
18:                 $< ts_2 = ts'_2 >$
19:             **end if**
20:             **if** $ts'_1 > ts_1$ **then**
21:                 $< ts'_1 = ts_1 >$
22:             **else**
23:                 **if** $ts'_2 - ts'_1 > T_{T4}$ **then**
24:                     $< ts'_1 = ts_1 >$
25:                 **else**
26:                     $< ts_1 = ts'_1 >$
27:                 **end if**
28:             **end if**
29:             $< c' = c + dc', c = c', dc' = 0 >$
30:         **end if**
31:         $< c = c', dc' = 0 >$
32:     **else**
33:         $< ts'_1 = ts_1, ts'_2 = ts_2 >$
34:         $< c' = c, dc' = 0, mark' = 0 >$
35:     **end if**
36: **end for**
37: **for each** (i, D_{addr}) in L_{DB} **do**
38:     **if** $M_{DB} \ni i, D_{addr}$ **then**
39:         $< ts_1 = ts'_1, ts_2 = ts'_2, c = c' >$
40:     **end if**
41: **end for**

Appendix B   Packet Filtering Procedures

Algorithm 2. Packet Filtering Procedures

1: <Lookup ts'_1, ts'_2, c for record (i, D_{addr}) in L_{DB} >
2: **if** record found **then**
3:     **if** $t - ts'_2 > T_{T1}$ **then**
4:         $ts'_1 = t, c' = 0, dc = 0, mark = 1$
5:     **end if**
6: **else**
7:     $ts'_1 = ts'_2 = t, c' = 0, dc = 0, mark = 0$
8: **end if**
9: $c' = c' + 1, dc = dc + 1, ts'_2 = t$
10: **if** $ts'_2 - ts'_1 > T_{T2}$ **then**
11:     **if** $c'/(ts'_2 - ts'_1) > T_{F1}$ **then**
12:         <Drop packet>
13:         <Send an overload warning>
14:     **end if**
15: **end if**
16: $ts_1* = \min_{u_i \in U_{D_{addr}}} ts_{1_i}'$
17: $ts_2* = \max_{u_i \in U_{D_{addr}}} ts_{2_i}'$
18: $c* = \Sigma_{u_i \in U_{D_{addr}}} (c_i + dc_i)$
19: **if** $ts_2* - ts_1* > T_{T3}$ **then**
20:     **if** $c*/(ts_2* - ts_1*) > T_{F2}$ **then**
21:         <Drop packet>
22:     **end if**
23: **end if**
24: <forward packet>

References

1. Klaba, O.: Octave Klaba Twitter (2016). https://twitter.com/olesovhcom/status/778830571677978624
2. Hilton, S.: Dyn Analysis Summary of Friday October 21 Attack (2016). https://dyn.com/blog/dyn-analysis-summary-of-friday-october-21-attack/
3. Krebs, B.: KrebsOnSecurity Hit With Record DDoS (2016). https://krebsonsecurity.com/2016/09/krebsonsecurity-hit-with-record-ddos/
4. Kolias, C., Kambourakis, G., Stavrou, A., Voas, J.: DDoS in the IoT: Mirai and other botnets. Computer **50**(7), 80–84 (2017)
5. Luo, J., Yang, X., Wang, J., Xu, J., Sun, J., Long, K.: On a mathematical model for low-rate shrew DDoS. IEEE Trans. Inf. Forensics Secur. **9**(7), 1069–1083 (2014)
6. Macia-Fernandez, G., Diaz-Verdejo, J.E., Garcia-Teodoro, P.: Mathematical model for low-rate DoS attacks against application servers. IEEE Trans. Inf. Forensics Secur. **4**(3), 519–529 (2009)
7. Guirguis, M., Bestavros, A., Matta, I., Zhang, Y.: Reduction of quality (RoQ) attacks on Internet end-systems. IEEE Infocom. **2**, 1362–1372 (2005)

8. Shameli-Sendi, A., Pourzandi, M., Fekih-Ahmed, M., Cheriet, M.: Taxonomy of Distributed Denial of Service mitigation approaches for cloud computing. J. Netw. Comput. Appl. **58**, 165–179 (2015)
9. Sharma, M., Arora, B.: Detection and prevention of DoS and DDoS in IoT. In: Singh, P.K., Wierzchoń, S.T., Tanwar, S., Ganzha, M., Rodrigues, J.J.P.C. (eds.) Proceedings of Second International Conference on Computing, Communications, and Cyber-Security. LNNS, vol. 203, pp. 845–855. Springer, Singapore (2021). https://doi.org/10.1007/978-981-16-0733-2_60
10. Mahjabin, T., Xiao, Y., Sun, G., Jiang, W.: A survey of distributed denial-of-service attack, prevention, and mitigation techniques. Int. J. Distrib. Sens. Netw. **13**(12) (2017)
11. Wang, J., Yang, X., Long, K.: A new relative entropy based app-DDoS detection method. In: The IEEE Symposium on Computers and Communications (2010)
12. Mirkovic, J., Reiher, P.: D-WARD: a source-end defense against flooding denial-of-service attacks. IEEE Trans. Dependable Secure Comput. **2**(3), 216–232 (2005)
13. Høiland-Jørgensen, T., et al.: The express data path: fast programmable packet processing in the operating system kernel. In: CoNEXT 2018, pp. 54–66. ACM (2018)
14. Francois, J., Aib, I., Boutaba, R.: FireCol: A Collaborative Protection Network for the Detection of Flooding DDoS Attacks. ACM (2012)
15. Rashidi, B., Fung, C., Bertino, E.: A collaborative DDoS defence framework using network function virtualization. IEEE Trans. Inf. Forensics Secur. **12**(10), 2483–2497 (2017)
16. Lee, S.B., Kang, M.S., Gligor, V.D.: CoDef: collaborative defense against large-scale link-flooding attacks. In: CoNEXT 2013, pp. 417–428. ACM, New York (2013)
17. Yu, S., Zhou, W., Doss, R., Jia, W.: Traceback of DDoS attacks using entropy variations. IEEE Trans. Parallel Distrib. Syst. **22**(3), 412–425 (2011)
18. Xiang, Y., Li, K., Zhou, W.: Low-rate DDoS attacks detection and traceback by using new information metrics. IEEE Trans. Inf. Forensics Secur. **6**(2), 426–437 (2011)
19. Yu, S., Tian, Y., Guo, S., Wu, D.O.: Can we beat DDoS attacks in clouds? IEEE Trans. Parallel Distrib. Syst. **25**(9), 2245–2254 (2014)
20. Gilad, Y., Herzberg, A., Sudkovitch, M., Goberman, M.: CDN-on-demand: an affordable DDoS defense via untrusted clouds. In: NDSS (2016)
21. Tsai, S.-C., Liu, I.-H., Lu, C.-T., Chang, C.-H., Li, J.-S.: Defending cloud computing environment against the challenge of DDoS attacks based on software defined network. In: Advances in Intelligent Information Hiding and Multimedia Signal Processing. SIST, vol. 63, pp. 285–292. Springer, Cham (2017). https://doi.org/10.1007/978-3-319-50209-0_35
22. Idziorek, J., Tannian, M.F., Jacobson, D.: The insecurity of cloud utility models. IT Prof. **15**(2), 22–27 (2013)
23. Fouladi, R.F., Kayatas, C.E., Anarim, E.: Frequency based DDoS attack detection approach using naive Bayes classification. In: 2016 39th International Conference on Telecommunications and Signal Processing (TSP), pp. 104–107 (2016)
24. Bertin, G.: XDP in practice: integrating XDP in our DDoS mitigation pipeline (2017). https://netdevconf.info/2.1/session.html?bertin
25. Suricata: eBPF and XDP (2019). https://suricata.readthedocs.io/en/latest/capture-hardware/ebpf-xdp.html
26. Shirokov, N.V.: XDP: 1.5 years in production. Evolution and lessons learned (2018). http://vger.kernel.org/lpc-networking2018.html

27. Fleming, M.: A thorough introduction to eBPF (2017). https://lwn.net/Articles/740157/
28. Miller, D.: [GIT] Networking (2016). https://lore.kernel.org/lkml/20160727.010753.2221383279830501569.davem@davemloft.net/
29. Thingsboard: Thingsboard (2020). https://thingsboard.io/
30. Mainflux: Open Source IoT Platform (2020). https://www.mainflux.com/
31. Kekki, S., et al.: MEC in 5G networks. ETSI White Paper **28**, 1–28 (2018)
32. Giust, F., et al.: MEC deployments in 4G and evolution towards 5G. ETSI White Paper **24**(2018), 1–24 (2018)
33. Agrawal, D., El Abbadi, A., Das, S., Elmore, A.J.: Database scalability, elasticity, and autonomy in the cloud. In: Yu, J.X., Kim, M.H., Unland, R. (eds.) DASFAA 2011. LNCS, vol. 6587, pp. 2–15. Springer, Heidelberg (2011). https://doi.org/10.1007/978-3-642-20149-3_2
34. Jimenez-Peris, R., Patino-Martinez, M., Kemme, B., Alonso, G.: Improving the scalability of fault-tolerant database clusters. In: Proceedings 22nd International Conference on Distributed Computing Systems, pp. 477–484 (2002)
35. Page, L.M.: BPF - perform a command on an extended BPF map or program (2020). https://man7.org/linux/man-pages/man2/bpf.2.html
36. Miano, S., Doriguzzi-Corin, R., Risso, F., Siracusa, D., Sommese, R.: Introducing SmartNICs in server-based data plane processing: the DDoS mitigation use case. IEEE Access **7**, 107161–107170 (2019)
37. Shelby, Z., Hartke, K., Bormann, C.: The Constrained Application Protocol (CoAP). RFC, June 2014. http://www.rfc-editor.org/rfc/rfc7252.txt
38. Linux Kernel Team: BPF Documentation. The Linux Kernel documentation, August 2020. https://www.kernel.org/doc/html/latest/bpf/index.html
39. Linux Kernel Team: BPF-HELPERS (2020). https://man7.org/linux/man-pages/man7/bpf-helpers.7.html
40. Sanfilippo, S., Noordhuis, P., Rediger, J.: Hiredis (2020). https://redislabs.com/lp/hiredis/
41. Espressif: ESP32 (2020). https://www.espressif.com/en/products/socs/esp32
42. Pycom: FiPy (2020). https://pycom.io/product/fipy/
43. Arm: Arm TrustZone Technology (2020). https://developer.arm.com/ip-products/security-ip/trustzone
44. Pinto, S., Santos, N.: Demystifying arm TrustZone: a comprehensive survey. ACM Comput. Surv. **51**(6), 1–36 (2019)
45. Shinagawa, T., et al.: BitVisor: a thin hypervisor for enforcing I/O device security. In: VEE 2009, pp. 121–130. ACM, New York (2009)
46. Turull, D., Sjödin, P., Olsson, R.: Pktgen: measuring performance on high speed networks. Comput. Commun. **82**, 39–48 (2016)
47. Bhuyan, M.H., Elmroth, E.: Multi-scale low-rate ddos attack detection using the generalized total variation metric. In: 2018 17th IEEE International Conference on Machine Learning and Applications (ICMLA), pp. 1040–1047 (2018)
48. Zhijun, W., Qing, X., Jingjie, W., Meng, Y., Liang, L.: Low-rate DDoS attack detection based on factorization machine in software defined network (2020)
49. Fussell, S.: The All-Seeing Eyes of New York's 15,000 Surveillance Cameras (2021). https://www.wired.com/story/all-seeing-eyes-new-york-15000-surveillance-cameras/

Industrialising Blackmail: Privacy Invasion Based IoT Ransomware

Calvin Brierley(✉) ⓘ, Budi Arief ⓘ, David Barnes ⓘ,
and Julio Hernandez-Castro ⓘ

School of Computing, University of Kent, Canterbury, UK
{C.R.Brierley,B.Arief,D.J.Barnes,jch27}@kent.ac.uk

Abstract. Ransomware (malware that threatens to lock or publish victims' assets unless a ransom is paid) has become a serious security threat, targeting individual users, companies and even governments, causing significant damage, disruption and cost. Instances of ransomware have also been observed stealing private data and blackmailing their victims. Worryingly, the prevalence of Internet of Things (IoT) devices and the massive amount of personal data that they collect have opened up another avenue of attack. The main aim of this paper is to determine whether *privacy invasion based* ransomware would be a viable vector for attackers to use on IoT devices. The secondary aim is to identify countermeasures that can be implemented to prevent such attacks from being used. To accomplish these aims, we examined how private data accessible via IoT devices could be obtained, processed and managed by a ransomware attacker. We identified a number of data sources on IoT devices that can be used to access private data, such as audio and video feeds. We then investigated methods to interpret such data in order to blackmail the device's owner. We then produced proof of concept malware for multiple IoT devices, including an external "collator" that manages the valuable data collected, demonstrating that an attack could be performed at scale. This research shows that attackers can use the functionality of an infected device to invade the privacy of the device's owner, as part of a ransomware attack. We have demonstrated that, given suitable infrastructure, attackers would be able to ransom users for values higher than the cost of the compromised device, as well as heavily damage the trust in the device itself, which would cause further negative impact on the device manufacturer. Finally, we highlight the need for proactive measures to deter this style of attack by applying the suggested countermeasures.

Keywords: Security · Privacy · IoT · Ransomware · Malware · Cloud services · Cybercrime · Blackmail

1 Introduction

The increasing popularity of the Internet of Things (IoT) has lead to a corresponding increase in attacks on IoT devices. While IoT devices themselves are

© Springer Nature Switzerland AG 2021
N. Tuveri et al. (Eds.): NordSec 2021, LNCS 13115, pp. 72–92, 2021.
https://doi.org/10.1007/978-3-030-91625-1_5

used for many different purposes – such as light bulbs, digital video recorders, and fridges – when infected, they are typically used to perform either Distributed Denial of Service (DDoS) attacks [2], or to mine cryptocurrency [48]. However, ransomware has also become increasingly prevalent [5,9,41], and its success has garnered significant interest in carrying out ransomware attacks on IoT devices.

The volume and the relative insecurity of IoT devices make them a potentially profitable target for ransomware authors. To evaluate the potential threat of IoT ransomware, researchers have developed proof of concepts investigating how IoT devices could be attacked [6,26]. However, as IoT devices rarely store files that their user may consider essential, typical crypto ransomware may not be as effective as they would be on regular personal computers. Instead, early IoT ransomware strains typically "lock" infected devices, preventing them from working correctly unless a payment is made [6]. While this method of ransom may be effective, there are a number of limitations (discussed later in this paper), which may dissuade ransomware operators from using it. Attackers are likely to explore other methods of monetising IoT-based ransomware in the future. One such method involves extracting private data from and/or using the IoT device, which can then be used to extort the user under threat of public release.

In this paper, we aim *to determine the viability of ransomware attack leveraging privacy invasion techniques on IoT devices,* and *devise countermeasures that can be implemented to prevent such attacks from being used by cybercriminals.*

Contributions. The key contributions of our paper are: **(i)** a demonstration of how attackers may identify and extract private data accessible via IoT devices to facilitate ransomware; **(ii)** an overview of how such an attack might be structured and managed; **(iii)** an identification of possible weaknesses that may be introduced by attackers when performing such an attack; **(iv)** a list of countermeasures that could be used to hinder or prevent such an attack.

The rest of the paper is organised as follows. Section 2 covers previous privacy based ransomware attacks and IoT privacy research. Section 3 investigates data sources commonly found on IoT devices, and how they could be accessed by attackers. Section 4 describes how attackers could interpret exfiltrated data to identify private information. Section 5 shows how attackers could collate information extracted from IoT devices during a ransomware campaign. Section 6 demonstrates some of the privacy-invasion techniques on IoT devices with differing sensors and uses. Section 7 discusses countermeasures that could be used to prevent such attacks, the limitations of the current work, and further research that could be performed. Finally, Sect. 8 summarises our findings.

2 Background and Related Work

Ransomware is class of malware that uses a number of techniques to restrict access to assets owned by users, typically requiring a payment in cryptocurrency to be made for access to be returned [30,34]. As ransomware continues to evolve, new methods have been used to ransom victims more effectively. One of the latest trends is for ransomware operators to steal sensitive data and to threaten the owners with its release, unless a ransom demand is paid. This method is particularly effective if the stolen data is confidential or embarrassing in nature, as it could be severely damaging if made public.

Multiple companies have already been impacted by this method. In February 2021, CD Projekt Red, a games development company, was subjected to a ransomware attack. As part of the ransom note, the attackers claimed to have stolen source code, employee details and accounting information, which they threatened to release if payment was not made within 48 h [8]. After CD Projekt Red refused to pay the ransom, the source code was put up for auction [38]. It was later revealed that portions of the data were potentially being leaked online [15]. In December 2020, the Scottish Environmental Protection Agency (SEPA) was also subject to a ransomware attack, with the attackers stealing approximately 1.2 GB of files. After refusing to pay the ransom, the attackers publicly released over 4,000 documents on the dark web, including emails and databases used for contracts and commercial services [39,45].

2.1 IoT Based Ransomware

As both IoT devices and ransomware have become more popular, it is not surprising to see an increased interest in IoT based ransomware – from both security researchers and attackers. Initial attempts to produce IoT based ransomware have implemented various "locking" methods to ransom users, i.e., preventing infected devices from functioning correctly until a payment is made [6,28,51]. More complex types of ransomware may require persistence, which while possible, may be difficult to achieve, depending on the design of the device [7].

While these techniques may work in certain circumstances, consumer IoT devices impose two obvious limitations for successful crypto- and locker-based ransomware: *replaceability* (most IoT devices are designed to be relatively "cheap" when compared to traditional desktop targets – as such, users may instead opt to simply replace the device rather than pay a ransom); and *lack of valuable files* (IoT devices rarely contain files that are essential to the user, so crypto-based ransomware is unlikely to be as effective). However, as IoT devices are often designed to have access to data associated with their user's personal environment, they thereby may provide a unique opportunity for attackers. In what follows, we describe how IoT devices may be used by attackers to invade the privacy of their users.

2.2 Privacy Invasion

IoT devices often have direct access to sensors within a user's home, which has lead to a significant amount of research into the privacy of data that they manage or create [29,42,43]. This is especially important as IoT devices are, by design, required to be connected to the Internet. Therefore, if a device is found to be exploitable, this information may be exposed to remote attackers.

Previous research has investigated how attacks on IoT devices may impact users, including case studies that demonstrate the possible methods attackers could use to track user activity [3]. Various attacks have also been performed "in the wild"; for instance, there have been numerous instances of attackers accessing network cameras exposed to the Internet, allowing them to view video feeds inside homes and, in some cases, sell obtained "adult content" to others [47]. In one instance, an attacker used a camera's speaker to threaten victims and demand a ransom of 50 bitcoin [1].

It is therefore straightforward to see that the natural progression of ransomware attack strategy would be to threaten to leak data belonging to victims in order to encourage payment. It may be possible for attackers to exploit IoT devices' access to sensors – e.g., by monitoring or turning on a microphone or camera without the owner's knowledge – in order to capture personal or potentially embarrassing data. In the next section, we will discuss the possible sources of private information that could be exploited by an attacker.

3 Data Sources

Many IoT devices – such as wearables, smart toys, and medical devices – process or generate private data that their legitimate users may not want to be publicly exposed. Below, we discuss the data sources commonly found on such IoT devices, and how they could be used by a malicious attacker:

- *In-built Sensors.* An IoT device typically uses sensors to measure aspects of its environment in order to function. Some of the most commonly available sensors are cameras (which are often used in Internet-connected security systems), microphones (which are sometimes used for communication and control) and geolocation sensors (which can be used to determine the current location of the user).
- *Network Data.* IoT devices, by definition, must be able to connect to the Internet, allowing them to communicate with other devices and their users. However, if the device has permissions to send, receive or view any sensitive data, attackers who exploit the device will gain the same privileges. It can lead to security and privacy issues such as passive monitoring, where if the infected device acts as a gateway to the internet (e.g. a router), the attacker may be able to "sniff" the packets sent through it. The attacker may also be able to scan the internal network of the device's local network, which could lead to the discovery of additional sources of personal information such as network accessible file storage or other vulnerable IoT devices.
- *Local Configuration settings.* While IoT devices are less likely to contain significant amounts of user-created data, they may still store personal information that is of value. An IoT device may request information from their users during the device's set-up stage – such as their name or email address – which is often stored within the device's configuration settings. If the location of this information is known to the attacker, it could be extracted to facilitate communication with, or intimidate, the victim. The attacker could also scan the memory of local processes or storage for data with a recognisable structure, such as email addresses or dates, using regular expressions.

4   Identifying Private Data

For privacy based ransomware attacks to be successful, the attacker must first be able to extract data from IoT devices, but more importantly, identify data of value which could be used to extort their victims. For large ransomware campaigns, it is infeasible to manually search through large volumes of collected data to pick out relevant information. Instead, it would be necessary for attackers to develop methods to categorise and sift through the available data automatically and efficiently. Below, we discuss some the methods that could be used.

4.1   Malicious Use of Machine Learning

IoT devices typically have access to various types of structured data, such as configuration settings, which would be relatively easy for attackers to access and interpret. However, raw data collected from IoT devices' sensors will first need to be processed before its "value" can be determined. One approach is to use machine learning tools to automatically classify input data, drastically lowering the amount of manual intervention required by the attacker. This method could exploit two data sources commonly found on IoT devices, as shown below.

Identifying Private Images with Image Recognition. Cameras are often considered as a vector to invade a user's privacy, as if an attacker is able to gain access, they would also be able to extract images from within a victim's home without their knowledge. However, the attacker must be able to identify which images are likely to be "valuable". The process for selecting potentially ransomable images could be performed manually by the attacker, but it would be a time-consuming process that would not scale well. Therefore, automating this process would be desirable for the attacker. There are various different models that may assist in identifying ransom-able images, such as:

- *Theme/Object Recognition.* If certain themes or objects are detected – such as cars, buildings, or crowds – it could indicate that the infected device is stationed outside, and are likely to produce images of "low value". If people or objects likely to be inside, such as furniture, are detected, they will raise the potential value of the images extracted from the device.
- *Face Detection.* Face detection could be used to confirm the presence of human victims within obtained images. If a victim is confirmed to be within the image, it could be very valuable when used in a ransom note as proof of exploitation, especially if the victim was caught in a compromising position.
- *Explicit Content Detection.* Some online services offer explicit content detection for uploaded images/videos. A typical use case would be to prevent the upload/transmission of explicit content on "safe-for-work" platforms. An attacker could use this maliciously by scanning for explicit content taken without the victim's consent, which could then be used to ransom the victim.

Identifying and Transcribing Private Conversations. The possibility of eavesdropping via vulnerable IoT devices has been explored in previous research [13,50] but not in the context of ransomware. For this method, the attacker aims to transcribe using speech-to-text engines private conversations held by the victim. Once the audio has been transcribed, the attacker can use automated methods to search for keywords, such as those related to potentially exploitable activity.

4.2 Network-Based Privacy Invasion

There are several techniques that attackers could use to extract private information by interacting with the local network using compromised IoT devices.

Intercepting Browsed Domains. If an attacker is able to intercept a user's Internet traffic via an infected device (such as a router), they may be able to extract sensitive information about the user's browsing habits. In this case, the attacker may intercept traffic passing through the device and extract domain names of any websites that the user visits from various protocols, such as DNS [33], HTTP [14] or HTTPS [10]. The websites can then be compared against a list of domains associated with illegal or compromising activities. If a match is found, details could then be logged to a Command and Control (C&C) server.

Intercepting Web Content. It may also be possible to intercept the content of visited web pages, and the content of websites with known structures could be read to extract important information, such as video titles, usernames or personal information. For HTTP traffic, this is relatively simple, as communication is typically performed in plaintext, allowing attackers to access any transferred content. Increasingly, web traffic is using HTTPS, which encrypts the communication between the client and server when transmitting web content [11,18]. However, it could still be possible to gain access to encrypted content using "man in the middle" (MitM) attacks, such as `SSLStrip`, which allows attackers to intercept and modify victim's web requests to bypass HTTPS encryption [32]. This allows the attacker to catch inattentive users unaware and extract plaintext communication from typically encrypted traffic. A similar style of attack has been previously implemented by the IoT malware `VPNFilter` to extract usernames, passwords and logins [24].

Identifying Device Locations via WiFi Positioning. The location of the infected device could be used to determine the address of the user. However, in order to ascertain the location of the infected device, the attacker must make use of the available data sources. Some devices need to be aware of their current position in order to function correctly, such as fitness trackers, which may need to periodically acquire the current location of the device to track a user's running activity and route. Ideally, this type of information would be acquired using a

Global Positioning System (GPS), however, most IoT devices are unlikely to implement GPS sensors, especially if they are not designed to be moved often.

Online WiFi Positioning systems allow users to triangulate their current position by comparing a scan of local WiFi signals to a list of known signal locations stored in an online database. The accuracy of this measurement is dependant on various factors, such as the number of detected signals, or matches found in the service providers' database.

If an infected device has wireless capabilities, attackers may be able to perform a scan to discover the SSIDs, MAC addresses and signal strengths of nearby routers, which can then be sent to the C&C server. The attacker could then upload it to an online service such as Mozilla Location Services or the Google Cloud platform to obtain an estimate of the device's location [22,36].

Internal Network Structure. Infected devices could provide attackers with access to other devices on the local network which would be otherwise inaccessible from the Internet. The attackers would then be able to scan or attack previously inaccessible devices, potentially gaining access to further private data.

4.3   Data Processing

Once data has been successfully extracted from the device, it must then be processed to identify any potentially ransomable information. For network data, which is typically well structured, this is a computationally inexpensive process.

Less structured data, such as that which is collected from device sensors, can be much more difficult to interpret. While the use of machine learning can significantly reduce the amount of manual effort required to identify ransomable data, there are some logistical issues that attackers may need to overcome before it can be considered viable. Many IoT devices are unlikely to have the hardware to run the required machine learning models, and IoT devices' internal memory is often limited to only what is required to run the system, which may prevent collected data from being locally stored.

To circumvent these issues, attackers may instead process, classify, and store images collected by infected devices on remote systems. For example, attackers could choose to process collected data on their own server using publicly available models. However, this may not scale well, and a large ransomware campaign may cause immense network strain on the attacker's infrastructure, which could be quite costly to maintain. Therefore, it may become necessary to outsource processing to a third party, such as cloud services.

5   Data Collation

The privacy invasion methods we have discussed present possible avenues for ransomware authors to extract private information from IoT devices. However, using the extracted information to perform a ransomware attack in a large campaign presents multiple challenges, such as how to manage the collected data, how to generate an effective ransom note, and how the information could be published should the ransom not be paid. In this section, we will examine how these challenges may be approached by future attackers.

5.1 Data Management

As demonstrated in the previous section, there are various methods attackers may use to extract private data from victims. However, the collected data must be correctly managed for threats of publication to be effective. As part of this research, we created a basic proof of concept collator that allows the attacker to manage data collected from various compromised devices. An abstract view of the collator's operating structure can be found in Appendix A.1 (Fig. 4).

The collator exposes an API for infected devices to interact with, allowing various types of private data to be uploaded, such as images, audio recordings or browsing history. Once data is received by the collator, it can be processed using the appropriate method, such as those described in Sect. 4.3. Each data point is associated with the infected device's MAC address, as it is an easily available unique identifier that is unlikely to change, even through reboots.

The attacker can then access the data processed by the collator via a web interface, shown in Appendix A.2 (Fig. 5a). Additional features, such as highlighting particularly interesting collected information, such as valuble words in audio transcripts or private browsing activity, could also be implemented.

5.2 The Ransom

Once adequate personal information has been collected, a ransom note demanding payment can be generated and displayed to the victim. If any contact information has been extracted from the device, such as an email address, the ransom note could be sent directly to the user. Alternatively, the attacker could attempt to display the ransom note by hijacking communication methods native to the device, such as attached screens or network services [6].

Typically for ransomware attacks, the ransom note would likely contain a description as to what has occurred, a timer, and instructions for paying the ransom. However, unlike ransomware that prevents users from accessing their resources, privacy invasion ransomware threatens to release private information unless a ransom is paid before a certain time. Therefore, including select private information in the ransom note that has been obtained throughout the collection stage may provide sufficient evidence to force the victim into making a payment. By "personalising" ransom notes in this manner, it may lead less technically-aware victims to conclude that the attack was a manual effort made to target them specifically, which may further encourage payment.

5.3 Publishing Private Information

As part of a privacy-based ransomware attack, the victim is threatened with the release of their private information unless a payment is made. Private information could be publicised in a number of ways, varying in complexity.

Centralised Publication. One method attackers could use to publicise information is to create a centralised "leaking platform" available via a publicly accessible website. Any victims that do not make a payment would have their information published to the website for anyone to view. As part of the ransom note, victims would be encouraged to visit the website for further information or to facilitate payment, acting as form of advertisement. Previous victims' private information would be visible to the "new users", which would serve as proof that the attacker will follow through with threats to publicise.

"Direct" Publication. Attackers could use information previously gathered about the victim to determine who would be most impacted by its release, such as friends, family or co-workers. For example, if the attacker identifies the victim's social media accounts during the information gathering stage, they may be able to enumerate people that the victim associates with. They could then attempt to use the same social media platforms to distribute the victim's private information, such as through the use of automated chat-bots. If this technique is used alongside the aforementioned leaking platform method of distribution, these messages could also serve to advertise it.

While this approach could drastically increase the impact of publicising information, it may also increase the complexity of the ransomware, as the attacker would need to automate account identification, enumeration and distribution for supported social media platforms.

5.4   Scale of Operation

Previously, such malware would require significant manual oversight. The automation steps outlined above, such as the use of machine learning and managing large volumes of data with a collator, would allow attacks to be performed without needing costly manual labour.

6   Proof of Concepts

To test the viability of privacy-based ransomware on IoT devices, we attempted to extract private information from a number of different device types, then collated it such that it could be used to ransom a user. For an attack to succeed, it is assumed that the attacker is able to access the vulnerable service such that they are able to exploit it remotely.

6.1   Netgear R6250 Router

As routers often act as the main gateway for Internet traffic in a network, we determined that they would be ideal for testing the network data extraction techniques discussed in Sect. 4.2. We chose to use a Netgear R6250 router for testing, which could be exploited using a previously discovered command injection vulnerability [31,37].

Domain Extraction. To test extracting data from network activity, we created a program to sniff local packets using the `libpcap` library [25], which was cross-compiled to be compatible with the target router's architecture. The program intercepts any packets destined for port 80 or 443 (the default ports for HTTP and HTTPS), extracts visited domain names and compares them against a hard-coded list. If a match is found, an API call is made to the collator, which records the visited domain, a timestamp of the visit, and the device's MAC address.

We created a network consisting of the R6250 router, a phone and a desktop computer. After exploiting the router, we uploaded and ran the application, then browsed various websites using the connected devices. The application successfully identified and reported domains visited using both HTTP and HTTPS to the collator, which the "attacker" was then able to view. For this proof of concept, we did not implement interpretation of any web content, but this could theoretically be implemented by a dedicated attacker in the future.

WiFi-Positioning. While the router did exhibit wireless capabilities, we were not able to scan for nearby SSIDs and MAC addresses. This may be due to limitations imposed by the expected usage of the device. However, we were able to view the local MAC address and SSID of the router, which could then be used to query a WiFi-Positioning service. While only one "signal" would be available for reference, which may reduce the result's accuracy, it should still allow attackers to make an approximate guess of the user's location, as WiFi signals have a limited range within which they can be detected.

Configuration Extraction. During the investigation of the device, we attempted to identify where user settings were being stored. We found that user settings were being saved to the second partition on the flash chip, which was accessible via the `/dev/mtdblock1` file. By using a simple `grep` command,

```
# head /dev/mtdblock1 | grep 'wlg_passphrase\|http_username
\|http_passwd\|wla_passphrase\|pppoe_username\|pppoe_passwd
'
wlg_passphrase=adminlol
http_username=admin
ipv6_pppoe_username=
wla_passphrase_backup=
http_passwd=adminlol
wlg_passphrase_2=
wla_passphrase_2=
wla_passphrase_3=
wla_passphrase_4=
ipv6_pppoe_passwd=
pppoe_passwd=examplepw123
wlg_passphrase_backup=
pppoe_username=exampleemail@isp
wla_passphrase=adminlol
```

Fig. 1. Extracting configuration data

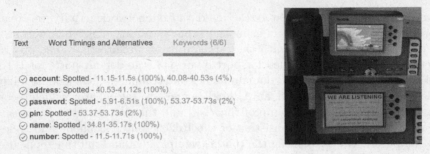

(a) IBM demo recognising keywords   (b) Ransom note hijacking the screen

Fig. 2. Attacking the Yealink SIP-T38g

we were able to view sensitive configuration data that was stored in plain text, as shown in Fig. 1.

Ransom Note. Previous research has shown that it was possible to redirect DNS requests made to a compromised router [6]. Using this technique, an attacker could redirect users browsing the internet to a webpage containing a ransom note. In addition to traditional ransomware elements, such as a timer and a demand for payment, it could also include select personal information collected by the malware to act as "proof of compromise". An example of how the ransom note could be presented is shown in Fig. 5b in Appendix A.2.

6.2   Yealink SIP-T38g Phone

The SIP-T38g is an Internet connected IP phone with a built in LCD screen. As the device is designed for direct communication, we used it to test the audio extraction techniques described in Sect. 4.1.

Private Conversation Extraction. The first step for extracting private conversations is to obtain audio from the device when a call is made. While we could have potentially recorded audio directly from the device's microphone, we instead chose to extract call data from the device's network activity, as this would allow us to hear *both* sides of the conversation. To do this, we used VoIPong [4,12], an open source tool that allows the interception and decoding of VoIP calls.

We modified, configured, and cross-compiled a custom version of VoIPong such that it would be able to run natively on the phone. We then exploited the device using a command injection vulnerability present in its web interface, allowing us to upload and run the application, which would then save calls to a pre-defined folder. Unfortunately, the phone had limited storage, with only a collective 60 MB of space across all the available partitions. To overcome this, we hosted a Network File System (NFS) share on the collator server, which the phone could then mount and modify as if it were a local directory. The collator then periodically checked for "file close" events within the share folder such that, when recordings were finished, conversations could be transcribed.

When the audio is ready to be processed, it is passed to a speech-to-text service for transcription. Initially, we attempted to use a local instance of Mozilla's "deepspeech" engine with a pre-trained model and scorer [35]. However, audio extracted from the intercepted calls were sampled at a rate of 8 kHz, also known as "narrowband", while the Mozilla model expected a sample rate of 16 kHz, which lead to unsatisfactory performance. While a new model could be trained to understand narrowband audio, it was considered to be out of scope for this paper. Instead, we tested various online services to transcribe the call accurately.

The Google Cloud Services API [23] successfully transcribed conversations with higher accuracy. We also tested using an "IBM Watson Speech to Text" demo [27] (which included support for narrowband audio), to successfully extract key components of the conversation. This demo also featured keyword identification, which could be used by attackers to listen for subjects of interest, as shown in Fig. 2a. Finally, we were able to upload the call to YouTube after converting it to a video format. Approximately ten minutes after the initial upload, captions had been automatically added, and could be scraped from the source of the video's webpage. Given that YouTube provides this feature for free, it could potentially be used by attackers to avoid paying for the use of cloud services.

After the conversation has been transcribed, the text and audio file can be inserted into the collator. The attacker can then search for "valuable" words in the text, such as "password" or "address", as potential blackmail material. This entire process can be fully automated without giving the victim any indication that they are being monitored, until the ransom note is triggered.

Ransom Note. As with the R6250 router, the attacker could hijack the device's web server to display a ransom note, including "proof of compromise" such as recordings of the victim. However, as the web server is unlikely to be accessed in day to day usage, they could also hijack the connected screen [6], as shown in Fig. 2b. It could be possible to expand to other communication media, such as using the speakers to play back recorded conversations, but this is unlikely to be unnecessary if the previous approaches are successful.

6.3   DCS-932L Camera

The DCS-932L is an Internet connected camera designed by D-Link. We selected this device to test WiFi-positioning based location extraction, and image based privacy invasion.

WiFi-Positioning. During our testing, we found that when the camera uses WiFi to connect to the Internet, it was possible to scan for nearby SSIDs and MAC addresses. We used a previously discovered buffer overflow exploit [44] to upload and run a WiFi scanning application, which returned information on three nearby access points. By uploading the access point information to Google Cloud Services we were able to determine our location within 15 m.

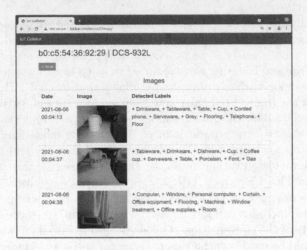

Fig. 3. Labelling images extracted from an infected DCS-932L Camera

Table 1. Privacy invasion methods used for each device

Device	Domain extraction	Config extraction	Audio transcription	Image recognition	Location identification
Netgear R6250	✓	✓	-	-	Partial[a]
Yealink SIP-T38g	-	-	✓	-	-
D-Link DCS-932L	-	-	-	✓	✓

[a]Unfortunately, we were unable to fully test the WiFi-positioning method for the R6250 router, as it was only powered when performing our analysis, preventing its MAC address from being detected or stored by any WiFi-positioning services.

Image Extraction. As the camera is intended to be used for surveillance, this device was ideal for testing image based privacy invasion techniques. We found that during normal operation, the device would provide a snapshot from the camera to the user when they visited the web server. After infecting the device, we were able to make direct requests to this snapshot at `/image.jpg` on the local webserver. We uploaded an application that would save, encode and transfer images to the collator, which would then use Google Cloud services [16] to label recognised objects, locations and activities [21]. As shown in Fig. 3, the platform was able to recognise and correctly label objects within the extracted images. If required, other services such as face detection [20] or explicit content detection [19] could also be applied with minimal changes.

Ransom Note. The DCS-932L camera did not contain many methods to communicate with the user. As most interaction with the device was performed via the web service (which displays the current view from the camera), the attacker could use the same method as described in Sect. 6.1 to hijack the webserver to display a ransom note.

6.4 Summary

In this section, we demonstrated practical examples of how private information could be extracted from various IoT devices of differing types: router-based information, audio data and image data. We have also shown how the collected data could feasibly be analysed, organised, and used by an attacker to facilitate privacy invasion based IoT ransomware.

Table 1 provides a summary of the six privacy invasion methods that can be used, namely *Domain Extraction*, *Config Extraction*, *Audio Transcription*, *Image Recognition*, and *Location Identification*. Additionally, Table 1 also shows how these methods fare when applied against the three IoT devices we included in our proof of concepts.

While using IoT devices to invade the privacy of users has been theorised in the past, it has rarely been explored as a practical option for the average attacker. Here, we have shown several examples as to how such privacy invasions could potentially be monetised using ransomware, and how such attacks could be implemented at scale.

7 Discussion

Privacy-based IoT ransomware could have very negative impacts on users and their perception of IoT devices. Therefore, it is important to investigate potential countermeasures. Additionally, some limitations of our current work is discussed, along with several ideas for future research.

7.1 Countermeasures

There are a number of countermeasures that could be implemented by device developers, cloud providers, or IoT device users, as discussed below.

Domain Interception Protections. As shown in Sect. 6.1, it is possible for an attacker to extract the domains of websites that victims visit. While users can protect themselves by using privacy tools such as VPNs or Tor [46], it is unrealistic to suggest every user use such tools just in case one of their devices is infected with such malware. Alternative methods to secure communication between users and web services must instead be implemented by website hosts.

As HTTP traffic is designed to be unencrypted by default and requires the domain to be included within the headers, it is very simple to extract information from any traffic generated by the victim. By using HTTPS, the user can limit the information that an attacker can extract through the use of encryption. However, as mentioned in Sects. 4.2 and 4.2, it is still possible to extract the visited domain or perform downgrade attacks. These attacks can be prevented through the use of:

- *Encrypted Server Name Indication (ESNI).* While the contents of HTTPS communication is encrypted, the domain can be extracted from the SNI portion of HTTPS handshake packets. Encrypting this portion of the header using a compatible DNS server will prevent the attacker from being able to discern the visited domain [10]. Encrypted Client Hello (ECH), a more recent protection mechanism, could also be used to prevent domain extraction in the future [40].
- *HTTP Strict Transport Security (HSTS).* In Sect. 4.2, HTTPS downgrade attacks were highlighted as a possible method for intercepting the contents of web service communications. HSTS allows web hosts to force clients to only use HTTPS when visiting their domain, preventing such downgrade attacks. Some of the most popular browsers even contain hard-coded lists of HTTPS-only websites by default [17].

Malicious Activity Detection in Cloud Services. Currently, attackers may find it difficult to natively implement software on infected IoT devices that can process data collected from its sensors, such as object recognition on captured images. While this may change in the future – either through more cost-efficient machine learning algorithms, or more resources being made available on the average IoT device – attackers are currently more likely to rely on outside processing, such as online cloud services. As such, attackers may need to use these cloud services at scale in order to adequately manage the throughput of infected devices. Cloud providers may be able to detect such malicious behaviour through the measuring of various metrics, such as:

- An account using multiple IP addresses to call the API, which may imply that functions are being called directly from infected IoT devices.
- "Privacy related" functions being called excessively or in certain sequences, such as facial or object recognition followed by nudity detection.
- Whether a trial account is being used, as it may imply that the attacker is aiming to reduce costs by using free processing without payment.

If the cloud service provider is able to identify a user as malicious, banning or shutting down the associated account may delay the operation of the malware campaign. A more extreme approach may be to prevent accounts from accessing certain functionality commonly associated with privacy based ransomware until the owner has provided sufficient proof of identity.

Data Devaluation. If a victim is threatened with the public release of their private data, there are very few steps that they can take to reduce the impact, as they do not have any method to remove the stolen data from the attacker's storage. However, it may be possible to reduce the trustworthiness of information attained by the attackers by providing false data to the C&C server, thus reducing the overall value of files that are released. This may also waste the attacker's time and resources, as they would need to receive, store and analyse any data sent by the fake "victim".

Updating. While this has often been mentioned, it is worth re-enforcing the principle that applying updates and patches, and changing default passwords, are important steps in securing IoT devices against possible compromise.

7.2 Limitations and Further Work

Countermeasure Creation. Due in part to the variety in the design of IoT devices, the creation of universal countermeasures is not a simple process. While the countermeasures discussed above can be effective, it could be argued that some are only applicable in certain scenarios. This work highlights the need for further research as to how IoT devices can be designed to limit the effectiveness of privacy-invasion based malware.

Native Malicious Machine Learning. Currently, the identification and management of data presents a significant hurdle that attackers must overcome in order to create effective privacy invasion based ransomware. The infrastructure required to transfer, store, and process collected data may dissuade malicious actors from attempting to perform these types of attacks. However, as the hardware present in IoT devices continues to improve, and machine learning techniques become increasingly efficient, it may eventually be possible to run machine learning tools natively on infected devices rather than outsourcing the data processing. It may be beneficial to investigate the viability of such native tools, as it may heavily reduce the costs when running a large malware campaign.

Psychological Effects. Unlike other malware, which typically targets the restriction of information, privacy based ransomware instead threatens to expose it, which has the potential of being very distressing for victims. A study of the psychological effects of this malware could reveal the non-monetary costs of infection, such as how public perception may change concerning IoT devices, should this affect a significant number of devices.

ARP Poisoning. In Sect. 4.2 we described techniques that intercept network traffic to extract private information. Typically, these require the infected device to be positioned such that it is a "man in the middle" (MitM), with the user's network activity passing through it. Routers are perfectly positioned for this type of attack. However, devices that do not hold this position, such as network cameras, will only be able to examine their own network activity.

A possible way that infected IoT devices could use is an Address Resolution Protocol (ARP) poisoning attack, which would allow attackers to insert themselves in-between the network gateway and another target [49]. If IoT devices are shown to be capable of performing such attacks, they may be able to use MitM attacks on other devices on the same network without acting as the gateway.

8   Conclusions

In this paper we investigated how IoT devices could be used to facilitate privacy-invasion based ransomware targeting consumers. To do this, we first examined various data sources commonly found on IoT devices and how they could be leveraged by attackers to extract data. We then proposed methods attackers could use to identify and process that data to extract sensitive user information for the purpose of performing a ransomware attack. We discussed how automated machine learning and data collation could be used to manage data collected from vulnerable IoT devices to perform ransomware attacks at a large scale.

We showed how some of the privacy-invasion techniques could be realised on three IoT devices with differing sensors and data sources. During the demonstration, we were able to extract various mock "private data" and send it to a remote data collation service, such that an attacker could easily track and process it.

We then discussed potential countermeasures that could be implemented by users or IoT developers to prevent or reduce the impact of such attacks, before finally identifying the work's limitations and opportunities for future research.

A   Appendices

A.1   Data Collator Structure

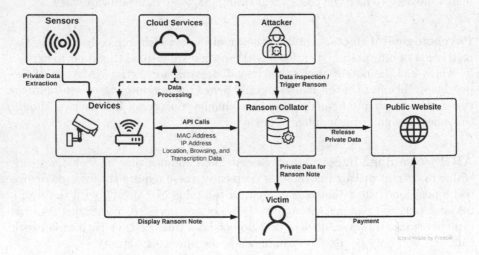

Fig. 4. Data collator structure

A.2   Collator and Ransom Note

(a) IoT Collator summarising information collected from a router

(b) An example ransom note, including proof of compromise

Fig. 5. Collator and example ransom note

References

1. abcNEWS: Terrifying video of family's hacked ring camera system (2019). https://abcnews.go.com/GMA/News/video/terrifying-video-familys-hacked-ring-camera-system-67704081/. Accessed June 2021
2. Antonakakis, M., et al.: Understanding the Mirai botnet. In: 26th USENIX Security Symposium (USENIX Security 2017), pp. 1093–1110 (2017)
3. Arias, O., Wurm, J., Hoang, K., Jin, Y.: Privacy and security in internet of things and wearable devices. IEEE Trans. Multi-Scale Comput. Syst. **1**(2), 99–109 (2015)
4. Balaban, M.: Voipong user's manual (2005). http://www.enderunix.org/voipong/manual/. Accessed April 2021
5. Bitdefender: Security 2020 consumer threat landscape report (2021). https://www.bitdefender.com/files/News/CaseStudies/study/395/Bitdefender-2020-Consumer-Threat-Landscape-Report.pdf. Accessed July 2021
6. Brierley, C., Pont, J., Arief, B., Barnes, D.J., Hernandez-Castro, J.: PaperW8: an IoT bricking ransomware proof of concept. In: Proceedings of the 15th International Conference on Availability, Reliability and Security, pp. 1–10 (2020)
7. Brierley, C., Pont, J., Arief, B., Barnes, D.J., Hernandez-Castro, J.: Persistence in linux-based IoT malware. In: Asplund, M., Nadjm-Tehrani, S. (eds.) NordSec 2020. LNCS, vol. 12556, pp. 3–19. Springer, Cham (2021). https://doi.org/10.1007/978-3-030-70852-8_1

8. @CDPROJEKTRED: Important update (2021). https://twitter.com/CDPROJEKTRED/status/1359048125403590660. Accessed June 2021

9. Internet Crime Complaint Center: Internet crime report 2020 (2021). https://www.ic3.gov/Media/PDF/AnnualReport/2020_IC3Report.pdf. Accessed July 2021

10. Chai, Z., Ghafari, A., Houmansadr, A.: On the importance of encrypted-SNI (ESNI) to censorship circumvention. In: 9th USENIX Workshop on Free and Open Communications on the Internet (FOCI 2019) (2019)

11. Let's Encrypt: Let's encrypt stats. https://letsencrypt.org/stats/. Accessed July 2021

12. EnderUNIX: Voipong (2011). https://github.com/EnderUNIX/VoIPong. Accessed July 2021

13. Fabian Bräunlein, L.F.: Smart Spies: Alexa and Google Home expose users to vishing and eavesdropping (2019). https://www.srlabs.de/bites/smart-spies. Accessed July 2021

14. Fielding, R., et al.: RFC2616: Hypertext transfer protocol-http/1.1 (1999)

15. Goodin, D.: CD projekt red does an about-face, says ransomware crooks are leaking data (2021). https://arstechnica.com/gadgets/2021/06/cd-projekt-red-says-its-data-is-likely-circulating-online-after-ransom-attack/. Accessed June 2021

16. Google: Cloud computing services — Google Cloud. https://cloud.google.com/. Accessed July 2021

17. Google: HTTP strict transport security. https://www.chromium.org/hsts/. Accessed July 2021

18. Google: HTTPS encryption on the web. https://transparencyreport.google.com/https/overview. Accessed July 2021

19. Google: Detect explicit content (safesearch) (2021). https://cloud.google.com/vision/docs/detecting-safe-search. Accessed Aug 2021

20. Google: Detect faces (2021). https://cloud.google.com/vision/docs/detecting-faces. Accessed Aug 2021

21. Google: Detect labels (2021). https://cloud.google.com/vision/docs/labels. Accessed Aug 2021

22. Google: Geolocation API (2021). https://developers.google.com/maps/documentation/geolocation/overview. Accessed July 2021

23. Google: Method: speech.recognize (2021). https://cloud.google.com/speech-to-text/docs/reference/rest/v1/speech/recognize. Accessed July 2021

24. Talos Intelligence Group: VPNFilter update - VPNFilter exploits endpoints, targets new devices (2018). https://blog.talosintelligence.com/2018/06/vpnfilter-update.html. Accessed July 2021

25. The TCPDUMP Group: TCPDUMP/LIBCAP public repository (2021). https://www.tcpdump.org/. Accessed July 2021

26. Hron, M.: The fresh smell of ransomed coffee (2020). https://decoded.avast.io/martinhron/the-fresh-smell-of-ransomed-coffee/. Accessed July 2021

27. IBM: Speech to text demo. https://speech-to-text-demo.ng.bluemix.net/. Accessed July 2021

28. Ilascu, I.: Hacker used ransomware to lock victims in their IoT chastity belt (2021). https://www.bleepingcomputer.com/news/security/hacker-used-ransomware-to-lock-victims-in-their-iot-chastity-belt/. Accessed June 2021

29. Kalbo, N., Mirsky, Y., Shabtai, A., Elovici, Y.: The security of IP-based video surveillance systems. Sensors **20**(17), 4806 (2020)

30. Kharraz, A., Robertson, W., Balzarotti, D., Bilge, L., Kirda, E.: Cutting the Gordian knot: a look under the hood of ransomware attacks. In: Almgren, M., Gulisano, V., Maggi, F. (eds.) DIMVA 2015. LNCS, vol. 9148, pp. 3–24. Springer, Cham (2015). https://doi.org/10.1007/978-3-319-20550-2_1
31. Land, J.: Multiple netgear routers are vulnerable to arbitrary command injection (2016). https://www.kb.cert.org/vuls/id/582384/. Accessed July 2021
32. Marlinspike, M.: New tricks for defeating SSL in practice. Black Hat DC 2 (2009)
33. Mockapetris, P.: Domain names - concepts and facilities (1987). https://datatracker.ietf.org/doc/html/rfc1034#section-5.3.2. Accessed July 2021
34. Mohurle, S., Patil, M.: A brief study of wannacry threat: ransomware attack 2017. Int. J. Adv. Res. Comput. Sci. 8(5), 1938–1940 (2017)
35. Morais, R.: Deepspeech 0.9.3 (2020). https://github.com/mozilla/DeepSpeech/releases/tag/v0.9.3. Accessed July 2021
36. Mozilla: Geolocate (2020). https://ichnaea.readthedocs.io/en/latest/api/geolocate.html. Accessed July 2021
37. NIST: CVE-2016-6277 detail (2017). https://nvd.nist.gov/vuln/detail/CVE-2016-6277. Accessed July 2021
38. Orland, K.: CD projekt red source code reportedly sells for millions in dark web auction [updated] (2021). https://arstechnica.com/gaming/2021/02/cd-projekt-red-source-code-reportedly-sells-for-millions-in-dark-web-auction/. Accessed June 2021
39. Palmer, D.: Hackers publish thousands of files after government agency refuses to pay ransom (2021). https://www.zdnet.com/article/hackers-publish-thousands-of-files-after-government-agency-refuses-to-pay-ransom/. Accessed July 2021
40. Patton, C.: Good-bye ESNI, hello ECH! (2020). https://blog.cloudflare.com/encrypted-client-hello/. Accessed July 2021
41. SonicWall: Sonicwall cyber threat report (2021). https://www.sonicwall.com/medialibrary/en/white-paper/2021-cyber-threat-report.pdf. Accessed July 2021
42. Sun, K., Chen, C., Zhang, X.: "Alexa, stop spying on me!" speech privacy protection against voice assistants. In: Proceedings of the 18th Conference on Embedded Networked Sensor Systems, pp. 298–311 (2020)
43. Surbatovich, M., Aljuraidan, J., Bauer, L., Das, A., Jia, L.: Some recipes can do more than spoil your appetite: analyzing the security and privacy risks of IFTTT recipes. In: Proceedings of the 26th International Conference on World Wide Web, pp. 1501–1510 (2017)
44. tacnetsol: CVE-2019-10999 (2019). https://github.com/tacnetsol/CVE-2019-10999. Accessed July 2021
45. Tidy, J.: Cyber criminals publish more than 4,000 stolen sepa files (2021). https://www.bbc.co.uk/news/uk-scotland-55757884. Accessed June 2021
46. Tor: Tor project — anonymity online. www.torproject.org/. Accessed July 2021
47. TrendMicro: Exposed video streams: how hackers abuse surveillance cameras (2018). https://www.trendmicro.com/vinfo/us/security/news/internet-of-things/exposed-video-streams-how-hackers-abuse-surveillance-cameras. Accessed June 2021
48. TrendMicro: Over 200,000 mikrotik routers compromised in cryptojacking campaign (2018). https://www.trendmicro.com/vinfo/nl/security/news/cybercrime-and-digital-threats/over-200-000-mikrotik-routers-compromised-in-cryptojacking-campaign. Accessed July 2021
49. Whalen, S., Engle, S., Romeo, D.: An introduction to ARP spoofing. Node99 [Online Document] (2001). https://www.cavalcantetreinamentos.com.br/blog/material-sala-de-aula/SegurancaemRedes/Outros/arp_spoofing_slides.pdf

50. Zhang, N., Mi, X., Feng, X., Wang, X., Tian, Y., Qian, F.: Understanding and mitigating the security risks of voice-controlled third-party skills on Amazon Alexa and Google Home. arXiv preprint arXiv:1805.01525 (2018)

51. Zhang, Y., et al.: A11 your PLCS belong to me: ICS ransomware is realistic. In: 2020 IEEE 19th International Conference on Trust, Security and Privacy in Computing and Communications (TrustCom), pp. 502–509. IEEE (2020)

Machine Learning and Security

SQL Injections and Reinforcement Learning: An Empirical Evaluation of the Role of Action Structure

Manuel Del Verme[1,2]([⊠]), Åvald Åslaugson Sommervoll[3], László Erdődi[4], Simone Totaro[2,5], and Fabio Massimo Zennaro[3]

[1] McGill University, Montreal, Canada
[2] Mila, Montreal, Canada
[3] Department of Informatics, University of Oslo, Oslo, Norway
[4] Department of Information Security and Communication Technology, Norwegian University of Science and Technology, Trondheim, Norway
[5] Université de Montréal, Montreal, Canada

Abstract. Penetration testing is a central problem in computer security, and recently, the application of machine learning techniques to this topic has gathered momentum. In this paper, we consider the problem of exploiting SQL injection vulnerabilities, and we represent it as a capture-the-flag scenario in which an attacker can submit strings to an input form with the aim of obtaining a flag token representing private information. We then model the attacker as a reinforcement learning agent that interacts with the server to learn an optimal policy leading to an exploit. We compare two agents: a simpler structured agent that relies on significant a priori knowledge and uses high-level actions; and a structureless agent that has limited a priori knowledge and generates SQL statements. The comparison showcases the feasibility of developing agents that rely on less ad-hoc modeling and illustrates a possible direction to develop agents that may have wide applicability.

Keywords: Reinforcement learning · Penetration testing · Capture the flag · SQL injection

1 Introduction

In recent years several works have explored applications of machine learning to computer security problems, ranging from anomaly detection models used to sift through large network data sets [12,26] to language models trained on code repositories to spot malicious programs [23,29]. In all these cases, whenever a problem could be fit into one of the paradigms of machine learning, and sufficient data and computational resources could be provided, machine learning has delivered statistical models able to produce accurate and fast predictions.

A relevant area in the field of computer security is penetration testing (PT). Loosely speaking, PT embraces a large set of activities carried out by legitimate

© Springer Nature Switzerland AG 2021
N. Tuveri et al. (Eds.): NordSec 2021, LNCS 13115, pp. 95–113, 2021.
https://doi.org/10.1007/978-3-030-91625-1_6

or ethical hackers in order to test the security of a system. Simulations of PT often takes the form of security capture-the-flag (CTF) challenges, that is, competitions in which penetration testers compete to detect, and possibly exploit, vulnerabilities on systems specifically configured for such an event. CTFs constitute not only a useful learning resource for human hackers, but they also provide well-defined and legitimate environments that may be used to train artificial agents. Formalizing PT is a topic of interest in the academia and the industry, as witnessed, for instance, in the development of CTF challenges for autonomous agents, such as the DARPA Cyber grand challenge[1].

We consider the reduction of a representative CTF challenge to a reinforcement learning (RL) problem, and we analyze how agents trained using different approaches fare on this task. Specifically, we take into consideration the emblematic problem of SQL injection (SQLi), in which an agent tries to craft a malicious string that, once embedded in a SQL statement, leads to some form of unwanted information disclosure. Exploiting SQLi vulnerabilities is a non-trivial problem which requires a hacker to detect a potential vulnerability, probe the target system, collect information from the responses, and finally submit the malicious input. In our work, we develop RL agents designed to try to automate the process of SQLi. Assuming the existence of a vulnerability has been already detected, we deploy our agents in an environment containing a vulnerable system, and we let them work out a SQLi through interaction and inference. We compare two different models: agents relying on a priori knowledge, and agents endowed with a more restricted knowledge about the environment. The first type of agent, which we name *structured agent*, relies on user-injected knowledge of SQL syntax and the form of queries run by the target system; this model closely resembles the model presented in [11]. The second type of agent, which we name instead *structureless agent*, has a more limited knowledge of SQL syntax or of the target system; it builds its SQLi from SQL tokens and alphanumeric characters.

We compare these two approaches, the structured and the structureless, on a common CTF task representing a simple yet realistic instance of SQLi vulnerability. Although the two agents have significant differences hindering a direct comparison, we evaluate both of them in terms of their performance (measured on the task they are trained to solve), flexibility and cost (evaluated in terms of a trade-off between level of generalization of the model, need for encoding of a priori knowledge, and computational resources).

Our results advance the research on the development of RL agents for PT and CTF-like problems, contributing to a better understanding of the role of structure and shedding light on possible future lines of development. While results on structured agents have already been presented in the literature [11], this work extends existing results by considering the application of structured agents to a more realistic settings (using a real instance of a SQL server instead of a simulated server), by deploying more sophisticated agents (relying on actor-critic agents instead of value-based agents), and by providing the agent with a richer feedback (returning a more nuanced error message). More importantly, the paper

---

[1] https://www.darpa.mil/program/cyber-grand-challenge.

introduce a new approach to solve the CTF problem that relies on significantly less prior knowledge, delegating the task of building such a knowledge to the RL agent itself. This RL agent shows the feasibility of training machine learning models for security that could learn in a strongly autonomous way; by requiring less ad-hoc modelling and injection of knowledge, these agents thus hold the promise to be easily deployable across many different problems. Finally, we offer a comparison between the structured and the structureless agent along the line of [32], by contrasting the advantages and disadvantages of both approaches.

The rest of the paper is organized as follows: in Sect. 2 we define the main concepts related to RL and SQLi; in Sect. 3 we review existing work on the topic of automating PT and solving SQL-based problems; in Sect. 4 we explain our methods, including the environment and the agents we designed; in Sect. 5 we present and discuss the results of our experiments. Finally, Sect. 6 contains ethical consideration about this work, while Sect. 7 summarizes our work and points to future developments.

2 Background

We review the main ideas from RL and PT relevant to this work. We provide the definition of a RL problem and of RL agents, and we discuss the generation of strings at character level within a RL context; for PT, we illustrate CTF problems and we explain the specific instance of SQLi.

2.1 Reinforcement Learning

We first recall the main aspects of the RL problem. RL provides a framework to train agents in a dynamic environment by letting them perform actions and observe the consequences of their choices; through a trial-and-error process, the agents infer a strategy (or policy) that allow them to achieve high long-term returns. Formally, a typical RL problem is embedded in a Markov Decision Process (MDP) $\mathcal{M}$. An MDP is defined via the tuple $\langle \mathcal{S}, \mathcal{A}, r, \mathcal{P}, d_0 \rangle$, where $\mathcal{S}$ and $\mathcal{A}$ are the state and action space set, which are possibly large but finite and discrete; $r : \mathcal{S} \times \mathcal{A} \to \mathcal{R}$ is the reward function used to encode a description of the desired behaviour, often chosen by the practitioner; $\mathcal{P} : \mathcal{S} \times A \to \Delta(\mathcal{S})$ is the transition dynamics of the environment (or simply dynamics) which provides a probabilistic description of how the environment transitions from a given state upon an action of the agent; d_0 is a distribution over the initial state of the environment. A solution of the RL problem is a policy $\pi^* : \mathcal{S} \to \Delta(\mathcal{A})$ that maximizes a long-term cumulative objective, for example the expected cumulative discounted reward. More formally:

$$\pi^*(a|s) = \arg\max_{\pi \in \Pi} \mathbf{E}_\pi \left[\sum_{t=0}^{\infty} \gamma^t r(s_t, a_t) \mid s_0 \right] \quad s_0 \sim d_0, \quad (1)$$

where Π is the space of probability distributions, the expectation $\mathbf{E}_\pi$ is with respect all possible trajectories starting from s_0 following policy π, and $\gamma \in [0, 1)$ is a factor discounting future rewards.

Actor-Critic Methods. One approach to solving Eq. 1 is via direct policy optimization, where we parametrize the policy π_θ via a set of parameters θ:

$$\theta^* = \arg\max_{\theta \in \Theta} \mathbf{E}_{\pi_\theta} \left[\sum_{t=0}^{\infty} \gamma^t r(s_t, a_t) \mid s_0 \right] \quad s_0 \sim d_0, \tag{2}$$

where Θ is now the space of parameters, and the expectation $\mathbf{E}_{\pi_\theta}$ is with respect to the parametrized policy π_θ. Policy gradient methods optimize this objective directly via gradient ascent. In order to reduce variance, actor-critic methods optimize this objective while at the same time learning an estimate of the reward $r(s_t, a_t)$; the actor module is responsible for the optimization of π_θ, while the critic module estimates the return in terms of a value function $V^\pi(s) = \mathbf{E}_\pi[\sum_{t=0}^{\infty} \gamma^t r(s_t, a_t)|s_0 = s]$, an action-value function $Q^\pi(s, a) = \mathbf{E}_\pi[\sum_{t=0}^{\infty} \gamma^t r(s_t, a_t)|s_0 = s, a_0 = a]$, or an advantage function $A^\pi(s, a) = Q^\pi(s, a) - V^\pi(s)$.

Proximal Policy Optimization. Proximal Policy Optimization (PPO) [25] is a state-of-the-art actor-critic algorithm which has been proven successful on a variety of complex tasks. PPO, in its proximal form, maximizes the following objective via multiple iteration of gradient ascent:

$$\pi_{\theta_{k+1}} = \arg\max_{\theta \in \Theta} \mathbf{E} \left[\frac{\pi_{\theta_k}}{\pi_{\theta_{k+1}}} A^{\pi_{\theta_k}}(s, a) \right] - \eta \mathbf{E} \left[\mathrm{KL}(\pi_{\theta_{k-1}}, \pi_{\theta_k}) \right], \tag{3}$$

where π_{θ_k} is the parametrized policy using the parameter values at time k, η is a regularization hyper-parameter, and $KL(p, q)$ is the Kullback-Leibler (KL) divergence from distribution p to q. The KL penalty guarantees that the size of the steps in every gradient ascent iteration remains bounded.

Alternatively, the optimization in the PPO agent may be reformulated using a clipping operator:

$$\pi_{\theta_{k+1}} = \arg\max_{\theta \in \Theta} \mathbf{E} \left[\min(z(\pi_{\theta_k}) A^{\pi_{\theta_k}}(s, a), \mathrm{clip}(z(\pi_{\theta_k}), 1 - \epsilon, 1 + \epsilon) A^{\pi_{\theta_k}}(s, a)) \right],$$
$$\tag{4}$$

where $z(\pi_{\theta_k}) = \frac{\pi_{\theta_k}}{\pi_{\theta_{k+1}}}$, and the $\mathrm{clip}(a, 1 - \epsilon, 1 + \epsilon)$ operator clips the value a to force it within the interval $[a(1 - \epsilon), a(1 + \epsilon)]$, with $\epsilon \in \mathbb{R}$. The clipping operator in the new objective achieves the same aim of KL divergence, by keeping the update at every gradient ascent iteration bounded.

Direct policy parametrization and a simple optimization procedure make policy gradient methods interesting candidates for high dimensional state and action space, such as the text-based setting that we discuss next.

2.2   Word Level RL

The appealing property of policy gradient method stems from the temporal decomposition of the log-likelihood. The idea is to consider a sentence as an action made of a sequence of tokens and model the policy as a conditional distribution over that sequence. More formally, let $\mathbf{a} = (a_0, \ldots, a_k)$ be a sequence of tokens, and let policy $\pi_\theta(\mathbf{a}|s)$ be a joint distribution on $\mathbf{a}$ conditioned on s. Note that $\log \pi_\theta(\mathbf{a}, s) = \sum_{i=0}^{T} \log \pi_\theta(a_i \mid s, a_{i-1})$, where the starting is simply an empty token i.e. $a_{-1} = \epsilon$. Plugging in the new objective in Eq. 3, and substituting the expected value with the empirical average, we can rewrite the objective as follows:

$$\hat{\mathcal{L}}(\theta) = \frac{1}{N+1} \sum_{n=0}^{N} \frac{1}{T_n} \sum_{i=0}^{T_n} \frac{\pi_{\theta_k}(a_i \mid s_n)}{\pi_{\theta_{k+1}}(a_i \mid s_n)} A^{\pi_{\theta_k}}(s_n, \mathbf{a}) + \eta \mathbf{E}\left[\mathrm{KL}(\pi_{\theta_{k-1}}, \pi_{\theta_k})\right], \quad (5)$$

where N is the number of samples for estimating the empirical average, T_n is the number of tokens in the nth sample. Note that the advantage function, which provides the update direction of the policy gradient, depends on the complete sequence of tokens. Furthermore, in sparse reward settings like the one we will be considering, the gradient of the policy is effectively zero until a positive return is found. This optimization objective thus presents two significant challenges: exploration and credit assignment. We discuss here a heuristic exploration inspired by Thompson sampling, which proved to work well in practice, and leave credit assignment for future work.

Exploration. Typical heuristics rely on reward shaping either via sub-goals [2,4] or on an entropic regularizer that promotes exploration [14,20]. Both solutions change the optimal policy. Here, we take inspiration from Thompson sampling [18], and propose a "prior" distribution over sentences that ensure meaningful exploration of the query space. While the injection of knowledge in the form of a "prior" tailored by a user is appealing, it does explicitly introduce bias in the exploration process of the agent. Instead, we propose to learn a prior distribution over sequences by maximizing its entropy. More formally, let $\nu_\theta(\mathbf{a}, s)$ be a parametric distribution over sequences which maximizes the following objective:

$$arg \max_\theta H(\nu_\theta) = arg \max_\theta - \sum_i^{T} \nu_\theta(a_i \mid s) \log \nu_\theta(a_i \mid s) \quad (6)$$

Over a finite domain, as in the case of our actions, the solution of this optimization problem is the uniform distribution. If θ is parametrized by a neural network with softmax activation, then achieving a uniform distribution is not trivial. We nonetheless add this contribution to our loss, and finally obtain the objective:

$$\hat{\mathcal{L}}(\theta) = \frac{1}{N+1} \sum_{n=0}^{N} \frac{1}{T_n} \sum_{i=0}^{K_j} \nu_{\theta_k}(a_i, s_n) \frac{\pi_{\theta_k}(a_i \mid s_n)}{\pi_{\theta_{k+1}}(a_i \mid s_n)} A^{\pi_{\theta_k}}(s_n, a_n) + \eta \mathbf{E}\left[\mathrm{KL}(\pi_{\theta_{k-1}}, \pi_{\theta_k})\right]$$

$$(7)$$

The prior distribution ν effectively slows down the optimization process, by reducing the magnitude of the importance ratio in (7) preventing the policy from becoming deterministic too quickly, while maintaining the optimal policy intact.

This form of Thompson Sampling is in contrast with the standard Bayesian literature, as we attempt to learn a suitable prior distribution from data, instead of handcrafting from prior knowledge.

2.3 Penetration Testing

The complexity of modern computer systems and networks entails the existence of several types of vulnerabilities which could be exploited by malicious actors with varying forms of motivation and expertise. An effective way to discover and patch vulnerabilities consists in penetration testing, that is mimicking the behaviour of attackers; indeed checking a system from the perspective of an attacker may reveal serious security deficiencies that could have been otherwise overlooked.

Capture the Flag. A prototypical example of penetration testing, used for education and training, are CTF-style security challenges, in which systems with simulated vulnerabilities are set up and probed by penetration testers. CTFs provide a simple and usable abstraction of a technical security challenge. The exploitation of a security vulnerability (or a chain of vulnerabilities) is rewarded in a non-ambiguous way in the form of a flag token. A flag is just a string in a special format that is easy to recognize and that can be gained by an attacker only after carrying out all the steps necessary to exploit a vulnerability. The capture of the flag is the criterion of success in a CTF, with no further exploitation required. According to the vulnerability under considerations, CTF challenges may be categorized in different groups, such as web hacking challenges or binary exploitation challenges. As human factors are normally excluded from these challenges, penetration testers are expected to rely only on their expertise and logic. CTFs thus constitute a relevant model for artificial agents, since these challenges may be framed as games with enumerable sets of actions, clear success conditions, and strategies that may be derived through reasoning and inference.

SQL Injection. In this work, we restrict our attention to web hacking CTFs. More precisely, we consider a simple CTF made up of a dynamic website with a SQLi vulnerability. Dynamic websites are common websites designed to offer rich user experiences on the web; they normally receive and store large amounts of data in order to improve and customize the experience of the users (for instance, they may store sensitive data to perform user authentication). For reasons of efficiency this data is often stored in dedicated relational databases, such as mysql, mssql, or posgresql. The website can query the database server using the standard *Structured Query Language (SQL)*. Simple queries for data retrieval (using a `SELECT` command along with a `WHERE` clause) or advanced statements (concatenating, for instance, multiple SQL queries with a `UNION` statement) allow the website to extract the necessary information. To customize these queries the website may embed in the query some user input. The possibility for a SQLi vulnerability opens when user input is not properly validated and directly embedded in a pre-generated query. In such a case, a malicious user may craft an input string allowing her to get full or partial control over the query. In the least threatening case, the attacker can modify the expression evaluation of the query to disclose information; in more severe cases, a determined attacker may be able to write local files to or even run operating system instructions. Even if there are no clearly defined methodologies to perform SQLi exploitation, a typical approach involves a first exploratory phase aimed at uncovering the character-istics of the vulnerability (identifying the vulnerable web input parameter, the type of input parameter, restrictions and filtering of the input, structure of the pre-generated query, SQL answer presentation from the website), and then an exploitation phase in which the vulnerability is exploited and the flag captured.

3   Related Work

In this section we review both previous work related to using automation, arti-ficial intelligence and machine learning to tackle the PT problem, and exist-ing work related to RL agents dealing with textual actions or with SQL-based problems.

Automated tools for PT. Automating PT is an old challenge in computer security. The most immediate way to automate the process of PT is to develop tools that can follow scripted directives and quickly execute repetitive and menial tasks. Security scanners like Nessus[2] or applications like sqlmap[3] fit in this cat-egory. These tools distill human knowledge, encode it in an executable script, and execute it; as such, they do not perform any learning, and their adaptability to new scenarios depends on how foreseeing and inclusive are their codes.

Planning for PT. Symbolic approaches to AI and optimal planning offered a higher-level approach to the PT problem: instead of encoding solutions, it is possible to express a problem in a rigorous formalism and produce a solution through a solver. Models of interest include plans [6], attack graphs [3], MDPs, partially observable MDPs [24], Stackelberg games [27], and Petri nets [5]. [16] provides a taxonomy of these models along the dimensions of uncertainty in the model and property of the agent actions. Whenever a problem has a limited dimensionality, these models may be solved exactly, providing an optimal solu-tion. The drawback of this approach is that it requires a rigorous modelling of the problem, and that the complexity for solving the model may quickly diverge, making it unfeasible to solve realistic challenges.

RL for PT. A more versatile approach to solve larger and less formalized PT problems is provided the RL paradigm. While the problem environment can still be expressed in terms of a MDP or a POMDP, its solution is not achieved through exact planning, but through learning via inference. The idea of training RL to solve PT problems goes back, at least, to the work of [10,22] and [13], all considering different levels of abstraction of the PT problem and different RL agent algorithms. More recently [9] analyzed the problem of automating the development of RL environments for PT, [32] considered trade-offs in providing

---

[2] https://www.tenable.com/products/nessus.
[3] http://sqlmap.org/.

RL agents with a priori knowledge, and [19] extended the application of RL agents to modelling post-exploitation actions. Finally, a more fine-grained modelling of the specific PT problem of SQLi is studied in [11], which also offers a preliminary evaluation of RL agents tackling this challenge. The current paper follows that line of work, studying and analyzing more realistic challenges and agents.

Interactive Fiction. The problem of generating strings to exploit a SQLi vulnerability has resemblances with the problem of solving interactive fiction games (IF). In IF, a player is presented with text describing a situation; the player can then interact with the environment by taking actions; these actions are processed by the system which provides a new textual description of the consequences of the actions and the new state of the environment. There are some obvious similarity between IF games and SQLi challenges: they both require actions in forms of strings (natural language in IF, SQL in SQLi) and the agent is provided a textual description of the state of the world (natural language description of a situation in IF, HTML responses in SQLi). Moreover, it is possible to distinguish two types of IF games that may be further put in relation to our work. The first type is *choice-based IF*, in which a player can choose actions from a restricted set of pre-defined textual actions. RL agents have been proposed that embed and process the textual description of the environment and the actions, and then estimate the value of actions [15,31]. Our structured agent adopts a similar approach to the SQLi problem, in the sense that it selects its action from a set of strings; however, it does not currently perform any embedding or processing of textual inputs (such as, HTML responses). The second type is *parser-based IF*, in which a player can autonomously generate a textual description of the action it wants to undertake; this provides the player with a much larger degree of freedom, although the large majority of IF games has parsers able to process a very limited number of commands based on an elementary verb-object syntax. RL agents have been developed that again embed and process the textual description of the environment, and then exploit the verb-object structure of commands to generate actions [17,21,30]. Our structureless agent has some similarities with these approaches, in the sense that it generates its actions in the form of strings. However, beyond the surface similarity, there is a significant difference in the underlying environment in IF and SQLi. In IF games, the environment tends to be very rich in structure, with a complex interrelated set of states; this constitutes an exploratory challenge of its own, which has been addressed with several techniques such as rewarding the discovery of new states [30], defining sub-tasks [17], learning admissible actions in different states [17], or identification of bottleneck states [1]. In our SQLi problem, instead, the environment tends to have little structure and to provide responses that are minimally informative; a challenge for the agent is to capture this structure, without which the problem could turn to a trivial brute-forcing or a bandits problem [18].

SQL semantic parsing. Finally, a last line of work that may bear some relation to our work is SQL semantic parsing. In SQL semantic parsing a RL agent is trained to generate correct SQL queries given a natural language description of the desired output [28,33]. Once again, this setup has some correspondence with SQLi challenges, especially when using a structureless agent: actions are SQL strings, and the state has a textual description (natural language in SQL semantic parsing, HTML responses in SQLi). Differences are noticeable too: although often trained using RL, the finalized SQL semantic parsing agent is required to produce outputs without interacting with an environment; moreover, significant guidance to the SQL semantic parsing agent is given through the natural language input, while the SQLi agent lacks such hints for discovering a vulnerability.

4 Methods

In this section we present the environment we designed for our experiments, we provide details on the agents we developed, and offer some consideration about the role of structure (or its absence).

4.1 Environment

We construct an artificial environment with a union SQLi vulnerability. In designing such an environment we make a trade-off between two desiderata: (i) an environment that guarantees some degree of realism; and, (ii) an environment that would allow us to seamlessly train our agents.

Concerning the first aim, we decided to devise a CTF-like environment in which agents are required to perform some degree of information-gathering analogous to the one carried out by real hackers; specifically, our challenge requires the agent to perform exploratory actions aimed at discovering the type of input necessary for SQLi and the underlying structure of the pre-generated query. Inferring these characteristics is essential in order to achieve a SQLi in a reasonable number of steps.

Concerning our second aim, we chose to create a challenge that would allow us to train and test both our structured agent which relies on strong a priori knowledge of the task (SQL syntax, format of useful commands) and our structureless agents which is supposed to start with almost zero-knowledge (except for the knowledge that commands are made up by alphabetic characters and SQL keywords). By training both models on the same challenge, this allows us to highlight the strengths and the weaknesses of each agent. Although the two models learn different action policies (the structured agents develop an action policy over the finite set of pre-made SQL strings available, while the structureless agents learn to generate syntactically correct SQL statements to exploit SQLi), the identical environment allows us to compare them by analyzing how they achieve their objective and by considering the trade-offs that they offer in terms of abstraction, versatility, and efficiency. Next, we describe the setup of our webserver environment, and the form of SQLi it admits.

Setup. We instantiate a mock webserver hosting a dynamic page populated by sending queries to a back-end database a SQL query is composed by using pre-generated string appended with a provided input. The definition of the pre-generated query opens up the possibility of a SQL injection.

The back-end database contains two tables: a `Users` table, containing data meant to populate the page hosted by the webserver, and a `Private` table containing confidential information. The basic schema of the two tables is presented in Table 1 and Table 2. The content of the table `Private` is the information that the agent aims to disclose through a SQL injection. In CTF terms, the content of the table `Private` constitute the *flag* the agent aims to retrieve.

Table 1. `Users` table schema.

ID	username	firstName	lastName	age	nationality	create_at
...	...	...	...	...	...	

Table 2. `Private` table schema.

ID	user	account
...	...	...

The pre-generated query accessing the database takes one of the following forms:

> `SELECT` *cols* `FROM Users WHERE firstName =`"<*input*>"
>
> `SELECT` *cols* `FROM Users WHERE nationality =`'<*input*>'
>
> `SELECT` *cols* `FROM Users WHERE age =`<*input*>

where *cols* corresponds to a list from one to three column names, and <*input*> is a user-defined string. Given the absence of any processing of the *input* string, an agent can exploit the intrinsic SQL injection by crafting a malicious input.

Exploit. To successfully exploit the SQL injection vulnerability in these queries, the agent has to submit a *input* string of the form: [0|"|'] `UNION SELECT account[,NULL]`* `FROM Private` − − where [0|"|'] denotes the choice of the right escape character, with 0 being an arbitrary integer; [,`NULL`]* denotes the repetition from zero to an arbitrary number of times of the keyword `NULL` in order to match the number of columns with the `UNION` command; − − is a comment operator to ignore the rest of the pre-generated string. An SQL command with a union operator can only be evaluated if the number of selected columns are the same for the queries that are concatenated by the union. In order to match the number of columns with the original query we add null values to the attacker created selection. For instance, if the server is instantiated with the pre-generated query: `SELECT firstName, lastName, age FROM Users WHERE nationality =`'*input*' then the correct input for SQL injection would be: '`UNION SELECT account,NULL,NULL FROM Private` − −.

4.2 Structured Agent

The structured agent relies on a priori knowledge of the form of the pre-generated SQL query running on the target server. This shrinks the search space to well-formed SQL statements that would match the pre-generated query.

Action Space. We then generate a small finite action space $\mathcal{A}$ containing 25 actions. These actions can roughly be partitioned into four sub-sets of actions depending on their aim: (i) exploratory SQL statements aimed at probing the escape character in the pre-generated SQL statement (6 actions); (ii) exploratory SQL statements aimed at guessing the number of columns necessary for the SQLi (9 actions); (iii) exploitative SQL statements attempting a SQLi (9 statements); (iv) other actions (1 action). Refer to Appendix A.1 for the complete list of actions and their partitioning.

Implementation. The structured agents is implemented as a PPO agent using the formulation in Eq. 4. The actor develops its own parametric policy π_θ over the finite set of actions in $\mathcal{A}$. After choosing an action a, the input string is sent to the server, embedded in the pre-generated query and sent to SQL server. The response of the server is a HTML page that could be handled by a static parser; since this parsing is not relevant to our study, we abstract it away and just provide the agent with a numeric code corresponding to the result of the action. This code allows to discriminate between an action that was syntactically wrong and generated a SQL error, an action that was syntactically correct and returned an empty string, an action that was syntactically correct and returned some content, and an action that successfully performed the SQLi.

Optimal Policy. While a brute-forcing agent may guess the right SQLi by simply trying out all the actions, this approach would be extremely inefficient; if we assume the agents simply goes through all his action until it finds the right SQLi statement, this procedure would require on average 12.5 actions[4]. In addition, the scalability of finding the right syntax with brute-forcing is extremely bad. As the learning environment becomes more complex, using brute-forcing is not an option. We also would like to emphasize that this approach is not similar to the activity of fuzzing. With fuzzing the attacker tries to discover the vulnerability by sending the right input to trigger the vulnerability, whilst the aim of our approach is to learn the optimal policy for the exploitation of the vulnerability. Sending random input in the beginning of the learning phase is normal with the applied ML paradigm. Through interacting with the environment, the RL agent is expected to learn the structure underlying its exploratory actions, and use it efficiently to find out the information necessary to perform the SQLi. Notice that, given the overlap between exploratory and exploitative SQL statements, a human agent is expected to achieve SQLi in less than 5 actions (using at most 2 actions to find the escape, and 3 actions to guess the correct number of columns).

---

[4] A completely random agent would use an average of 17 actions.

Thus, the structured agent learns a reasonable distribution of probability over the given SQL commands which allows it to efficiently solve and to generalize to all problems of the form presented in our environment.

4.3 Structureless Agent

The structureless agent assumes limited knowledge of the environment. It is not provided with pre-generated SQL statements; instead it learns by trial-and-error to form syntactically correct inputs, the aim of this agent is to exploit the system to the fullest extent, restricting ourselves to correct SQL statements would prevent the agent from exploiting bugs in the SQL implementation.

Action Space. The most generic action space $\mathcal{A}$ for the structureless agent is defined by a set of all strings that may be generated by sampling tokens from a generic alphabet $\mathcal{A}$. The alphabet $\mathcal{A}$ contains letters $\{a, b, c, ...\}$, numbers $\{0, 1, 2, ...\}$, linguistic tokens including space $\circ$, empty string ϵ, escape characters, end-of-string symbols and other punctuation marks $\{\circ, \epsilon, ', '', \text{EOF}, ,, ...\}^5$, and SQL keywords $\{\text{UNION}, \text{SELECT}, \text{NULL}, \text{FROM}, --, ...\}$. An atomic action by the structureless agent is then a list $\mathbf{a}$ of elementary tokens; for instance the SQLi string in the example above would correspond to the 28-element list: $\mathbf{a} = [', \text{UNION}, \circ, \text{SELECT}, \circ, a, c, c, o, u, n, t, ,, \text{NULL}, ,, \text{NULL}, \circ, \text{FROM}, \circ, P, r, i, v, a, t, e, \circ, --]$. Such a list can then be parsed into an actual SQL statement.

Solving a RL problem with a large alphabet like $\mathcal{A}$ requires substantial resources. Therefore, we decided to investigate first of all the actual feasibility of learning with our structureless agent given alphabets with smaller cardinality. Tuning the number of tokens will allow us to control the complexity and the training time of the agents, while at the same time validate our structureless approach. This setup also exposes a natural setting for curriculum learning, where the complexity of the task at hand may be fixed according to the length of the shortest valid sequence to achieve the SQLi.

Implementation. We instantiate a PPO agent implementing the loss function in Eq. 7. At every interaction, the agent first observes a response from the server, converts the text into tokens, processes the sequence of token with a GRU [8] based autoregressive model, and finally it produces a latent vector. The latent vector is then fed into the actor-critic network, which is provided with a policy head, a value head and a prior head. The value head is used by the critic to output a single scalar per sentence, the policy head generated the actor output in the form of a vector of a fixed length, and the prior head also outputs a vector of a fixed length encoding our exploration prior. We found this approach to be more stable than using another auto regressive model as output. A sequence of tokens is then converted into a readable string, sent to the SQL engine, embedded in the pre-generated query, and processed by the SQL server. In return, the agent receives a new state and a reward upon completion.

---

[5] $\circ$ represents the concatenation symbol, space characters and, a comma character.

Optimal Policy. Generating successful actions over such a large alphabet is very challenging. While the structured agent could still achieve a solution in reasonable time by brute forcing and simply trying all the options in its finite action space, this approach is infeasible for the structureless agent. Given an alphabet even of modest size, the combinatorial explosion of strings that may be generated with the available tokens quickly becomes unmanageable. Moreover, a large number of these randomly generated string would consist of syntactically wrong or meaningless SQL statements. The structureless agent is not provided any a priori knowledge about the structure of a SQL statement. In order to learn how to perform SQLi, it has to learn first the basics on how to generate legal SQL statement, and then learn how to craft the necessary input to achieve an exploit. The structureless agent is expected to learn a useful distribution over characters and SQL tokens that will lead to the instantiating of string that may lead to a SQL injection in the type of problems on which it was trained.

Role of Structure. Priori knowledge about the SQL syntax has often been argued to be a good design choice, for instance the case of SQL parsing in [28]. Although at first not knowing the basic SQL syntax may look like a weakness, we want to remark that it constitutes one of the main desirable traits of the structureless approach. Providing knowledge in the form of a fixed SQL query pattern may be problematic; while this makes sense in the case of SQL parsing when the agent is required to form well-behaving complete SQL statements [28], this does not hold in our case, where the agent has to create snippets of SQL statements that in isolation would be incomplete, but that embedded in a pre-generated query may lead to an exploit. Providing patterns bias the agents towards standard solutions, while, we would like the agent to discover new exploits, for instance, to the specific way in which an implemented SQL server may handle inputs.

5   Experiments

In this section we run the structured and the structureless agents on the environment described in Sect. 4. The environment has been developed following the RL standards of OpenAI gym [7], while the agents have been implemented relying on standard libraries. The code for all experiments is openly available[6].

5.1   Reference Agents

Solving the task by bruteforce (given the same dictionary as the structureless agent) would take an average of 110 trial per successful flag retrieval, while common tools like sqlmap[7] can not solve the task without expertly picked flags.

---

[6] https://github.com/manuel-delverme/sql_env.
[7] https://github.com/sqlmapproject/sqlmap.

5.2   Structured Agent

Setup. We run a PPO agent complying to the formulation in Eq. 4 from a standard library[8]. We use default hyperparameters in the library for our PPO agents, in particular a learning rate of $3 \cdot 10^{-4}$ and a clipping value $\epsilon = 0.2$. To collect reliable statistics we trained 10 PPO agents for 10^6 episodes, with a maximum number of iterations per episode set at 30.

Results. Figure 1a shows the evolution of the performance of the agent during training. At the beginning the performance of the agent is similar to a guessing agent, but after 10^4 episodes the mean number of queries that the agent executes settles between 1 to 5. Towards the end of the training, an increase in standard deviation suggests more exploratory actions on the side of the agent.

Figure 1b shows the performance statistics of each individual agent at the end of training. After 10^6 episodes of training, each agent was further tested on 10^3 episodes, and the distribution of the number of queries required to perform SQLi is reported. All the agents present a very similar distribution.

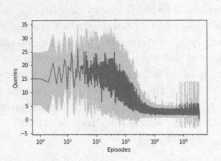

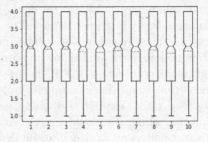

(a) Mean # of queries to perform SQLi executed by the 10 PPO agents during (log) training, shaded is deviation.

(b) Number of queries required to SQLi by each of the 10 trained PPO agents. In orange, the median, green for mean; the notches give a 95% confidence interval; the boxes and the whiskers mark the 25th and 50th percentiles respectively.

Fig. 1. Performance of the structured agent.

Discussion. The PPO agent was able to learn an effective policy to achieve SQLi across the set of problems presented in our environment. As discussed above, it was expected that an optimally trained structured agent would take up to five queries before finding the flag. Surprisingly, all the agents consistently

---

[8] https://stable-baselines3.readthedocs.io/en/master/.

took between one and four queries, with the same median of three across all of them. The structured agent is able to reach this optimal behaviour by learning to exploit information present in the error messages returned by the server. In particular it is able to distinguish between empty and error results, providing valuable information in the choice of the next action. This distinction voids the necessity for explicit exploratory actions, allowing the agent to gain information about the escape and the number of rows while using exploitative actions that may immediately lead to success. The feedback information thus allows the agent to develop a more effective policy than the one originally presented in [11].

5.3 Structureless Agent

Setup. We run a PPO agent implementing the formulation in Eq. 7. We use customized hyperparameters documented in the online implementation. We trained the agent on two environments with a different level of complexity, defined by the alphabet $\mathscr{A}$ available to the agent. The first environment with complexity 3 uses an alphabet of size 6, while the second environment with complexity 4 uses an alphabet of size 7. Refer to Appendix A.2 for details on the alphabets. In our experiments we use a complexity of 3 and 4, for each of them we evaluate each sub task, from 1 to 3 column index. The key difference between 1 to 2 or three column indexes is the randomness of the initial condition. To collect statistical data we train the same PPO agents with 10 seeds. Each episode has a maximum duration of 30 queries, after which it is reset by sampling a new pre-generated query made by an escape character and the number of columns.

Results. Figure 2a shows the average cumulative return, averaged across seeds, and the maximum return averaged in a window of the latest 10 episodes. Recall that the reward is binary: 1 in case of success and 0 in case of failure. When running an environment with complexity 3, some of the agents do successfully learn a policy; instead, when running an environment with complexity 4, only one or two agents on average manage to learn a policy leading to SQLi.

In Fig. 2b we show the return in an environment with complexity of 4 as a function of the number of columns necessary to perform the SQLi. The plot highlights the drop in performance of the agent as the problem gets more challenging with the increase of the number of columns to consider in the union SQLi. When using 3 columns, the return points to a failure in learning.

Discussion. The structureless PPO agent showed a degree of success in solving simple SQLi problems in an environment with low complexity. Increasing the complexity turned out to be problematic; the instability of policy gradient proved to be a challenge as it prevents the agent to advance in its curriculum.

6 Ethical Considerations

While developed for legitimate defensive purposes, PT tools carry with them the risk of misuse; in particular, the same tools that may be used to guarantee

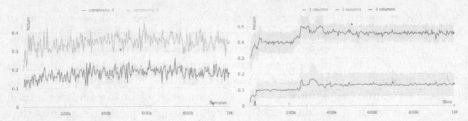

(a) Average reward across seeds during. The shaded region gives the standard deviation.

(b) Average reward across the number of columns during training when running on an environment with complexity 4.

Fig. 2. Performance of the structureless agent.

the safety of a system, may also be adopted by malicious actors to probe and exploit vulnerable targets. The authors of this research strongly condemn any use of their results for criminal or illegal activities, or for the development of autonomous agents to be used in the context of conflict[9].

7   Future Work and Conclusions

In this paper we modeled the problem of learning how to perform SQLi as a RL problem. We considered two approaches for solving the problem: one based on a structured agent provided with relevant a priori knowledge about the problem, and one based on a structureless agent with limited a priori knowledge. We then designed an environment on which we empirically tested both agents. The structured agent was able to quickly learn an effective policy, but its success strongly depended on the expert coding of the action space. On the other hand, the structureless agent presents a more promising approach, as it does not require the hardcoding of a specific action space, nor it is affected by any bias implicitly or explicitly introduced by an expert defining the action space. However, learning in this scenario turns out to be much more challenging, as the space of possibilities is extremely large. Our PPO agents managed to learn in a low-complexity setting, but scaling up to more realistic scenarios would require more computational power and tuning. We observed that the use of a prior in the loss function helps preventing the policy of the agent to collapse on a deterministic policy too quickly; however it does not solve the exploration problem nor the the credit assignment. More versatile agents like the structureless one represent a useful direction of development. On one hand, future work will be directed to shed some of the structure still coded in the structureless agent. On the other hand, research will focus on the problem of improving the learning of the agent, and deploying it to solve more realistic CTF challenges.

---

[9] https://futureoflife.org/awos-signatories/.

A   Implementation Details

A.1   Structured Agent

The following is the list of actions available to the structured agent:

1. ϵ
2. 1' or 1=1 –
3. 1' or 1=2 –
4. 1' union select NULL –
5. 1' union select NULL, NULL –
6. 1' union select NULL, NULL, NULL –
7. 1' union select account from private –
8. 1' union select account, NULL from private –
9. 1' union select account, NULL, NULL from private –
10. 1" or 1=1 –
11. 1" or 1=2 –
12. 1" union select NULL –
13. 1" union select NULL, NULL –
14. 1" union select NULL, NULL, NULL –
15. 1" union select account from private –
16. 1" union select account, NULL from private –
17. 1" union select account, NULL, NULL from private –
18. 1 or 1=1 –
19. 1 or 1=2 –
20. 1 union select NULL –
21. 1 union select NULL, NULL –
22. 1 union select NULL, NULL, NULL –
23. 1 union select account from private –
24. 1 union select account, NULL from private –
25. 1 union select account, NULL, NULL from private –

where ϵ denotes an empty string. Actions are partitioned in SQL statements aimed at probing the escape character in the pre-generated SQL statement (action number $2, 3, 10, 11, 18, 19$), SQL statements aimed at guessing the number of columns necessary for the SQLi (action number $4, 5, 6, 12, 13, 14, 20, 21, 22$), SQL statements attempting a SQLi (action number $7, 8, 9, 15, 16, 17, 23, 24, 25$), other actions (action number 1).

A.2   Structureless Agent

The following are the alphabets at different levels of complexity. For complexity three we use the following alphabet: $\mathscr{A}_3 = \{$∘UNION ∘ SELECT∘,∘NULL$_9$∘,, ∘1∘, ∘'∘,∘"∘, ∘"∘, ∘"∘, ∘a FROM p − −∘, $\epsilon\}$ where a and p are aliases for account and private, respectively. For complexity four we use the following alphabet: $\mathscr{A}_4 = \{$∘UNION ∘ SELECT∘,, ∘NULL$_9$∘, ∘a∘, ∘1∘, ∘'∘, ∘"∘, ∘ FROM p − −∘, $\epsilon\}$

References

1. Ammanabrolu, P., Tien, E., Hausknecht, M., Riedl, M.O.: How to avoid being eaten by a grue: structured exploration strategies for textual worlds. arXiv preprint arXiv:2006.07409 (2020)
2. Andrychowicz, M., et al.: Hindsight experience replay. In: Proceedings of the 31st International Conference on Neural Information Processing Systems, pp. 5055–5065 (2017)
3. Applebaum, A., Miller, D., Strom, B., Korban, C., Wolf, R.: Intelligent, automated red team emulation. In: Proceedings of the 32nd Annual Conference on Computer Security Applications, pp. 363–373 (2016)
4. Bellemare, M., Srinivasan, S., Ostrovski, G., Schaul, T., Saxton, D., Munos, R.: Unifying count-based exploration and intrinsic motivation. In: Advances in Neural Information Processing Systems, vol. 29, pp. 1471–1479 (2016)
5. Bland, J.A., Petty, M.D., Whitaker, T.S., Maxwell, K.P., Cantrell, W.A.: Machine learning cyberattack and defense strategies. Comput. Secur. **92**, 101738 (2020)
6. Boddy, M.S., Gohde, J., Haigh, T., Harp, S.A.: Course of action generation for cyber security using classical planning. In: ICAPS, pp. 12–21 (2005)
7. Brockman, G., et al.: Openai gym (2016)
8. Cho, K., van Merriënboer, B., Bahdanau, D., Bengio, Y.: On the properties of neural machine translation: encoder-decoder approaches. In: Proceedings of SSST-8, Eighth Workshop on Syntax, Semantics and Structure in Statistical Translation, pp. 103–111 (2014)
9. Chowdary, A., Huang, D., Mahendran, J.S., Romo, D., Deng, Y., Sabur, A.: Autonomous security analysis and penetration testing. In: The 16th International Conference on Mobility, Sensing and Networking (MSN 2020) (2020)
10. Elderman, R., Pater, L.J., Thie, A.S.: Adversarial reinforcement learning in a cyber security simulation. Ph.D. thesis, Faculty of Science and Engineering (2016)
11. Erdődi, L., Sommervoll, Å.Å., Zennaro, F.M.: Simulating SQL injection vulnerability exploitation using q-learning reinforcement learning agents. J. Inf. Secur. Appl. **61**, 102903 (2021). https://doi.org/10.1016/j.jisa.2021.102903. https://www.sciencedirect.com/science/article/pii/S2214212621001290
12. Gardiner, J., Nagaraja, S.: On the security of machine learning in malware C&C detection: a survey. ACM Comput. Surv. (CSUR) **49**(3), 1–39 (2016)
13. Ghanem, M.C., Chen, T.M.: Reinforcement learning for efficient network penetration testing. Information **11**(1), 6 (2020)
14. Haarnoja, T., Zhou, A., Abbeel, P., Levine, S.: Soft actor-critic: off-policy maximum entropy deep reinforcement learning with a stochastic actor. In: International Conference on Machine Learning, pp. 1861–1870. PMLR (2018)
15. He, J., et al.: Deep reinforcement learning with a natural language action space. In: Proceedings of the 54th Annual Meeting of the Association for Computational Linguistics (Volume 1: Long Papers), pp. 1621–1630 (2016)
16. Hoffmann, J.: Simulated penetration testing: from "Dijkstra" to "Turing Test++". In: Twenty-Fifth International Conference on Automated Planning and Scheduling (2015)
17. Jain, V., Fedus, W., Larochelle, H., Precup, D., Bellemare, M.G.: Algorithmic improvements for deep reinforcement learning applied to interactive fiction. In: Proceedings of the AAAI Conference on Artificial Intelligence, vol. 34, pp. 4328–4336 (2020)

18. Lattimore, T., Szepesvári, C.: Bandit Algorithms. Cambridge University Press, Cambridge (2020)
19. Maeda, R., Mimura, M.: Automating post-exploitation with deep reinforcement learning. Comput. Secur. **100**, 102108 (2021)
20. Mnih, V., et al.: Asynchronous methods for deep reinforcement learning. In: International Conference on Machine Learning, pp. 1928–1937. PMLR (2016)
21. Narasimhan, K., Kulkarni, T.D., Barzilay, R.: Language understanding for text-based games using deep reinforcement learning. In: Proceedings of the Conference on Empirical Methods in Natural Language Processing (2015)
22. Pozdniakov, K., Alonso, E., Stankovic, V., Tam, K., Jones, K.: Smart security audit: reinforcement learning with a deep neural network approximator. In: 2020 International Conference on Cyber Situational Awareness, Data Analytics and Assessment (CyberSA), pp. 1–8. IEEE (2020)
23. Raff, E., Barker, J., Sylvester, J., Brandon, R., Catanzaro, B., Nicholas, C.K.: Malware detection by eating a whole exe. In: Workshops at the Thirty-Second AAAI Conference on Artificial Intelligence (2018)
24. Sarraute, C., Buffet, O., Hoffmann, J.: Penetration testing== pomdp solving? In: Workshop on Intelligent Security (Security and Artificial Intelligence) (2011)
25. Schulman, J., Wolski, F., Dhariwal, P., Radford, A., Klimov, O.: Proximal policy optimization algorithms. arXiv preprint arXiv:1707.06347 (2017)
26. Shone, N., Ngoc, T.N., Phai, V.D., Shi, Q.: A deep learning approach to network intrusion detection. IEEE Trans. Emerg. Top. Comput. Intell. **2**(1), 41–50 (2018)
27. Speicher, P., Steinmetz, M., Hoffmann, J., Backes, M., Künnemann, R.: Towards automated network mitigation analysis. In: Proceedings of the 34th ACM/SIGAPP Symposium on Applied Computing, pp. 1971–1978 (2019)
28. Xu, X., Liu, C., Song, D.: SQLNet: generating structured queries from natural language without reinforcement learning. arXiv preprint arXiv:1711.04436 (2017)
29. Xue, H., Sun, S., Venkataramani, G., Lan, T.: Machine learning-based analysis of program binaries: a comprehensive study. IEEE Access **7**, 65889–65912 (2019)
30. Yuan, X., et al.: Counting to explore and generalize in text-based games. arXiv preprint arXiv:1806.11525 (2018)
31. Zelinka, M.: Baselines for reinforcement learning in text games. In: 2018 IEEE 30th International Conference on Tools with Artificial Intelligence (ICTAI), pp. 320–327. IEEE (2018)
32. Zennaro, F.M., Erdodi, L.: Modeling penetration testing with reinforcement learning using capture-the-flag challenges: trade-offs between model-free learning and a priori knowledge. arXiv preprint arXiv:2005.12632 (2020)
33. Zhong, V., Xiong, C., Socher, R.: Seq2SQL: generating structured queries from natural language using reinforcement learning. arXiv preprint arXiv:1709.00103 (2017)

Secure Collaborative Learning
for Predictive Maintenance
in Optical Networks

Khouloud Abdelli[1,2], Joo Yeon Cho[1(✉)], and Stephan Pachnicke[2]

[1] ADVA Optical Networking SE, Fraunhoferstrasse 9a, 82152 Martinsried, Germany
{KAbdelli,JCho}@adva.com
[2] Christian-Albrechts-Universität zu Kiel, Kaiserstr. 2, 24143 Kiel, Germany
stephan.pachnicke@tf.uni-kiel.de

Abstract. Building a reliable and accurate machine learning (ML) model is challenging in optical networks when training datasets are business-sensitive. We propose a framework of secure collaborative ML learning for predictive maintenance on cross-vendor datasets. Our framework is based on federated learning and multi-party computation technologies. Each vendor builds a local ML model based on its own private data. A server builds a global ML model by aggregating multiple local ML models in a private-preserving way. The server computes only the sum of the local models but cannot see any local model individually by the multi-party computation technique. The vendor-confidential dataset is never exposed to the server or other vendors. Moreover, after the global ML model is deployed in optical networks, the measured data compared to the prediction are privately distributed to the local model owners, which is beneficial to vendors. We applied our framework to the remaining useful life (RUL) prediction of laser device. Our experiments show that an accurate ML model can be built using sensitive datasets in a federated learning setting.

Keywords: Federated learning · Multi-party computation · Machine learning · Predictive maintenance · Optical network

1 Introduction

Machine learning (ML) and artificial intelligence (AI) have received tremendous attention recently in many applications, e.g. from self-driving cars and language translators to disease diagnosis and anomaly detection systems, to name a few. The widespread use of mobile devices accelerates the development of AI-supported applications based on rich and sensitive user data. While ML and AI cannot solve every problem, there are many sets of well-defined applications that are suited to this approach.

ML methods have been emerging as a promising tool for predictive maintenance in manufacturing industry and communication networks. Fiber optic networks build the spine of telecommunication networks today due to their high

© Springer Nature Switzerland AG 2021
N. Tuveri et al. (Eds.): NordSec 2021, LNCS 13115, pp. 114–130, 2021.
https://doi.org/10.1007/978-3-030-91625-1_7

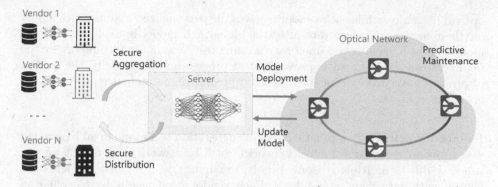

Fig. 1. ML-based predictive maintenance process in federated learning

capacity of data transmission. Proactively predicting the degradation of hardware components of optical networks and maintaining their supply chain can help prevent outages of services.

It is challenging to build an accurate and reliable ML model in optical networks. Since hardware network elements are usually manufactured by small and medium-sized companies, an ML model is often built based on the limited amount of training data. This situation can be relieved, if the training dataset can be aggregated from multiple vendors and consolidated in a central location to build a collaborative ML model. Since collaborative learning allows to train a model on larger datasets rather than the dataset available in any single vendor, it leads to a higher quality and more accurate ML model.

However, such collaboration is not straightforward in reality since vendors are not willing to share their training data with external companies. Training data are often company-confidential and the data sharing itself may violate privacy protection regulations in their home countries. With the federated learning (FL) technique, the training data is not required to be centralized, but can instead remains with the data owners.

Our Contribution. In this paper, we propose a framework of secure collaborative learning for predictive maintenance on cross-vendor datasets. We assume that each vendor manufactures the same type of hardware and competes each other to offer the hardware to an optical network operator. Note that our framework can be extended to a scenario based on heterogeneous type of hardware, predicting not a specific type of hardware but an overall hardware failure rate of the target network.

A training dataset remains in the vendor's domain and is never exposed to other companies. A global ML model is built by aggregating local ML models from multiple vendors in a secure way by multi-party computation (MPC) technology. An aggregation server is assume to be located in the domain of optical network and controlled by the network maintenance operator. A global model is used to predict the maintenance work for the hardware components running in optical networks, while each vendor receives the personalized maintenance report on their hardware failure rate after the global ML model is deployed. Since a local dataset is usually obtained by the aging test, a maintenance report by the field test can be useful to improve the test process and, eventually, the quality of products. An overview of the ML-based predictive maintenance process in FL is shown in Fig. 1.

Related Work. In [5] a practical secure aggregation technique in an FL setting was proposed over large mobile networks. Such framework does not fit for our use case due to multiple reasons. Firstly, in our use case, a global model is not shared with data owners (vendors). Each vendor gets benefit by receiving an individual maintenance result (e.g. the difference between the prediction and the real failure) after the global model is deployed and hardware degradation is predicted. Secondly, the scalability is not important since the number of vendors are not very large and dropouts are expected to be rare. On the other hand, secure aggregation is critical since the disclosure of the private training dataset may give negative impact on the data owner's business.

Another interesting work on collaborative predictive maintenance was presented in [16], where a combination of blockchain and federated learning techniques was applied. We apply a multi-party computation technique for data privacy since it is more suitable for our use case. Details are given in Sect. 2.

The rest of this paper is structured as follows: first, the background technologies are briefly explained. Then, our framework is described. Next, the experimental results are presented. Finally, we conclude the paper.

2   Background

Predictive Maintenance by ML. Telecommunication networks rely on fully functional hardware components that run under optimal conditions. In order to reduce the risk of unplanned network interruption and service outage, it is important to estimate correctly the degradation of hardware network components using analyzing tools and techniques, by which the maintenance cost and resource allocation are determined.

ML-based prediction is an emerging method to improve the accuracy of estimation of maintenance work for large networks. ML techniques can be useful if a sufficiently large, diverse, and realistic set of training data exists. Since an ML model relies so heavily on good training data, the availability of such a dataset is a crucial requirement for this approach. However, it is challenging to develop a high-precision ML model for predictive maintenance mainly due to the lack of training data. Since the hardware failures or maintenance events do not occur frequently, it takes time until good and meaningful training data are collected. Hence, in reality, the accelerated aging test results (e.g. a life cycle under the extreme temperature or the over-powered condition) are usually used for training a model.

Federated Learning. Federated learning (FL) is a tool that enables distributed parties to work together to train machine learning models without sharing the underlying data or trusting any of the individual participants [6]. FL can be used to build an ML model from various companies for the purpose of predicting the failures, repairs, or maintenance of network systems. In FL, each vendor trains an ML model on their private data and using their own hardware. These models are then aggregated by a central server (e.g. a network operator) to build a unified global model that has learned from the private data of every vendor without ever directly accessing it. Hence, confidential training data (e.g. aging test results of products) are not visible to a server, nor other competitive vendors.

However, private data might be still extractable from the local models by so-called model inversion attacks [11]. It was demonstrated that extracted images from a face recognition system look suspiciously similar to images from the underlying training data. This type of attack can be mitigated by applying differential privacy techniques; adding noise to the local models before sending them to the server. However, such noise will degrade the overall model performance, which is not preferable to our use case. That's why the secure aggregation using an MPC protocol comes to play.

Secure Multi-Party Computation (MPC). MPC is a subfield of cryptography that allows a set of distrusting parties to jointly evaluate a function on their input without revealing any private input beyond the intended output [23]. MPC can be used to run machine learning models on data without revealing the data to the model owner and without revealing the model to the data owner. MPC protocols for an honest majority typically use a secret sharing scheme as a basic tool. Shamir's secret sharing scheme was published in 1979 [20]. A dealer wishes to share a secret amongst n parties. Any subset of $t + 1$ or more of the parties can reconstruct the secret, but no subset of t or fewer parties can learn anything about the secret. Since then, many different protocols have been developed for constructing secret sharing schemes with different properties, and for different settings.

Secure Aggregation. An important challenge in federated learning is to prevent a server or other vendors from reconstructing the private data of any vendor while collaborating. A secure aggregation protocol provides strong privacy guarantees even when vendors behave maliciously. Moreover, the protocols are robust against dropout during the operation, and resistant to the multi-round aggregation attack [21]. It is still an open question how to construct an efficient and robust secure aggregation protocol that addresses all the challenges.

There is a rich literature exploring secure aggregation in both the single-server setting (via additive masking [4], via threshold homomorphic encryption (HE) [12], and via generic secure multi-party computation (MPC) [7]) as well as in the multiple non-colluding servers setting [10]. Secure aggregation can also be approached using trusted execution environments, as presented in [13].

Among those, MPC allows multiple parties to jointly compute a function without revealing their inputs to each other. By taking an end-to-end approach to the system design, MPC allows multiple parties with complex economic relationships to safely collaborate on machine learning computation through the use of release policies and auditing, while also enabling users to achieve good performance without manually navigating the complex performance trade-offs between MPC protocols.

Gated Recurrent Unit (GRU). GRU, proposed by Cho et al. in 2014 as solution to the gradient vanishing problem [9], is a type of recurrent neural networks (RNNs) used to process sequential data and to capture long-term sequential dependencies. Compared to other RNNs such as long-short term memory, it requires less memory requirements. GRU has a simple structure: it contains two gates namely update gate and reset gate, controlling the flow of the information. The forward propagation of the GRU is expressed by the following equations:

$$z_t = \sigma(W_z \cdot x_t + W_z \cdot h_{(t-1)} + b_z) \tag{1}$$

$$r_t = \sigma(W_r \cdot x_t + W_r \cdot h_{(t-1)} + b_r) \tag{2}$$

$$h_t = z_t \circ h_{(t-1)} + (1 - z_t) \circ \tanh(W_h \cdot x_t + W_h \cdot (r_t \circ h_{(t-1)}) + b_h) \tag{3}$$

where z_t denotes the update gate, r_t represents the reset gate, x_t is the input vector, h_t is the output vector, W and b represent the weight and the bias matrices respectively. σ is the gate activation function and $tanh$ represents the output activation function. The '·' operator denotes a matrix multiplication, the 'o' operator represents the dot product.

3   Framework

We consider training an ML model in a federated learning setting, wherein each vendor maintains the private dataset of its own hardware. A global ML model is trained under the coordination of a central server based upon multiple local models that are built by different vendors. A server can get only a sum of the local models and does not see individual local models. Based on the global model, the maintenance work on optical networks is predicted and the replacement are prepared. Vendors can get benefit by receiving the personalized report on the discrepancy between the local model and the real failure rate that has been measured while the network is in operation.

3.1   Secure Aggregation Protocol

Secure aggregation enables each vendor to submit a local model privately and a server to learn nothing but the sum of the local models. A secure aggregation protocol for mobile networks was proposed in [6] and [3]. This method relies on a pairwise secret exchange and Shamir's t-out-of-n secret sharing scheme, focusing on the setting of mobile devices where communication is extremely expensive, and dropouts are common. Our use case is different in a sense that the number of local models are not very big, and the dropouts are very rare. If a dropout occurs, the protocol is reset and started again. Local models can be aggregated under the following two threat scenarios.

Semi-honest Behavior. The server and vendors are assumed to behave honestly but curiously. That is, all participants follow the protocol exactly as instructed but also try to retrieve the private data of other vendors, if possible. Under this assumption, the n-out-of-n secret sharing scheme is used.

Suppose N is the number of vendors and each vendor trains its own local model using its own private dataset. The i-th client generates a random linear mask s_i and sends $(f_i + s_i)$ to the server. In parallel, the s_i is divided into N additive shares, $\{p_{i1}, \ldots, p_{iN}\}$ where $s_i = \sum_{j=1}^{N} p_{ij}$. Note the size of shares are similar to s_i. These N shares are distributed to other vendors in such a way that each vendor receives a unique share out of N shares. In result, the i-th vendor receives $\{p_{1i}, \ldots, p_{Ni}\}$. Finally, the i-th vendor sends the sum of the shares $\sum_{j=1}^{n} p_{ji}$ to the server.

By aggregating one-time padded local models and the sum of the shares, the server can calculate the sum of the local models as follows:

$$\sum_{i=1}^{N}(f_i + s_i) - \sum_{i=1}^{N}\sum_{j=1}^{N} p_{ji} = \sum_{i=1}^{N} f_i + \sum_{i=1}^{N}(s_i - \sum_{j=1}^{N} p_{ij}) = \sum_{i=1}^{N} f_i \qquad (4)$$

Malicious Behavior. In this model, the corrupted vendors may arbitrarily deviate from the secure aggregation protocol. Though they are not major, some vendors may not behave honestly and provide an incorrect local model or shares. There are two strategies against malicious adversaries: verifiable secret sharing [18] and Byzantine-resilient FL [17]. This topic is beyond scope of this paper and will be addressed in a future publication.

3.2 Training Procedure

Suppose that a server (network provider) builds a global ML model for predictive maintenance with N vendors. The model training procedure is as follows.

1. **Setup:** A server selects N vendors that join the development of the global model in an FL setting. The selected vendors receive a model training software.
2. **Local models:** Each vendor locally trains a local model using its own dataset. Since each vendor has a different size of dataset, the weight of local models can be normalized or trained with a fixed size of data in multiple rounds.
3. **Secure aggregation:** Every vendor performs a secure aggregation protocol which is described in Subsect. 3.1. In results, the server receives the one-time padded local models and the sum of shares. Using Eq. (4) the sum of the local models can be calculated.
4. **Global model:** The server develops a global model by averaging the local models that have been received from vendors. The global model training can be done in multiple rounds.

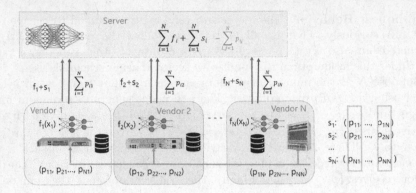

Fig. 2. Secure collaborative learning using FL and secret sharing

5. **Deployment:** The server deploys the global model on the network and performs predictive maintenance. When the degradation and failure of hardware components are observed, the prediction accuracy is measured and a global model is updated.
6. **Secure feedback:** The server produces the statistical results of the maintenance per vendor and sends them back to vendors individually.

An overview of the secure collaborative learning procedure is shown in Fig. 2 and the pseudo code of the training process is given in Algorithm 1.

4 Experiments

4.1 Description of Use Case

Semiconductor lasers are the most commonly used optical transmitters for high-speed data transmission due to their high efficiency, low cost, and compactness. Their reliability directly impacts the reliability and the availability of the whole optical communication system. Unexpected failure or sudden degradation of a laser device during operation can lead to high maintenance costs, excessive downtime, and optical network disruption.

Therefore, it is highly required to monitor the performance of the laser device while in operation, and to predict the remaining useful life (RUL) defined as the estimated time before device failure, in order to plan an effective maintenance schedule. Hence, maximizing the operational availability, enhancing system reliability, and minimizing the maintenance costs.

Recently, data-driven approaches [1, 14], extracting useful insights from the operational collected data to learn the degradation trend and thus to perform the RUL estimation without requiring any specific knowledge or using any physical model, have gained popularity. The development of such models requires the availability of run-to-failure data sets modeling the normal operation behavior as well as the degradation process under different operating conditions. However, these data are often unavailable due the scarcity of the failures during the system operation and the long time needed to monitor the device up to failing and then to generate the reliability data. That's why accelerated aging tests are often used to collect run-to-failure data in a shorter amount of time by causing the device to fail more quickly under normal conditions by applying accelerated stress conditions resulting in the same degradation process leading to failure [8].

However, the burn-in aging tests are carried out just for a few devices due to the high costs of performing such tests. Hence, the amount of the run-to-failure data that can be derived from such tests, might be small, which can adversely impact the performance of the ML model [2]. Therefore, a secure FL framework, where many laser manufacturers collaborate with their small local dataset, derived from burn-in aging tests, stored at their premises, in order to build an accurate and reliable global RUL prediction model, can be a good solution to tackle the aforementioned problem.

We consider a FL system composed of a server and N vendors that collaboratively train a robust global predictive model, while keeping every vendor's data private. It is to be noted that the global model is run in a server hosted by an optical network operator owning the infrastructure in which the semiconductor lasers manufactured by the different vendors are deployed, and that the vendors might have different types of lasers with various characteristics resulting in different degradation trends, and thereby the data owned by each vendor can be different from the other vendors' data, leading to heterogeneous FL settings.

4.2   Data Generation and Preprocessing

To validate the FL framework proposed for the above-described use case, a dataset by combining experimental and synthetically generated data is built.

Experimental Data. To generate the experimental dataset, accelerated aging tests are performed for different laser devices operating at high temperature of 90 °C to strongly increase the laser degradation and thus accelerating the device failure. For each aging test, the current (e.g. degradation parameter) is monitored periodically up either to 2,000 h or 3,000 h (the end of the test) under constant output power. The time to failure of the device, denoted by t_f, is defined as the time at which the current has increased 20% of its initial value. The current measurements of the different devices, recorded from the beginning of the aging test until t_f of the device or the end of the test, are segmented with a sliding window of size 10. In total, an experimental data set of 278 samples is built.

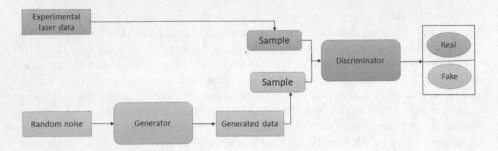

Fig. 3. Synthetic laser reliability data generation using GAN model

Synthetic Laser Data Generation. To increase further the amount of data, a generative adversarial network (GAN) model is used to synthetically generate realistic laser reliability data, from a random noise. The GAN model is trained with the experimental laser reliability data incorporating the 10-length sequences of current measurements. It is composed of two sub-models, namely the generator and the discriminator, competing against each other.

As shown in Fig. 3, the generator is trained to produce new data from the noise input, whereas the discriminator is trained to distinguish the fake data generated by the generator and the real data. This process continues till the generator can generate data samples that the discriminator can not differentiate them from real data. The architecture of the generator and the discriminator contains 3 GRU hidden layers with 16 cells. The loss function of GAN model, whereby the generator tries to minimize it and the discriminator tries to maximize it, can be formulated as follows:

$$L_{GAN} = \min_G \max_D [E_{x \sim pdata(x)}[\log D(x)] + E_{z \sim p_z(z)}[\log(1 - D(G(z)))]] \qquad (5)$$

where D and G denote the discriminator and the generator models respectively. $p_{data}(x)$ represents the probability distribution of real training data. $p_z(z)$ is the probability distribution of the noise vector z.

Once the GAN model is trained, the generator sub-model is used to create synthetic data. To evaluate the quality of the synthetic data, the metrics namely root mean square error (RMSE), Fréchet distance (FD) and Percent root mean square difference (PRD), are adopted. RMSE is used to quantify the stability between the original data and the synthetic data. FD calculates the similarity between the real data and the generated data. PRD evaluates the difference between the real data and the generated data. Table 1 shows that the different evaluation metrics are so small, which proves that the synthetic data is very similar to the real data. To visually inspect how close the distribution of the synthetic data is to that of real data, the t-distributed stochastic neighbor embedding (t-SNE) visualization [22] is adopted. Figure 4 illustrates that the distribution of the synthetic data resembles that of the original experimental data, which proves the effectiveness of the generator in producing realistic data.

Table 1. Comparison of evaluation metrics

Metric	RMSE	FD	PRD
Value	0.03	0.05	0.31

FL Data Preprocessing. The experimental data is combined with the synthetic data to build a large dataset of 5162 samples. The RUL of each sample is estimated as the difference between t_f and the time t at which the RUL is predicted. The built dataset is normalized and randomly divided into a training (comprising of 80% of the samples used for training the local models) and a test dataset (the remaining 20% for testing). The training dataset is split then into 10 vendors with different parts of 350, 400, 500, 600, 382, 520, 450, 445, 300, and 380, respectively.

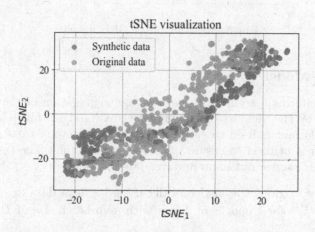

Fig. 4. t-SNE visualization of the synthetic and real data distributions

4.3 Local Models

The selected ML model of each vendor is GRU as it is good at pre-processing sequential data and to capture the dependency modeling the degradation trend. Figure 5 shows the architecture of the proposed local model. The GRU model takes as input a sequence of length 10 historical current measurements $\{I_{(t-9)}, I_{(t-8)}, \ldots, I_t\}$ and outputs the RUL_t at the time t. It is composed of 3 hidden layers of 64, 32 and 16 memory cells, respectively. Exponential linear unit (ELU) is selected as an activation function for the hidden layers. The loss function used to update the weights of the model based on the error between the predicted and the desired output is the mean square error (MSE). Adam is chosen as an optimization algorithm to update the weights of the local ML Model.

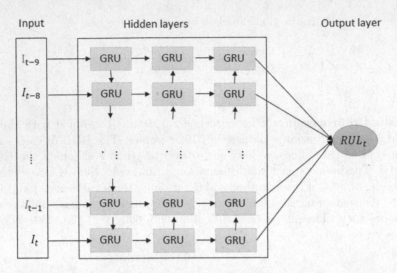

Fig. 5. Structure of the GRU model

4.4   Global Model

The server performs a secure weighted average aggregation of the local model updates sent by the vendors by combining FedAVG algorithm [15] and MPC: whereby the former is used to get the gradient information from the vendors, and the latter is utilized to ensure the secure aggregation. The training of the global model is carried out in an iterative process as follows:

- The vendor k trains the model locally using its local data x_k, and updates the model $f_k^{(t)}$ for b epochs of Adam with mini-batch size of B to compute $f_k^{(t+1)}$.
- The server securely aggregates each vendor's $f_k^{(t+1)}$ using MPC.
- A global model F is computed by summing $f_k^{(t+1)}$ for $k = 1, \ldots, N$.

The above-described process is repeated for multiple rounds to improve the performance of the global model. For our experiments, b, B and N_{round} are set to 16, 16 and 100 respectively. The pseudo code of the algorithm is given in Algorithm 1.

Algorithm 1. Federated averaging algorithm using MPC

Input The N vendors are indexed by i; x_i is the local training dataset; n_i is the size of the dataset; s_i is the linear mask; p_{ij} is the j-th share of the linear mask s_i; n is the size of the aggregated datasets of all the vendors; B is the local mini-batch size; and η is the learning rate.

Output A global ML model F

for round $t = 1, 2, \cdots$ **do**
    for $i = 1, 2, \ldots, N$ **do**
        $(f_i + s_i)^{t+1} \leftarrow LocalUpdate(i, f_i^t)$
        $q_i^{t+1} \leftarrow LocalShares(i)$
    end for
    $F^{t+1} \leftarrow \sum_{i=1}^{N} (\frac{n_i}{n} f_i + s_i)^{t+1} + \sum_{i=1}^{N} q_i^{t+1}$
end for

$LocalUpdate(i, f)$:
$\mathcal{B} \leftarrow$ (split x_i into batches of size B)
for each epoch B **do**
    for batch $b \in \mathcal{B}$ **do**
        $f \leftarrow f - \eta \cdot A(f, b)$
    end for
    $f \leftarrow f + s_i$
end for
return f_i to the server.

$LocalShares(i)$:
for $j = 1, 2, \ldots, N$ **do**
    $q_i \leftarrow \sum_{j=1}^{N} p_{ij}$
end for
return q_i to the server.

4.5 Performance Evaluation Metrics

The accuracy of the ML model RUL prediction is evaluated by using several evaluation metrics namely the root mean square error (RMSE), the mean absolute error (MAE), the standard deviation (SDEV), and the scoring function S [19] which are formulated respectively as follows:

$$RMSE = \sqrt{\frac{(RUL_{pred(i)} - RUL_i)^2}{N}} \tag{6}$$

$$MAE = \frac{\sum_{i=1}^{N} |RUL_{pred(i)} - RUL_i|}{N} \tag{7}$$

$$SDVE = \sqrt{RMSE^2 - MAE^2} \tag{8}$$

$$S = \begin{cases} e^{\frac{\sum_{i=1}^{N} RUL_{pred(i)} - RUL_i}{a_1}}, & \text{if } RUL_{pred(i)} < RUL_i \\ e^{\frac{\sum_{i=1}^{N} RUL_{pred(i)} - RUL_i}{a_2 \cdot}}, & \text{if } RUL_{pred(i)} \geq RUL_i \end{cases} \tag{9}$$

where RUL_i and $RUL_{pred(i)}$ denote the true RUL and the predicted RUL for the test sample i, respectively, and N represents the total number of test samples. The parameters a_1 and a_2 are user-defined parameters managing the asymmetric preference of underestimated predictions over overestimated predictions.

The RMSE and MAE metrics are used to calculate the closeness of the predicted RULs to the actual RULs by equally penalizing the underestimated and overestimated predictions, while the scoring metric penalizes overestimated cases more than the underestimated cases since if the predicted RUL is larger than the actual RUL, the maintenance plan will be scheduled later (after the failure of the device), leading not to predict the outage of the device and thereby resulting in higher costs.

5 Analysis

The performance of the FL approach is compared to the following two approaches:

- Centralized approach: the GRU model is trained with the aggregated training dataset $X = \sum_{i=1}^{N} x_i$: the dataset from each vendor is stored and aggregated at a centralized database and then the ML model is applied to that data;
- Decentralized approach: each vendor trains the GRU model on its local data without participating in the FL approach.

The performances of the different decentralized ML models trained with the local data of each vendor C_i are illustrated in Table 2. It can be observed that the small amount of local data ($x_i \leq 600$ samples) impacts badly the ML model's RUL

Table 2. Decentralized ML models

Vendor	MAE(h)	SDVE(h)
C_1	622.01	595.07
C_2	421.32	462.87
C_3	295.78	392.19
C_4	262.15	350.41
C_5	561.85	433.24
C_6	652.36	591.42
C_7	487.92	520.48
C_8	305.51	350.23
C_9	666.47	678.78
C_{10}	436.98	472.21

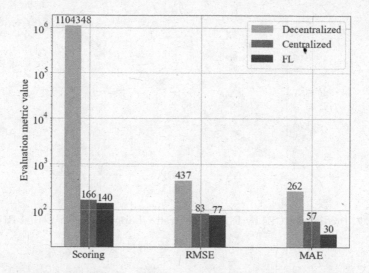

Fig. 6. Comparison of the federated (FL), centralized and decentralized approaches using RMSE, MAE and scoring metrics

prediction capability by yielding high MAE ($\geq$262 h) and SDVE ($\geq$350 h) scores. For the decentralized approach, the best model achieved by C_4 is selected as a reference to be compared with the other approaches. The different techniques are evaluated on the unseen test dataset and using the above-mentioned metrics. The results of the comparison, shown in Fig. 6, demonstrate that the FL framework outperforms the decentralized approach by yielding smaller values of all the evaluation metrics, and that the FL approach can achieve similar and even better performance than the centralized approach. As depicted in Fig. 7, the predicted RULs by the FL approach are very close to the true RUL values, which proves the effectiveness of the FL framework in accurately estimating RUL of the laser. The performances of the FL and centralized approaches are very similar, which demonstrates that the FL framework achieves good prediction capability while ensuring the data privacy and confidentiality. Figure 8 shows that the FL approach could achieve the same RMSE as the centralized approach after reaching 50 rounds. The results prove that the FL framework has good convergence and stability.

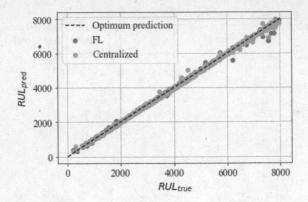

Fig. 7. Predicted RULs by FL and centralized approaches vs. actual RULs

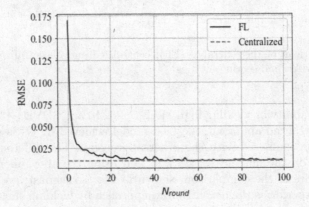

Fig. 8. Normalized RMSE of the FL approach with number of rounds. The dashed line represents the RMSE achieved by the centralized approach.

6   Conclusion

Optical networks often require a high level of reliability and sustainability. Machine learning techniques are expected to improve maintaining such networks efficiently. We showed that our framework would be a useful tool to build an accurate ML model for predictive maintenance by aggregating business-sensitive datasets in a private-preserving way. For the future work, we will apply our framework to other use cases and extend the threat model to malicious adversaries scenario.

Acknowledgment. This work has been performed in the framework of the CELTIC-NEXT project AI-NET-PROTECT (Project ID C2019/3-4), and it is partly funded by the German Federal Ministry of Education and Research (FKZ16KIS1279K).

References

1. Abdelli, K., Griesser, H., Pachnicke, S.: Machine learning based data driven diagnostic and prognostic approach for laser reliability enhancement, pp. 1–4 (2020)
2. A hybrid CNN-LSTM approach for laser remaining useful life prediction (2021)
3. Bell, J., Bonawitz, K.A., Gascón, A., Lepoint, T., Raykova, M.: Secure single-server aggregation with (poly)logarithmic overhead, Cryptology ePrint Archive, Report 2020/704 (2020). https://ia.cr/2020/704
4. Bonawitz, K.A., et al.: Practical secure aggregation for federated learning on user-held data. CoRR abs/1611.04482 (2016)
5. Bonawitz, K., et al.: Practical secure aggregation for privacy-preserving machine learning. In: Proceedings of the 2017 ACM SIGSAC Conference on Computer and Communications Security, CCS 2017, pp. 1175–1191 (2017)
6. Bonawitz, K., et al.: Practical secure aggregation for privacy preserving machine learning, Cryptology ePrint Archive, Report 2017/281 (2017). https://ia.cr/2017/281
7. Burkhart, M., Strasser, M., Many, D., Dimitropoulos, X.: SEPIA: Privacy-preserving aggregation of multi-domain network events and statistics. In: 19th USENIX Security Symposium (USENIX Security 10) (Washington, DC), August 2010
8. Celaya, J.R., Saxena, A., Saha, S., Goebel, K.F.: Prognostics of power mosfets under thermal stress accelerated aging using data-driven and model-based methodologies, September 2011
9. Cho, K., et al.: Learning phrase representations using RNN encoder-decoder for statistical machine translation (2014)
10. Corrigan-Gibbs, H., Boneh, D.: PRIO: private, robust, and scalable computation of aggregate statistics. In: Proceedings of the 14th USENIX Conference on Networked Systems Design and Implementation, NSDI 2017, pp. 259–282 (2017)
11. Fredrikson, M., Jha, S., Ristenpart, T.: Model inversion attacks that exploit confidence information and basic countermeasures. In: Proceedings of the 22nd ACM SIGSAC Conference on Computer and Communications Security, CCS 2015, pp. 1322–1333 (2015)
12. Halevi, S., Lindell, Y., Pinkas, B.: Secure computation on the web: computing without simultaneous interaction. In: Rogaway, P. (ed.) CRYPTO 2011. LNCS, vol. 6841, pp. 132–150. Springer, Heidelberg (2011). https://doi.org/10.1007/978-3-642-22792-9_8
13. Lie, D., Maniatis, P.: Glimmers: Resolving the privacy/trust quagmire. CoRR abs/1702.07436 (2017)
14. Liu, Z., Wang, Q., Song, C., Cheng, Y.: Similarity-based difference analysis approach for remaining useful life prediction of GAAS-based semiconductor lasers. IEEE Access 5, 21508–21523 (2017)
15. Brendan McMahan, H., Moore, E., Ramage, D., Hampson, S., Agüera y Arcas, B.: Communication-efficient learning of deep networks from decentralized data (2017)
16. Mohr, M., Becker, C., Möller, R., Richter, M.: Towards collaborative predictive maintenance leveraging private cross-company data. In: Reussner, R.H., Koziolek, A., Heinrich, R. (eds.) INFORMATIK 2020, Gesellschaft für Informatik, Bonn, pp. 427–432 (2021)
17. Prakash, S., Hashemi, H., Wang, Y., Annavaram, M., Avestimehr, S.: Byzantine-resilient federated learning with heterogeneous data distribution (2021)

18. Rabin, T., Ben-Or, M.: Verifiable secret sharing and multiparty protocols with honest majority, STOC 1989, pp. 73–85 (1989)
19. Saxena, A., Goebel, K.: Phm08 challenge data set (2008)
20. Shamir, A.: How to share a secret. CACM 22(11), 612–613 (1979)
21. So, J., Ali, R.E., Guler, B., Jiao, J., Avestimehr, S.: Securing secure aggregation: Mitigating multi-round privacy leakage in federated learning. CoRR abs/2106.03328 (2021)
22. van der Maaten, L., Hinton, G.: Viualizing data using t-sne 9, 2579–2605 (2008)
23. Yao, A.C.-C.: How to generate and exchange secrets (extended abstract). In: 27th Annual Symposium on Foundations of Computer Science, Toronto, Canada, vol. 1986, pp. 162–167. IEEE Computer Society (1986)

Network Security

Gollector: Measuring Domain Name Dark Matter from Different Vantage Points

Kaspar Hageman[1]([✉])(iD), René Rydhof Hansen[2](iD), and Jens Myrup Pedersen[1](iD)

[1] Department of Electronic Systems, Aalborg University, Aalborg, Denmark
{kh,jens}@es.aau.dk
[2] Department of Computer Science, Aalborg University, Aalborg, Denmark
rrh@cs.aau.dk

Abstract. This paper proposes *Gollector*, a novel tool for measuring the domain name space from different vantage points. Whereas such measurements have typically been conducted from a single (or few) vantage point, our proposed solution combines multiple measurements in a single system. *Gollector* allows us to express the relative difference in the covered domain name space, and the temporal characteristics, as domain name *dark matter*. We leverage a three-week trace from four vantage points, by applying the tool to three security-related use cases: early domain registration detection, data leakage in a split-horizon situation, and a proposed method for subdomain enumeration. We release the *Gollector* source code to the research community to support future research in this field.

Keywords: DNS · TLS · Domain names · Measurements

1 Introduction

The Domain Name System (DNS) has historically played, and continues to play, a vital role in many different areas of network security research, including examining Internet censorship [31], spam detection [26,38], and identifying botnet communication [20]. The highly distributed nature of DNS, with information scattered across millions of domain name servers, means there exists neither a method to reliably observe all interactions with the DNS, nor a method to reconstruct the full domain name space. Consequently, researchers (implicitly or explicitly) choose one or more *vantage points*, e.g., network locations or network datasets, from which to conduct DNS measurements.

The (DNS) vantage point has a major impact on the DNS-related data that can be collected and processed. This is the case both for *passive* measurements, e.g., traffic monitoring of DNS resolvers that is highly dependent on physical location, but also for *active* measurements, e.g., due to geographical split horizons [11] or censorship [31]. We will refer to the part(s) of the domain name space that cannot be observed from a given vantage point as *DNS dark matter* (with respect to that viewpoint).

© Springer Nature Switzerland AG 2021
N. Tuveri et al. (Eds.): NordSec 2021, LNCS 13115, pp. 133–152, 2021.
https://doi.org/10.1007/978-3-030-91625-1_8

Different (partial) solutions have been deployed by the research community, including simply increasing the number of vantage points covered as well as including more different types of vantage points. However, to the best of our knowledge, there have been no studies focusing specifically on the impact of choosing different vantage points, and solutions discussed in the literature have been mostly ad-hoc. In this paper, we introduce the *Gollector* tool and framework as a step towards a more systematic and structured treatment of vantage points specifically, and DNS data collection and analysis in general. In particular, we intend *Gollector* to become the "one-stop-shop" for DNS collection and analysis. Therefore, we open-source the tool for the research community to use, and the source code can be found at:

https://github.com/aau-network-security/gollector

We start the paper by providing the relevant background (Sect. 2) and place our work in the context of prior research (Sect. 3). In the remainder of the paper, we present the main contributions of the paper:

- We provide an overview of the existing vantage points, describing their conceptual advantages and drawbacks (Sect. 4).
- We present a novel tool and framework, *Gollector*, which combines data collected from different vantage points, allowing for the comparison of each vantage point (Sect. 5).
- We apply the tool to a sample dataset (Sect. 6) and leverage the data (in Sect. 7) for three previously unexplored use cases related to *DNS dark matter*, and show that combining vantage points has a positive impact on DNS studies: *(i)* early domain detection, *(ii)* data leakage with split horizons and *(iii)* subdomain enumeration.

2   Background

Systems on the Internet are commonly addressed within two namespaces: the IP address name space and the domain name space. IP addresses are used by routing devices to forward network traffic to the correct host, whereas domain names are more user-friendly and are therefore used by humans to address hosts. The DNS has been facilitating the translation between these two namespaces since the 1980s [30]. The domain name space forms a tree structure, where each node in the tree is a label, and a domain name is a composition of all labels in a path of the tree from the root to a leaf. The nodes in the first layer are referred to as top-level domains (TLDs) and for the right-most label in a domain name (e.g., `.com` is the TLD for the domain `www.example.com`). A domain – sometimes referred to as a Fully Qualified Domain Name (FQDN) – can further be decomposed into an apex part and a subdomain part; the apex domain is the part that is registered at a domain registry, with the subdomain being the remaining part of the domain name. The higher levels of the domain name space are highly-regulated and reserved, and newly created domains (i.e., the apex domains) can be created under so-called public suffixes only [16]. A part of the domain name space that is managed by a particular organization is referred to as a zone. For instance, registries - the operators of the TLDs – are authoritative for the zone which comprises all domains under that TLD, and maintains a zone file in which all mappings between the domain and IP name space are stored, or DNS records. The content of these zone files is served by *authoritative name servers* to DNS clients, answering queries with the appropriate DNS records if the name server is authoritative for the queried data, or with a reference to another name server if not. Clients commonly rely on intermediate DNS servers, referred to as resolving name servers or *resolvers*, to resolve DNS queries on their behalf while caching data locally to increase the performance of the DNS ecosystem as a whole.

The functionality of the DNS forms a fundamental basis for the workings of many other protocols on the Internet, including the Hypertext Transfer Protocol (HTTP) and Transport Layer Security (TLS). HTTP and TLS form the secure communication channel used by web browsers and web servers to communicate. Documents are exchanged by requesting specific locations identified by (among others) the domain name of the server that hosts the resource. TLS, providing the encryption layer to this exchange, relies on digital certificates exchanged between the browser and server which are used by clients to verify the authenticity of the web server [33]. These digital certificates embed a set of domain names in them, which denote the domains for which the certificate is valid. A certificate is signed by one of hundreds of trusted third parties, the Certificate Authority (CA), who is tasked to verify the identity of an owner behind a certificate request before issuing the certificate. Due to two major incidents in which a CA erroneously issued a certificate [1,32], the Certificate Transparency (CT) was developed to audit the issuance behavior of each CA [29]. In this framework, CAs submit newly issued certificates to publicly available, append-only logs, and as such, any third party can monitor these logs.

3   Related Work

Given the ubiquitous nature of domain names on the Internet, the vast majority of applications interact with them in one way or another, including applications with malicious intent. For example, phishing websites are commonly hosted on typosquatted domains (i.e., a catch-all term for domain names that are similar-looking to benign domains) [37] and bots within a botnet rely on the DNS as a communication channel to dynamically identify the location of their bot masters [36]. As such, the security community has relied on data collected through domain name measurements to better understand and mitigate such types of malicious behavior. Relying on network traces, including DNS and TLS, to build extensive domain name-related datasets has been an ongoing process for many years. Passive DNS was proposed in 2004 as a method to support DNS data recovery, by collecting DNS queries in the wild, thereby being able to replicate the state of zone files at a particular point in time [40]. The ISC implemented a version of these ideas in 2012 [25], which resulted in the commercialization of the framework in 2013 under the company Farsight Security [21].

The ENTRADA project focuses on collecting passive DNS traffic from the perspective of authoritative name servers instead [41]. Alternatively, researchers relied on active measurements for creating longitudinal datasets. The OpenIntel project collects a fixed set of DNS records for all apex domains within a set of TLD zones daily [34]. In their paper, the authors have collected data from three general TLD zone files comprising 50% of the apex domain name space, but have since then expanded to more general TLDs and sixteen country-code TLDs[1] [10]. Hohlfeld [27] expands upon this approach, by both collecting more than only DNS records (e.g., TLS support and particular TCP settings) and by relying on more domain name sources besides zone files (i.e., passive DNS and domains extracted from CT logs). Similarly, Project Sonar scans the IPv4 address space for (among others) TLS certificates, reverse DNS misconfigurations, and various TCP and UDP services [15].

Reconstructing the full domain name space is a complex task due to the distributed nature of the DNS. For many TLDs, access to zone files is controlled through the Centralized Zone Data Service (CZDS) [13], whereas access to other TLDs is more restricted, available ad-hoc involving non-disclosure agreements [27], making a full replication of the apex domain space difficult. Several techniques have been used to circumvent this, such as "zone-walking" for DNSSEC-enabled zones [18,35] or abusing misconfigurations of DNS name servers, that allowed for a full zone file disclosure through zone transfer request [23]. Alternatively, these zones can be partially reconstructed by relying on other data sources, including certificate transparency [39] and the aforementioned passive DNS [25,40]. Even though passive DNS collects FQDNs (in addition to apex domains), mapping out the full FQDN domain name space is even more complex than the apex domain name space. The penetration testing community has relied on domain enumeration as one method of "reconnaissance", or information gathering about a particular target. As a result, a number of tools exist that support subdomain enumeration or DNS-based reconnaissance [2,3,5–7]. Typically, these subdomains are identified by scraping third-party sources that have collected this information prior (e.g., search engines) [22] or by generating candidate FQDNs [3,5,7].

Gollector stands apart because it is intended to collect passive domain name-related data from more vantage points than any of these research or commercial initiatives. Furthermore, the tool is unique in the sense that it specifically emphasizes the *differences* between vantage points, allowing us to evaluate the relative dark matter between each vantage point. Lastly, in contrast to tools from the penetration testing community, *Gollector* collects traffic from a global perspective, rather than focusing on a small set of individual domain names.

4   Vantage Points

When passively collecting traffic in the DNS (i.e., capturing traffic generated by a client population, rather than generating own DNS traffic) the measurement

---

[1] as of July 2021.

vantage point is a determining factor for what fraction of the total DNS traffic
one can observe, as illustrated by Fig. 1. Similarly, TLS traffic (prior to version
1.3) can be passively collected to observe the certificate (and other parameters)
exchanged during a TLS handshake, which suffers from the same vantage point
limitation as passive DNS collection. Alternatively, domain name related information can be extracted from other data sources that are not related to passive
traffic. Besides active measurement – the process of actively probing servers
for their responses to acquire information – sources are available that provide
insight into the management and operation of a domain name. TLD zone files
act as the ground-truth for all domains registered directly under a TLD, and
can be used to infer registrations and domain expirations. The CT framework
is an alternative source of TLS certificates, as it provides researchers access to
publicly available, append-only logs of newly issued certificates by CAs. The logs
guarantee that new certificates are published within a certain time frame – the
Maximum Merge Delay (MMD) – such that the logs remain up to date with the
latest issued certificates.

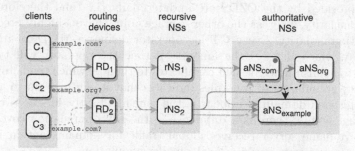

Fig. 1. The different vantage points (denoted by •) from which to conduct passive
DNS measurements. Each arrow represents a DNS query send between two devices,
where the colors indicate from which client the request originated. The various vantage
points have different observations based on the querying behavior of the three clients:
RD_1 observes $\{C_1, C_2\}$, rNS_2 observes $\{C_1, C_3\}$ and aNS_{com} observes $\{C_2, C_3\}$. (Color
figure online)

Even though these vantage points have their inherent differences, there is a
commonality between them: the part of the domain name space they observe
and the timing of those observations. Certain domain names or even full TLDs
may be observed from one vantage point, but would never be observable from
another. As such, a part of the domain name space can be considered dark
matter for the latter. Out of our previously-discussed vantage points, we identify
four vantage points that significantly differ from each other[2]: passive DNS from

---

[2] The difference between data collected from a routing device from a network operator
and a DNS resolver may be insignificant if both vantage points are owned by the
same party, in the case of an ISP.

a resolver, passive DNS from an authoritative name server, CT logs, and zone files. We can compare these vantage points according to the following properties. The WIDTH indicates how many TLDs the vantage point is capable of capturing domains across. The DEPTH shows what part of the FQDN a vantage point is capable of collecting domain names from. The TIME GRANULARITY represents the precision at which particular events are registered. A related dimension is the MAXIMUM TIME DELAY, which denotes how long it takes, worst case, for an event to be registered by a particular vantage point. Lastly, for the vantage points that passively collect data from a number of clients, the POPULATION COVERAGE illustrates the size of the overall population that is being covered by the vantage point.

Table 1 shows an overview of the four vantage points and their dimensions. Both a DNS resolver and CT logs are capable of observing across a variety of TLDs, although it depends on the DNS client population and certificate issuers, respectively, which TLDs are actually observed. The domains covered by the zone file of a TLD are registered at an apex domain level, and thereby this vantage point does not cover FQDNs as opposed to the others. Furthermore, the zone files provided by the CZDS are updated daily [12], and therefore have a one-day granularity, whereas the other vantage points have a highly precise (i.e., sub-second) granularity. Every CT log operator defines a MMD, or maximum merge delay, which denotes the amount of time the operator will take as a maximum to publish newly issued certificates to the log, which tends to be 24 h. The one-day granularity of zone files indicates that it can take up to a day for a newly registered domain to appear in the zone file. Lastly, for the two passive DNS vantage points, there is a difference in the DNS population coverage; an authoritative name server receives global traffic for domains within its zone, whereas a resolver serves only a local, smaller population.

Table 1. Summary of vantage points

| | **Dimension** | | | | |
Vantage points	WIDTH	DEPTH	TIME GRANULARITY	MAXIMUM TIME DELAY	POPULATION COVERAGE
CT logs	All TLDs	FQDN	Precise	MMD	–
Resolver	All TLDs	FQDN	Precise	–	Local
Authoritative NS	One TLD	FQDN	Precise	–	Global
TLD Zone file	One TLD	Apex	Daily	One day	–

5   Design

The current state-of-the-art tooling lacks the possibility of conducting analyses between vantage points at a full domain name space scale. Based on this, we derived a set of design goals that shaped the design and implementation of

Gollector. We first present these design goals, followed by an overview of the architecture of *Gollector* describing how each of the individual goals is met.

Firstly, the main purpose of *Gollector* is to allow for the data collection of DNS and domain name-related information from different vantage points (G_1). The design of the tool must allow the collection from new vantage points to be added at a future point in time (G_2). Given the large number of existing domain names, and the volume of DNS and TLS data that is generated on the Internet, the tool should handle data collection at a large scale and remain highly performant (G_3). The data structures in which the data is stored must allow for post-collection analysis (G_4). The collection of DNS traces may contain sensitive information, which third-party data sources may be hesitant to share with researchers, and may only be willing to do so in an anonymized form. However, the anonymization of data may make post-collection analysis more difficult, and less detailed, and as such we would like to preserve the relationship between unanonymized data and anonymized data in *Gollector* (G_5).

5.1   Architecture

To meet G_1, the architecture of *Gollector* consists of modular components: (1) a set of data collectors, (2) a data sink, and (3) a database for persistent data storage (see Fig. 2a). Each individual collector is a small component dedicated to collecting domain name-related data from one vantage point and sending the resulting data to the sink. So far, we implemented four collectors (see Sect. 5.2). The collectors and the sink communicate securely using gRPC, allowing the collectors and sink to operate on different machines and thereby collectors to operate in different network environments (i.e., collect data from different vantage points). The decoupling of collectors from the other components of *Gollector* allows new collector modules to be developed in the future, thereby meeting G_2.

The sink is designed to accept messages from the various collectors, extract database models from the messages and insert these models in the underlying database. As of now, we use PostgreSQL as the underlying database, as our database models naturally fit in a relational database model, and for future implementations, we can switch to a database intended for big-data analytics. The sink inserts new models in the database in batches rather than individual queries, resulting in a high-performance insertion rate (meeting G_3).

Domain names are stored in the database as a collection of database models (see Fig. 2b how the models relate to each other). Each collected FQDN is segmented in its parts, according to the domain name hierarchy (i.e., top-level domain, its public suffix, the apex domain, and the FQDN). Each segment is inserted as its separate row in its own table and has a foreign key to all parts higher in the hierarchy. The data in this database is enriched by adding more tables with pointers (i.e., foreign keys) to these domain-related tables; a timestamped certificate may point to an FQDN, whereas a timestamped zone file entry may point to an apex domain instead. This makes it easy to answer questions such as *"How many unique apex domains are observed under each TLD?"*

or *"For a given apex domain, how many certificates have we seen?"*, and thereby fulfills G_4.

Lastly, the segmented storage of domain names also applies to anonymized domain names. Instead of storing the domain name directly, we store an anonymized version of each segment by hashing[3] the segment after appending a salt to the segment. The database maintains a mirrored set of tables for anonymized segments, including the foreign keys from segments lower in the hierarchy to upper segments. To analyze data collected in both their anonymized and unanonymized form, we link the two sets of tables by adding a reference from the anonymized table to the unanonymized table (meeting G_5). This link will only exist if a particular segment has been seen in both an anonymized dataset and an un-anonymized dataset, and thus will not apply to all observed domain names. As such, this method only provides anonymity for segments that have only been seen in their anonymized form, and only until an unanonymized form is collected.

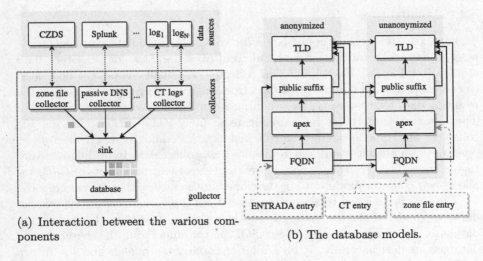

(a) Interaction between the various components

(b) The database models.

Fig. 2. Design of *Gollector*

5.2 Collectors

Each collector registers *events* related to a domain name. These events range from individual DNS queries to domain registrations. Depending on the collector, a collector may generate only one or a few events per domain or may generate many events over the course of a measurement. The current implementation of *Gollector* consists of the collectors described below.

---

[3] using SHA256.

Zone File Collection. This collector can fetch zone files from the CZDS [13] and zone files over HTTP from servers that provide access. The former is an API provided by ICANN that allows for a standardized way to access zone files of over a thousand gTLDs including .com and .net, whereas the latter is used to fetch the Danish .dk TLD. In both cases, the authentication is handled by the collector and is configured through a configuration file during startup. The collector automatically requests access for zone files daily when the granted access expires, ensuring that data collection continues during long measurements. All available zone files are then collected daily, and any changes between zone files of two consecutive days are tracked. Domain names that appear and disappear in the most recent zone file are considered new registrations and expirations/removals respectively. Furthermore, we collect all domain names observed on the first day but do not consider these to be registrations or expirations. *Gollector* stores the zone files both raw on disk as well as in a processed form in the underlying database, so it allows researchers to work with the raw zone file if needed.

Passive Resolver DNS. Gollector itself does not perform any passive DNS measurements itself, but rather relies on previously collected datasets instead. The supported format for parsing passive DNS data is in Splunk Stream [9] export data, which consists of a condensed form of individual DNS request-response pairs in a JSON format. From the logs, *Gollector* extracts the queried domain name and timestamp of the resolution, omitting any DNS-specific information, such as query types or resolved IP addresses.

CT Logs. Each CT log provides an HTTP API that can be used to fetch CT log entries. Such entries contain a full certificate chain of the newly-signed certificate, including the timestamp it was added to the log. *Gollector* traverses each log (as recognized by Google[4]), fetching all entries per log. This collector parses each entry, extracts the embedded domain names from the newly-signed certificate, and stores them with a timestamp when the certificate was submitted to the CT logs. Furthermore, the certificates are stored in their raw format in the underlying database, allowing for further, more in-depth, investigation when necessary.

ENTRADA. This collector interfaces with the dataset generated by ENTRADA, used to collect DNS resolutions at an authoritative name server level. This dataset comprises DNS-specific attributes of each resolution, such as the query type, the specific resolved IP address(es), and the IP addresses from which the query originates. We summarize this information by collecting some basic statistics related to an individual domain name that has been queried; the first time and the last time the domain was queried. As such, the information in *Gollector* is far smaller in size than the source dataset, at the cost of losing details.

---

[4] https://github.com/google/certificate-transparency-community-site/blob/master/docs/google/known-logs.md.

6   Dataset

We applied *Gollector* to four types of data sources, for which we implemented the aforementioned four collectors (Sect. 5.2). We collected the data over a time period of three weeks[5]. For our experiments, we collected the passive DNS traffic from our Danish university network (with 10 s of thousands of users) and the ENTRADA data from the Danish .dk TLD. We collected our certificate data from all recognized CT logs and attempted to retrieve all TLDs available from CZDS. Figure 2 illustrates the unique number of events, FQDNs, apexes, public suffixes, and TLDs observed per vantage point. Note that for the zone files, we only collected domains registrations and expirations, rather than all entries in the zone files. Since domains are registered at an apex domain level at a DNS registry, the collected zone files do not contain any FQDNs. Whereas our ENTRADA collector found the most unique FQDNs (161.5M), these FQDNs tend to be centralized under a relatively small set of TLDs (272) compared to the other vantage points. Conversely, our passive DNS collector identified the smallest number of FQDNs (6.0M), which is unsurprising given the relatively small number and homogeneity of clients the university network serves (i.e., primarily Danish students and academic staff). The CT log data spans most TLDs (1,087), which comprises 72.6% of all recognized TLDs [14].

Table 2. Overview of the collected data, denoting the unique number of events, FQDNs, apexes, public suffixes and TLDs observed per vantage point.

	Events	FQDNs	Apexes	Public suffixes	TLDs
Zone files	8,371,731	–	7,920,217	572	607
CT logs	114,182,670[a]	89,989,143	27,807,193	4,222	1,087
Passive DNS	200,146,260	6,046,480	1,213,405	1,125	580
ENTRADA	161,497,905	161,497,905	124,318,163	328	272

[a]We identify a CT event as a uniquely observed certificate.

We hypothesize that the ENTRADA and the passive DNS traffic are highly biased towards Danish traffic. To test this hypothesis, we analyze the distribution of unique apexes found per TLD for each of the vantage points. Table 3 shows for each vantage points, the percentage of apexes identified by that vantage point under a particular TLD, showing the top 10 TLDs per vantage point. The results show our hypothesis to be confirmed for ENTRADA, with nearly all apexes falling under the .dk TLD, whereas this is not the case for the passive DNS traffic. The passive DNS traffic contains a large number of apexes under reserved TLDs for internal use (i.e., mynet, my_net, home, lan [24]), and the .com TLD is more popular than the Danish TLD. The CT and zone file datasets are more in line with the general size of the TLDs; .com and .net are the largest TLDs.

---

[5] Between February 1st, 2021 and February 21st, 2021.

Table 3. The top ten TLDs per vantage point in terms of unique number of apex domains identified under the TLDs.

CT		Zones		Passive		ENTRADA	
TLD	%	TLD	%	TLD	%	TLD	%
com	44.3%	com	59.2%	mynet	23.9%	dk	100%
tk	4.5%	icu	10.7%	my_net	22.0%	arpa	0.0%
de	4.4%	net	4.4%	home	19.1%	com	0.0%
net	3.9%	xyz	3.9%	lan	16.5%	org	0.0%
org	2.9%	org	3.1%	com	4.9%	net	0.0%
uk	2.3%	wang	2.4%	dk	2.0%	se	0.0%
ru	1.6%	page	2.2%	localdomain	1.2%	0	0.0%
nl	1.6%	site	1.8%	net	1.1%	0	0.0%
br	1.5%	bar	1.0%	dlinkrouter	0.7%	0	0.0%
it	1.4%	club	0.8%	org	0.6%	0	0.0%

7   Use Cases

We demonstrate the utility of *Gollector* by diving deeper into three use cases. Firstly, we evaluate the impact of the time differences of the four vantage points by analyzing how effective they are in recognizing newly registered domains. Additionally, we leverage the relative dark matter differences between passive DNS measurements from a resolver and an authoritative name server perspective to investigate the split-horizon setup of our local university network. These two use cases showcase the benefits of multiple vantage points. Lastly, we leverage the full set of FQDNs for a domain name generation algorithm, as an alternative to brute-force subdomain enumeration techniques employed by penetration testing tools.

7.1   Early Detection of Domain Names

Various malicious actors rely on domain registrations for their operations, such as botnet operators (for domain fluxing) and phishers (for typo-squatting and hosting phishing sites in general). Prior work has demonstrated that the involved domains tend to be abused within a few days after their registration, after which they have already served their (malicious) purpose [42]. From a defense perspective, identifying such domains in the early part of their lifecycle is therefore of critical importance. A domain registration can be detected at different points of time depending on the vantage point. Zone files are a logical choice, as they originate from the party that registers new domains (i.e., registries) but have as a limitation that they are created with a one-day granularity[6]. We investigate

---

[6] Registries will have access to more accurate registration data than just the zone files, so this is a limitation for researchers who only have access to the zone files.

if other vantage points provide a more accurate – and thereby earlier – time of registration, especially focusing on CT logs, as they cover all TLDs rather than just one (which is the case for ENTRADA and to a lesser extent the passive DNS from university network).

We identified a registration of 4,438,966 domains over the course of 20 days[7] for an average of 221,948 domains per day. For each of these registrations, we identify if the other three vantage points (i.e., CT logs, passive DNS, and ENTRADA) observed the domains as well. Firstly, we identify if these vantage points observed the domain registrations *at all* in the full timeline. This serves as an indication to what extent domain registrations remain undetected and the coverage of the domain name space the vantage points have compared to zone files. We follow this up by identifying which of these domains were detected *before* the zone files registered these domains. For those domains, the one-day granularity of zone files is surpassed by the granularity of the other vantage point. Lastly, we identify the domains that were detected *within seven days* after the zone file identified the domain as registered. Wullink *et al.* [42] showed that phishing domains tend to be most active within the first seven days of their registration (based on the DNS traffic the domain receives). Therefore, identifying such domain registrations within seven days is highly beneficial for mitigation these attacks.

Table 4 shows the results, both in absolute numbers and the percentage of the total number of zone file registrations. Since the ENTRADA dataset operates at a single TLD's name server, we differentiate between the full dataset and the dataset for the .dk domains only. Across all TLDs, the CT logs have relatively high coverage, with almost one in four domain registrations being detected across the whole dataset. The passive DNS and ENTRADA datasets have a much smaller coverage, with only 0.01% and 1.1% of domain registrations being detected. Notably, CT logs provide earlier detection of domains compared to zone files for 13.8% of domains. When looking at the .dk domain only, all vantage points detect more registrations than the full dataset, with ENTRADA detecting nearly all registrations. Furthermore, of the domain registrations detected by the passive DNS dataset, almost all of them were .dk domains (with only 133 non-Danish registrations detected). In none of the cases, the percentage of identified registrations was significantly improved by including the first seven days after registration. For identifying new domain registrations, zone files are still primarily the best vantage points, but this can be supported by CT logs and ENTRADA for individual TLDs.

7.2   Split Horizon and Data Leakage

Large organizations commonly operate a *split-horizon* DNS infrastructure, where DNS resolutions receive different responses depending on the location of the requester. Use cases include load balancing, or protecting sensitive information that should only be accessible from within a corporate network [19]. Furthermore, the exposure of the existence of a particular hostname can already provide

---

[7] Since a registration is detected by computing the difference of the zone files of two subsequent days, we are missing the registrations on the first day of our measurement.

Table 4. Detection of newly registered domain names for non-zone files vantage points. The results for both the full set of TLDs and the `.dk` zone only are shown.

| | All TLDs | | | | | |
| | Absolute | | | Percentual | | |
	CT	Passive	ENTRADA	CT	Passive	ENTRADA
Overall	971,318	533	46,628	23.6%	0.01%	1.1%
Before	568,436	216	25,713	13.8%	0.01%	0.62%
Within 7 days	325,277	169	4688	7.9%	0.00%	0.11%
	.dk only					
Overall	16,476	63	46,495	34.9%	0.13%	98.5%
Before	0	0	25,673	0.00%	0.00%	54.4%
Within 7 days	639	3	4,601	1.35%	0.01%	9.74%

insight into an organization's inner workings and should potentially be protected against. We leverage our passive DNS data and ENTRADA dataset – both relatively biased towards the `dk` TLD – to investigate potential data leakage in our dataset. We identify which domain names are likely to be only used internally and what data is leaked outside the network through DNS queries. The split-horizon setup should result in particular domain names only being queried within the university network.

As a first step, we identify what apex domain names are likely to be owned by the university network. We assume that internal apex domains are heavily used for various services within the network, thereby having many different FQDNs in use. As such, we collect the unique number of FQDNs observed under each apex domain in our dataset. Table 5 shows this count for the 10 most prevalent apex domains, and also shows the percentage of total FQDNs observed in the passive DNS dataset it encompasses. FQDNs under `aau.dk` are seen most often (more than 63% of observed FQDNs fall under this apex), suggesting that this domain is used for internal systems within the network. Indeed, this domain is owned by the university, whereas the other domains in the table are related to background services such as advertisement/analytics (e.g., `googlesyndication.com`, `cedexis-radar.net`), or network management (e.g., `bbsyd.net`, `emnet.dk`), and are not associated with the university.

From our ENTRADA dataset, we found 18,499 FQDNs under the `aau.dk` apex domain, a much lower number than the 3,8M seen in the passive DNS dataset. Not all of these domain names are necessarily sensitive information, as some of the domains used by the university are likely used to host public websites. Therefore, we turn to the domains that have both been seen by the passive DNS and the ENTRADA dataset: this set of domains comprises 2,813 FQDNs, or 15.2% of the `aau.dk` FQDNs seen in the ENTRADA dataset. Since we have no ground truth of what is a sensitive domain and what is not, we compare this list of domains to the most common subdomains instead [8]. We found 435 (or

15.5%) of these domains is in the public list, leaving more than 2,300 subdomains potentially leaked. As a result of the anonymization practice of *Gollector*, we are unable to further investigate these potentially leaked domains, as these domains are anonymized and the unanonymized version can (deliberately) not be retrieved.

Table 5. The 10 apex domains with the most observed unique FQDNs in the passive DNS dataset collected from the university network.

Apex domain	Unique FQDN count	%
aau.dk	3,829,837	63%
googlesyndication.com	344,058	6%
technicolor.net	61,151	1.01%
cedexis-radar.net	44,771	0.74%
sophosxl.net	39,297	0.65%
bbsyd.net	36,758	0.61%
office.com	30,215	0.50%
emnet.dk	23,540	0.39%
obelnet.dk	22,909	0.38%
webspeed.dk	21,569	0.36%

7.3   Subdomain Enumeration

Part of the reconnaissance phase in penetration testing is subdomain enumeration, or the process of identifying all subdomains under a given apex domain. Strategies include scraping third parties or generating (i.e., brute-forcing) candidate FQDNs [3,5,7]. *Gollector* supports the former, as its database model allows to easily query all FQDNs observed under a particular apex domain. We present a method to support the latter as well. As opposed to the existing brute-forcing techniques, we infer a relationship between sets of subdomains, based on the co-occurrence of these subdomains under a shared set of apex domains. As a result, our proposed method generates accurate candidate FQDNs and identifies relationships between subdomains that otherwise would not be found. This inference is motivated by a particular use case in which subdomains are likely to co-occur under the same apex domain; cPanel defines a set of *Service Subdomains*, or subdomains exposed by cPanel to provide interfaces to external components [17]. Therefore, the existence of a cPanel subdomain may indicate that the other *Service Subdomains* are also "in use" under the particular apex domain, even if a DNS dataset has not identified its existence. Our proposed method consists of the following steps: (1) we convert our dataset of subdomains and apex domains in a graph, (2) we compute a clique cover of this graph, (3) we prune these cliques according to the weights in each clique to filter out nodes that are not relevant to the clique, and (4) we generate a set of candidate FQDNs, based on the pruned cliques.

As a first step, we split up our set of FQDNs into their subdomain and apex parts, and subsequently create a graph in which the subdomains are modeled as nodes. Edges between two subdomains express the measure of overlap of the sets of apex domains under which both subdomains have been seen. The edge weight is computed as the Jaccard index [28] of the set of apex domains under which the first subdomain has been seen and the set of apex domains under which the second subdomain has been. We prune the edges that have a weight of zero (i.e., between subdomains that are never seen under the same apex domain), and remove any nodes that are without edges (i.e., subdomains never seen under the same apex domain as another subdomain).

We split up the nodes in our graph into a *clique cover*. Cliques are induced subgraphs such that each node is adjacent to all other nodes in the subgraph. This implies that every subdomain within a clique has been observed under the same apex domain with all other subdomains at least once. By assigning each node to a clique we reach a clique cover, which we achieve by relying on the algorithm defined in Appendix A[8].

A clique cover ensures every subdomain falls in a clique, but this does not guarantee there is a strong connection between the nodes within the clique. Therefore, we prune each clique to remove nodes that are not considered relevant. We scale the edge weights in each clique such that the highest weight equals 1, and then prune the nodes whose maximum edge weight falls under a given threshold. In our experiments, we used a threshold value of 0.6, which we found through thorough experimentation.

For each clique, we can now generate a set of candidate FQDNs. We maintain a set for each subdomain, denoting the apex domains under which the subdomain has been observed, based on all FQDNs in our dataset. For each clique, we define the set of apex domains that *any* of the subdomains in the clique has been observed under. The Cartesian product of the apex domains and subdomains then forms the tuples of apex domains and subdomains representing the candidate FQDNs. The FQDNs already seen in data are left out from this set, forming the final set of candidate FQDNs.

We applied this methodology to a dataset of 2 million randomly sampled FQDNs from our dataset, In total, we identified 8,410 cliques comprising 22,519 subdomains. Appendix B shows several examples of subdomains that form a clique. These subdomains were previously seen under a set of 1,021,175 apex domains. Given our cliques, we generated 2,349,911 FQDN candidates, resulting in an average of only 2.3 FQDNs per apex domain. Out of these candidates, we could successfully resolve 1,396,129 FQDNs or 59% of candidates. Additionally, we also manually investigated some of the cliques to understand what the nature of these cliques is. This manual investigation was far from exhaustive, but we found cliques related to the software that runs on these domains (such as the

---

[8] There are potentially many clique covers, and our purpose is not to achieve a minimal clique cover.

cPanel example that drove this research) and cliques pointing to a specific organization. An example of the former clique type is cliques for subdomains used by Magento, a highly-popular open-source eCommerce platform [4]. We identified 470 cliques related to this platform with subdomains containing the keyword magento, often having shop or store as another keyword being embedded in one of the subdomains. The latter type includes a clique formed by subdomains under the apex domains fbcdn.net and whatsapp.net, containing 118 subdomains, indicating the relationship between Whatsapp and Facebook.

Our proposed method can be integrated into existing penetration testing tools as an alternative to wordlist-based domain generators. On top of that, our cliques can be used to identify shared domain name ownership, and to assist security researchers in identifying domains hosting the same services.

8   Conclusions

In this paper, we introduced *Gollector* as a novel platform for collecting domain name and DNS-related information. Through a thorough overview of the DNS and TLS ecosystem, we present a set of vantage points from which this information can be retrieved. Through three uses cases, we leverage the differences between these vantage points. Firstly, we show that that CT logs and passive DNS traffic collected at an authoritative name server can serve as a source for early domain registration detection. Zone files are outperformed by the CT logs in 13.8% of domains under all TLDs, and by the passive authoritative traffic in 54.4% of domains under the .dk TLD. Secondly, we compare passive DNS measurements from a university network with authoritative name server measurements to shed light on potential data leakage of subdomains under the main domain name in use by the university. Lastly, we present a method to generate potentially existing FQDNs, which infers these FQDNs based on the association of subdomains and apex domains.

Acknowledgments. This research was carried out under the SecDNS project, funded by Innovation Fund Denmark. We would like to express our gratitude to Finn Büttner and Erwin Lansing for their assistance in collecting our passive DNS datasets.

Appendix A   Clique Cover Algorithm

Algorithm 1 denotes the algorithm used to compute a clique cover for graph G. The intuition behind the algorithm is that two nodes – connected through an edge with the largest weight – have the largest priority to form a clique. The algorithm iterates over all edges in the graph and assigns a clique to each node in the graph based on the interactions that are observed through the edges. Depending on whether the source and destination nodes of the edge are already in a clique, the algorithm creates new cliques, adds nodes to existing cliques, or merges cliques. The output of the algorithm is a hashmap of the clique assigned to each node in the graph. The implementation of the algorithm includes several optimizations to reduce the edges to evaluate.

Algorithm 1: Clique cover algorithm

```
 1  Function cliqueCover (G);
    Input   : graph G of subdomain nodes
    Output: set of subdomain lists
 2  edges = edgeListFrom(G);
 3  edges = sortByWeight(edges);
 4  cliques = {};
 5  for edge in edges do
 6  │   src, dst = nodes in edge;
 7  │   cliqueSrc = cliques[src];
 8  │   cliqueDst = cliques[dst];
 9  │   if src not in clique and dst not in clique then
    │   │   /* both are without clique, create a new one        */
10  │   │   c = newClique(src, dst);
11  │   │   cliques[src] = c;
12  │   │   cliques[dst] = c;
13  │   else if src in same clique as dst then
    │   │   /* src and dst are already in the same clique        */
14  │   else if src not in clique and dst in clique then
    │   │   /* try to add dst to cliqueSrc                       */
15  │   │   if cliqueSrc.formsCliqueWith(dst) then
16  │   │   │   cliques[src].add(dst);
17  │   │   end
18  │   else if src in clique and dst not in clique then
    │   │   /* try to add src to cliqueDst                       */
19  │   │   if cliqueDst.formsCliqueWith(src) then
20  │   │   │   cliques[dst].add(src);
21  │   │   end
22  │   else if src and dst in different cliques then
    │   │   /* try to merge the two cliques                      */
23  │   │   if cliqueSrc.formsCliqueWith(cliqueDst) then
24  │   │   │   c = mergeCliques(cliqueSrc, cliqueDst);
25  │   │   │   cliques[src] = c;
26  │   │   │   cliques[dst] = c;
27  │   │   end
28  │
29  end
30  return cliques;
```

Appendix B   Examples of Cliques

Table 6 contains several examples of cliques. The table shows a general description of what the subdomains may be intended for, the number of subdomains in the clique, the number of apexes associated with these subdomains, and the list of subdomains comprised by the clique.

Table 6. Examples of cliques

Description	Subdomain count	Apex count	Subdomains
High-entropy subdomains	237	2	adfqjkxr, aeovrpvk, anhpfctcxzcp, asqzcggxiy, bdzvxofezaejku, ...
Email servers	5	34,249	imap, xwa, xas, pop, smtp
Western language-related subdomains	7	26,730	en, es, fr, pt, it, ru, de
More language-related subdomains	6	3,764	ko, zh, cs, nl, ar, ja
Content deliver network	9	5,197	cdn-1, cdn-3, cdn-2, cdn-5, cdn-7, ...

References

1. Comodo SSL affiliate the recent RA compromise. https://blog.comodo.com/other/the-recent-ra-compromise/. Accessed 23 July 2021
2. DNSdumpster. https://dnsdumpster.com/. Accessed 10 July 2021
3. DSNRecon. https://github.com/darkoperator/dnsrecon. Accessed 10 July 2021
4. Magento. https://magento.com/. Accessed 27 July 2021
5. OWASP/Amass. https://github.com/OWASP/Amass. Accessed 10 July 2021
6. Subfinder. https://github.com/projectdiscovery/subfinder. Accessed 10 July 2021
7. Sublist3r. https://github.com/aboul3la/Sublist3r. Accessed 10 July 2021
8. The most popular subdomains on the internet (2016). https://bitquark.co.uk/blog/2016/02/29/the_most_popular_subdomains_on_the_internet. Accessed 27 July 2021
9. About Splunk stream (2020). https://docs.splunk.com/Documentation/StreamApp/7.3.0/DeployStreamApp/AboutSplunkStream. Accessed 10 July 2021
10. Openintel - current coverage (2020). https://openintel.nl/coverage/. Accessed 10 July 2021
11. Using GeoIP with BIND 9 (2020). https://kb.isc.org/docs/aa-01149. Accessed 10 July 2021
12. About zone file access (2021). https://www.icann.org/resources/pages/zfa-2013-06-28-en. Accessed 30 Aug 2021
13. Centralized zone data service (2021). https://czds.icann.org/. Accessed 30 Aug 2021
14. List of top-level domains (2021). https://www.icann.org/resources/pages/tlds-2012-02-25-en. Accessed 30 Aug 2021
15. Project sonar (2021). https://opendata.rapid7.com/about/. Accessed 10 July 2021
16. Public suffix list (2021). https://publicsuffix.org/. Accessed 10 July 2021
17. value (2021). https://documentation.cpanel.net/display/CKB/Service+Subdomains+Explanation. Accessed 30 Aug 2021
18. van Adrichem, N.L.M., et al.: A measurement study of DNSSEC misconfigurations. Secur. Inform. 4(1) (2015). https://doi.org/10.1186/s13388-015-0023-y
19. Aitchison, R.: DNS techniques, pp. 163–207. Apress, Berkeley (2011). https://doi.org/10.1007/978-1-4302-3049-6_8
20. Alieyan, K., Almomani, A., Manasrah, A., Kadhum, M.M.: A survey of botnet detection based on DNS. Neural Comput. Appl. **28**(7), 1541–1558 (2017). https://doi.org/10.1007/s00521-015-2128-0
21. Behjat, A.: ISC spins off its security business unit (2013). https://www.isc.org/blogs/isc-spins-off-its-security-business-unit/

22. Bharath: A penetration tester's guide to subdomain enumeration (2018). https://blog.appsecco.com/a-penetration-testers-guide-to-sub-domain-enumeration-7d842d5570f6. Accessed 24 July 2021

23. Borges, E.: Wrong Bind configuration exposes the complete list of Russian TLD's to the Internet, March 2018. https://securitytrails.com/blog/russian-tlds. Accessed 30 Aug 2021

24. Eastlake, D., Panitz, A.: Reserved Top Level DNS Names, RFC ed. BCP 32, June 1999

25. Edmonds, R.: ISC passive DNS architecture (2012). https://mirror.yongbok.net/isc/kb-files/passive-dns-architecture.pdf

26. Hao, S., Kantchelian, A., Miller, B., Paxson, V., Feamster, N.: PREDATOR: proactive recognition and elimination of domain abuse at time-of-registration. In: Proceedings of the 2016 ACM SIGSAC Conference on Computer and Communications Security, CCS 2016, pp. 1568–1579. Association for Computing Machinery, New York (2016). https://doi.org/10.1145/2976749.2978317

27. Hohlfeld, O.: Operating a DNS-based active internet observatory. In: Proceedings of the ACM SIGCOMM 2018 Conference on Posters and Demos, SIGCOMM 2018, pp. 60–62. Association for Computing Machinery, New York (2018). https://doi.org/10.1145/3234200.3234239

28. Jaccard, P.: Distribution de la flore alpine dans le bassin des dranses et dans quelques régions voisines. Bull. Soc. Vaudoise. Sci. Nat. **37**, 241–272 (1901)

29. Laurie, B., Langley, A., Kasper, E.: Certificate Transparency, RFC ed. RFC 6962, June 2013

30. Mockapetris, P.: Domain Names - Implementation and Specification, RFC ed. STD 13, November 1987. http://www.rfc-editor.org/rfc/rfc1035.txt

31. Pearce, P., et al.: Global measurement of DNS manipulation. In: 26th USENIX Security Symposium (USENIX Security 2017), pp. 307–323. USENIX Association, Vancouver, August 2017. https://www.usenix.org/conference/usenixsecurity17/technical-sessions/presentation/pearce

32. Prins, J.: DigiNotar certificate authority breach "operation black tulip" (2011). https://media.threatpost.com/wp-content/uploads/sites/103/2011/09/07061400/rapport-fox-it-operation-black-tulip-v1-0.pdf. Accessed 23 July 2021

33. Rescorla, E.: The Transport Layer Security (TLS) Protocol Version 1.3, RFC ed. RFC 8446, August 2018

34. van Rijswijk-Deij, R., Jonker, M., Sperotto, A., Pras, A.: A high-performance, scalable infrastructure for large-scale active DNS measurements. IEEE J. Sel. Areas Commun. **34**(6), 1877–1888 (2016). https://doi.org/10.1109/JSAC.2016.2558918

35. Schlyter, J.: DNS Security (DNSSEC) NextSECure (NSEC) RDATA Format, RFC ed. RFC 3845, August 2004

36. Singh, M., Singh, M., Kaur, S.: Issues and challenges in DNS based botnet detection: a survey. Comput. Secur. **86**, 28–52 (2019). https://doi.org/10.1016/j.cose.2019.05.019. https://www.sciencedirect.com/science/article/pii/S0167404819301117

37. Szurdi, J., Kocso, B., Cseh, G., Spring, J., Felegyhazi, M., Kanich, C.: The long "taile" of typosquatting domain names. In: 23rd USENIX Security Symposium (USENIX Security 2014), pp. 191–206. USENIX Association, San Diego, August 2014. https://www.usenix.org/conference/usenixsecurity14/technical-sessions/presentation/szurdi

38. van der Toorn, O., van Rijswijk-Deij, R., Geesink, B., Sperotto, A.: Melting the snow: using active DNS measurements to detect snowshoe spam domains. In: NOMS 2018–2018 IEEE/IFIP Network Operations and Management Symposium, pp. 1–9 (2018). https://doi.org/10.1109/NOMS.2018.8406222

39. VanderSloot, B., Amann, J., Bernhard, M., Durumeric, Z., Bailey, M., Halderman, J.A.: Towards a complete view of the certificate ecosystem. In: Proceedings of the 2016 Internet Measurement Conference, IMC 2016, pp. 543–549. Association for Computing Machinery, New York (2016). https://doi.org/10.1145/2987443.2987462

40. Weimer, F.: Passive DNS replication. In: FIRST Conference on Computer Security Incident (2005)

41. Wullink, M., Moura, G.C.M., Müller, M., Hesselman, C.: ENTRADA: a high-performance network traffic data streaming warehouse. In: NOMS 2016–2016 IEEE/IFIP Network Operations and Management Symposium, pp. 913–918 (2016). https://doi.org/10.1109/NOMS.2016.7502925

42. Wullink, M., Muller, M., Davids, M., Moura, G.C.M., Hesselman, C.: ENTRADA: enabling DNS big data applications. In: 2016 APWG Symposium on Electronic Crime Research (eCrime), pp. 1–11 (2016). https://doi.org/10.1109/ECRIME.2016.7487939

Adversarial Trends in Mobile Communication Systems: From Attack Patterns to Potential Defenses Strategies

Hsin Yi Chen[1] and Siddharth Prakash Rao[1,2(✉)]

[1] Aalto University, Espoo, Finland
`hsin-yi.chen@aalto.fi`
[2] Nokia Bell Labs, Espoo, Finland
`sid.rao@nokia-bell-labs.com`

Abstract. Understanding attack patterns and attacker behavior has always been a prominent security research topic to provide insights into adversarial trends and defense strategies. In this paper, we demonstrate the process of analyzing adversarial trends in mobile communication systems using a conceptual threat modeling framework combined with graph analysis methodologies. We model 60 attacks using the Bhadra framework [30] and conduct graph-theory-based analysis to deduce insights. We observed the attack patterns, the diversity of attack paths given an attacker's ability or target impact, and the importance of each technique from a network graph viewpoint and discussed potential defense strategies that mobile operators can deploy accordingly. Our main contribution is demonstrating the potential of Bhadra for analyzing the security posture of an operator's network and simplifying the complexity of the mobile networks to communicate the security analysis results.

Keywords: Threat modeling · Mobile networks · Attack patterns

1 Introduction

As the threat landscape of mobile communication systems expands with the broader adoption of newer technologies and the involvement of more parties, threat intelligence sharing has become essential. As a response, the industry partners, including standardization and regulatory bodies (e.g., 3GPP, ENISA) and academia, have conducted many security analyses. However, there is a lack of common taxonomy and conceptual framework to gather all the knowledge in one place. In this work, we argue that such a framework is essential in understanding adversarial trends. It forms the first step in security communication towards threat intelligence sharing.

To our best knowledge, the recently proposed Bhadra framework [30] is the only conceptual threat and attack modeling framework that captures attack vectors in the end-to-end mobile communication systems from 2G to 4G. In this work, we demonstrate how a framework like Bhadra can be used to gain

© Springer Nature Switzerland AG 2021
N. Tuveri et al. (Eds.): NordSec 2021, LNCS 13115, pp. 153–171, 2021.
https://doi.org/10.1007/978-3-030-91625-1_9

insights on adversarial trends and provide potential defense strategies for mobile operators. In particular, we model individual attacks with Bhadra and apply graph-theoretic analysis on the modeled attack data. By visually representing our analysis, we discuss how operators can use similar methods to discover attack patterns, analyze the importance of techniques to the attackers and explore the possible impact given the attackers' capability. Our main contribution is to demonstrate how to use a framework like Bhadra for analyzing the security posture of an operator's network using readily available graph algorithms and simple visualizations.

Although threat modeling has always been an integral part of system security, it is mostly confined to using well-known frameworks – such as STRIDE [39] or MITRE ATT&CK [6] in recent years – on different types of systems. However, research on how to communicate threat modeling findings, especially graph analysis techniques, is far less explored. Some of the recent works [1,44] have used the MITRE ATT&CK framework for enterprise systems that initiated such a line of research. We continue to extend the research in the context of mobile communications systems and with the Bhadra framework. In this realm, one of our contributions is to explore Bhadra's potential in simplifying the complexity of mobile network security while building narratives for security communication.

The rest of the paper is organized as follows. Section 2 presents an overview of the mobile communication networks, the Bhadra framework, and existing research that summarizes analysis methods in attack patterns. Section 3 describes the methodology we used to collect attacks and conduct graph analysis. Section 4 presents the graph analysis results. Section 5 discusses limitations of our work and potential research directions in overcoming them. Finally, Sect. 6 contains concluding remarks.

2   Background

This section gives a high-level overview of mobile network topology to show the attack surface covered in the Bhadra framework. We discuss some of the known security weaknesses, specifically mobile network protocols, to illustrate the types of attack techniques that can be modeled using Bhadra. Then, we briefly introduce Bhadra and its design philosophy. Finally, we present related work in finding attack patterns and attack graph analysis.

2.1   Mobile Network Topology

Figure 1 shows a simplified version of mobile network topology that consists of the following components. *User Equipment (UE)* contains a Subscriber Identification Module (SIM) card that supports the identification of the subscriber to its mobile operator with the International Mobile Subscriber Identity (IMSI) stored in the SIM card. *Radio Access Network (RAN)* is the air interface that connects UEs to operators' networks. *Core Network (CN)* comprises components

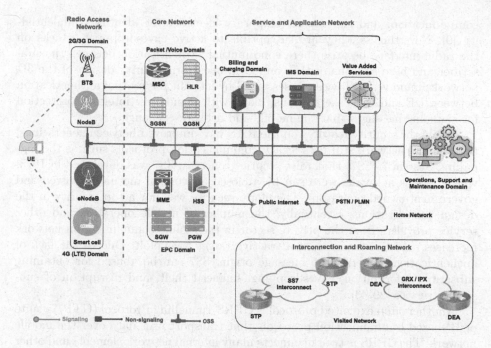

Fig. 1. Overview of mobile networks topology [4]

that are responsible for managing subscribers' authentication and mobility, initiating connections, and providing core telephony services such as SMS, voice calls, and Internet data.

Service and Application Network includes components that are responsible for billing and charging of the mobile service used by the subscribers. It also includes IP multimedia subsystem (IMS) and Value-added Services (VAS) that provide supplementary services to mobile subscribers on top of the core telephony services. In addition, *Interconnection and Roaming Network* enables roaming scenarios when a subscriber is outside their operator's serving area (i.e., home network). In a roaming scenario, the visited operator is connected to the subscriber's home network over the General Packet Radio Service (GPRS) roaming exchange or IP exchange carrier and retrieves the subscriber's profile from the Home Location Register (HLR) using signaling protocols.

2.2 Security Weaknesses

This section briefly describes some of the known security weaknesses in different mobile generation and communication protocols. Although these weaknesses are not exhaustive, we intend to help the readers to understand the techniques defined in the Bhadra framework or the attacks analyzed in this paper.

The 2nd generation (2G) or GSM networks offers three main security features, namely, subscriber authentication, encryption at the radio interface for communication, and the use of temporary identities for identity confidentiality [9]. Nevertheless, they are susceptible to active eavesdropping attacks on the radio interface because there is no mutual authentication between the subscriber and base stations of the connected operator. Security design of the 3G networks improves such weaknesses in 2G by introducing mutual authentication between UE and the base stations, along with mandatory integrity protection for signaling messages that the mobile and network exchange.

While the security features on the RAN have improved between generations, the 3G core network still uses legacy communication protocols such as the Signalling System 7 (SS7) that raise security concerns. SS7 was developed in 1975, where mobile networks were run by a closed network of mutually trusted and government-owned operators. Therefore, security was not a top priority in the design considerations. Eventually, the number of mobile operators and other service providers from the private sector in the mobile communication network increases, and SS7 become an attractive target to exploit. Due to the lack of authentication to verify the message origin, SS7 can be abused for obtaining subscriber information, eavesdropping, financial theft, and disruption of subscriber service [29, 43].

Another often exploited protocol is GPRS Tunnelling Protocol (GTP), a suite of IP-based communication protocols that transport user data over the mobile network. The GPRS network connects many internal network elements and other external networks such as the public Internet and other network operators, thus providing broad attack surfaces for attackers. However, since no built-in security mechanism is supported in GTP, operators are suggested to implement security protection such as IP Security (IPsec) at their network interfaces. Failing to do so may path the way for attackers to successfully carry out GTP attacks that leads to data interception, billing frauds, DoS against the network or user, and privacy leaks [41].

Session Initial Protocol (SIP) is yet another protocol with many known vulnerabilities. SIP is the underlying session control protocol used in IMS to provide multimedia communications services. Exploiting the vulnerabilities in SIP allows the attackers to, for example, send spoof SMS and perform Denial of Service (DoS) on SMS clients [42]. Commonly targeted IMS services include IMS-based Voice over IP (VoIP), Voice over LTE (VoLTE), SMS [42].

The 4G LTE network inherits several security weaknesses from 2G and 3G, mainly because it has to support backward compatibility. Also, since LTE contains several IP-based systems, attackers can now use IP-based penetration tools or exploit network components (e.g., DNS servers) they are more familiar with. This would naturally increase the attack surface and undermines the overall security. Among several other threats against Evolved Packet System (EPS) [9], jamming or flooding the radio channels of the mobile users to cause DoS is one of the common threats to LTE networks.

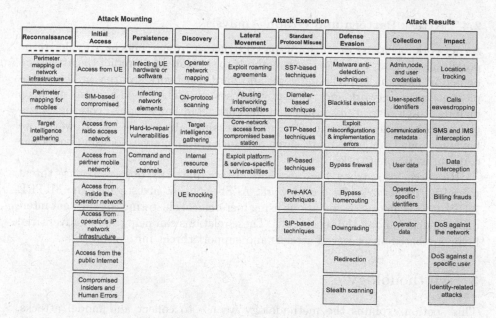

	Attack Mounting			Attack Execution			Attack Results	
Reconnaissance	Initial Access	Persistence	Discovery	Lateral Movement	Standard Protocol Misuse	Defense Evasion	Collection	Impact
Perimeter mapping of network infrastructure	Access from UE	Infecting UE hardware or software	Operator network mapping	Exploit roaming agreements	SS7-based techniques	Malware anti-detection techniques	Admin,node, and user credentials	Location tracking
Perimeter mapping for mobiles	SIM-based compromised	Infecting network elements	CN-protocol scanning	Abusing interworking functionalities	Diameter-based techniques	Blacklist evasion	User-specific identifiers	Calls eavesdropping
Target intelligence gathering	Access from radio access network	Hard-to-repair vulnerabilities	Target intelligence gathering	Core-network access from compromised base station	GTP-based techniques	Exploit misconfigurations & implementation errors	Communication metadata	SMS and IMS interception
	Access from partner mobile network	Command and control channels	Internal resource search	Exploit platform- & service-specific vulnerabilities	IP-based techniques	Bypass firewall	User data	Data interception
	Access from inside the operator network		UE knocking		Pre-AKA techniques	Bypass homerouting	Operator-specific identifiers	Billing frauds
	Access from operator's IP network infrastructure				SIP-based techniques	Downgrading	Operator data	DoS against the network
	Access from the public Internet					Redirection		DoS against a specific user
	Compromised Insiders and Human Errors					Stealth scanning		Identity-related attacks

Fig. 2. Bhadra threat modeling framework [30]

2.3 Bhadra Framework

Bhadra is a conceptual threat and attacks modeling framework that captures attack vectors in end-to-end mobile communication systems. Bhadra provides a taxonomy to map attacks and threats to 2G, 3G, and 4G mobile networks, where it describes the adversarial behaviors in terms of tactics and techniques. For more details about Bhadra, refer to the original paper [30].

Similar to the MITRE ATT&CK framework, Bhadra's taxonomy is arranged as a matrix (as shown in Fig. 2). The column titles are called *Tactics*, and they are essentially categories of *techniques*. Tactics are the attacker's intermediate or final goals, and techniques are the methods to accomplish those goals. Bhadra takes inspiration for its design philosophy from the ATT&CK framework and hence, shares several commonalities. Nevertheless, Bhadra's taxonomy covers techniques specific to network environment and protocols used in telecommunication systems, which are missing from the ATT&CK framework. For more complex mobile network attacks, one can use both Bhadra and ATT&CK in conjunction. This work solely uses the Bhadra framework.

Bhadra can be used for both attack and threat modeling. While modeling, the modeler would manually express the attack or threat as a set of tactic and techniques pairs which is referred to as *models* in this paper. Depending on the complexity of the attack, models may contain all or only a few tactics, and each tactic selected may contain more than one technique.

2.4   Attack Pattern and Graph Analysis

As network topologies are of graph-based structure, researchers have explored the possibility of using graph analysis methods to simulate and predict the attackers' behavior, assess risk in the network, and harden network security in, for example, enterprise network and cyber-physical systems. The graph analysis methods include graph algorithms, Bayesian networks, Markov models, cost optimization algorithms like game theory, and uncertainty algorithms [46]. However, we have not found any existing research in attack graph analysis focusing on mobile communication networks.

Research also exists that extracts attack patterns observed with threat modeling frameworks. In recent work, Al-Shear et al. investigated the MITRE ATT&CK techniques associations using hierarchical clustering to represent interdependencies among the techniques. These relations can help predict adversarial behavior based on observed attacks and support threat mitigation [1].

3   Methodology

This section explains the methodology we use to collect and model attacks. Moreover, we introduce the graph algorithms we use to associate with different aspects of the adversarial trends.

3.1   Attack Collection and Sampling

First, through a thorough literature review, we collected different types of attacks for modeling with the Bhadra framework. We mainly reused the broad literature presented in Bhadra's original paper [30]. It contains two groups of literature: *Group I* includes peer-reviewed papers that describe one or multiple attacks scenarios. *Group II* consists of security reports from standardization bodies (e.g., 3GPP, GSMA) and regulatory agencies (e.g., ENISA).

Out of this pool, we used the following three criteria for sampling the attacks for our study. (1) We selected multi-staged attacks that contain mounting, execution, and result collection stages. (2) We prioritized attacks where their descriptions clearly state at least the initial access and final impact along with some details on the attack procedures. (3) We picked attacks that cover different initial accesses, protocols, and network components for variety. The first and second criteria ensured that we could model the selected attacks using Bhadra as per its threat modeling procedure. At the same time, the third criteria allowed us to imitate a real-life scenario of an operator – where the observed attacks often consist of a variety of attack vectors – while seeking insights from the analysis. Our sampling yielded us 30 sources (i.e., attack papers) in total.

After the sampling, we further reviewed the selected attacks and found many similar ones with minor variants. In such attacks, the end goals and some intermediate steps were the same. However, the only varying aspect was the message types used for attacks, such as different Radio Resource Control (RRC) procedure messages in Pre-AKA techniques. We decided to count those as separate attacks while modeling even though they have a partially similar pattern. This way, we keep the graph analysis weighting more realistic as using different message types can be seen as different paths with which an attacker can reach the same end goals. We populated 60 attacks primarily from 30 of the sources that we had sampled. Table 2 in the appendix lists all the attacks that we considered.

It is important to note that the mobile operators rarely discuss actual attacks on their networks in public forums. Due to the lack of such attack data, we treat our collection of 60 attacks as if they were observed on a single operator's network premise for the rest of the paper. We believe that the attacks in our collection represent real-world scenarios (in terms of their practicality and variety), and an actual audit of an operator's network might yield a similar collection. This reasonable generalization helps us communicate our observations from graph analysis and potential defense strategies from an operator's point of view.

3.2   Attack Modeling

From our previous threat modeling experience with Bhadra, we observed that even with the clear technique description and examples that Bhadra provides, people may still come up with different models given the same attack scenario. This is because the results of any threat or attack modeling would vary based on the expertise (domain knowledge) of the person modeling it and of the details provided about the attack/threat. To minimize this effect, our modeling process involved the following two stages.

1. **Independent modeling**: In this stage, all the authors of this paper independently modeled all the attacks from our sample using Bhadra. While doing so, we first understood the attack and mapped their steps to the tactical objective as per Bhadra. We then tried to select at least one technique. Nevertheless, in some cases, depending on the details available about the attack, we had to select either all applicable techniques or none based on our reasoning.
2. **Discussion**: All the authors participated in a discussion where we jointly reviewed the attacks from our sample. Here, when conflicts were found (e.g., mismatch of techniques), we discussed until all the authors were convinced about the techniques applicable to the attack for final analysis. We found that such discussions helped us improve the reliability of our results as they collectively utilized the independent expertise of each author and compensated for the lack of details (if any) about a specific attack.

3.3   Graph Analysis

Our goal from graph analysis is to discover common attack patterns, importance, and diversity of techniques from our modeled attacks. After reviewing different methods, we chose graph algorithms because they had readily available algorithms that matched goals. We explain them in detail as follows. We used Python Networkx [12] package for our graph analysis.

Common Subpaths—Association of Techniques. We derived common subpaths (as an attack pattern) among the attack models to understand how the techniques are associated with each other. Networkx does not contain any readily available function to calculate common subpaths among paths. Hence, we wrote a simple python script to find common subpaths containing three to five nodes.

Connectivity—Importance of Techniques. Researchers have used graph connectivity to measure the communication network survivability [7]. We associate the similar idea to quantify the importance of a technique with the loss of average node connectivity after removing all the edges to and from the individual node. The more average connectivity loss, the lower the possibility an attacker would successfully finish all the tactics to finish his final goal covered in the impact tactical category.

Following the definition [2], we calculate average node connectivity $\bar{K}$ of a graph G as the average of local node connectivity over all pairs of nodes of G:

$$\bar{K}(G) = \frac{\sum_{u,v} K_G(u, v)}{\binom{n}{2}} \tag{1}$$

where $K_G(u, v)$, the local node connectivity for two non-adjacent nodes u and v, is the minimum number of nodes to be removed to disconnect the two nodes.

Unique Paths—Diversity of Attack Techniques. The number of unique paths to reach a certain goal has been used to infer the diversity of attack methods an attacker can choose [18]. We are particularly interested in visualizing the diversity of attack methods from a particular initial access point to a specific impact. Therefore, we calculate the number of simple paths between two nodes [38] given the attack graph built from our attack models using the built-in function in `NetworkX` [26].

4   Results

This section presents the graph analysis results based on the 60 attack models. We constructed an attack graph (as shown in Fig. 3) with the Python `Networkx` package.

Each node represents a technique, and each edge represents the connection of adjacent techniques used in the same attack. The thickness of each edge represents its weight, meaning how many times two nodes are connected in the attack models. We calculated and presented the weight in and out of a technique node in the figure. Also, each node is color-coded based on the number of unique connections where the node links next.

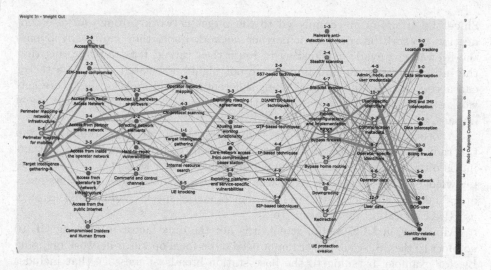

Fig. 3. Attack graph of the 60 modeled attacks

> **Strategy 1:** By visualizing basic graph analysis results, a security analyst can identify the strong association of techniques and the highly connected nodes as an information source to prioritize their defense. In Fig. 3, thickest edges represent the strong association of techniques. Similarly, the node with the highest value for the (weight-in, weight-out) pair represents the highly connected nodes.
>
> If Fig. 3 is treated like a real-life scenario of visualization of attacks observed on an operator's network, the operator's goal is to build defense strategies such that it either eliminate or reduce the thickest edges or reduce the (weight-in, weight-out) of the highly connected nodes.

We now highlight some insights derived from other results and explain the reason behind them with examples from the collected attack scenarios. Similar to the above example, we first describe our observation and then present a potential defense strategy.

4.1   Common Attack Patterns

Table 1 shows the common sub-paths of the modelled attacks. We observed a strong association of techniques that are used before and after exploiting roaming agreements. For example, attackers often use internal resource search or CN-protocol scanning in the discovery phase to gain information on the target network nodes. After initial access and discovery, attackers often misuse GTP, Diameter, and SS7 protocols and send crafted messages to exploit their target.

Since the attackers are connected to the target network through an interconnection network or spoof as a partner network node, they can easily bypass the firewall and evade blacklisting to reach their target. It is worth noting that the initial access point and impact are not highly associated since an attacker can access the roaming network using different techniques. Also, these core network attacks can target more broad attack surfaces and lead to various types of impact.

Another such association is the techniques used in attacks originated from the radio access network. In these attack scenarios, threat intelligence gathering is often required in the reconnaissance phase. Attackers need to gain some knowledge on the target UE (e.g., which operator it subscribes to) and its operators' network characteristics to find some operator-specific vulnerabilities, such as GUTI allocation mechanism [16].

Moreover, in LTE, signal strength is not the only factor in tricking UE to connect to the BS. An attacker might need to perform operator network mapping by, for example, listening to the base station broadcast message that includes frequency priority to adjust the fake BS configuration [25]. After the target UEs connect to the fake BS, an attacker often use the UE knocking technique that triggers the paging message by silent calls and messages to identify the location of a subscriber or spoof other paging message content and metadata. As we observed, Pre-AKA protocols are usually misused in radio attacks. For example, an attacker can send an identity request to the target UE to get the IMSI that links to identity-related attacks and location tracking. Besides, an attacker can also craft the RRC connection message or trigger NAS Detach Procedure to achieve denial of service or downgrading.

We observe some strong association in the attack patterns. Note that the distribution of the technique selection may not represent the actual number of incidents seen in the wild since we only modeled publicly available attack scenarios mostly from academic publications. Nevertheless, these associations can help prioritize defense deployment.

Strategy 2: Exploiting roaming agreements can be seen as a bottleneck that, if succeeded, could lead to a broader attack surface that allows an attacker to exploit signaling protocols such SS7, Diameter, or GTP. These protocols that do not have a secure mechanism to verify the sender and attacker can impersonate a benign roaming partner.

In this case, the operator's strategy would be to deploy the edge agents (if not already deployed) and impose strict policies for any traffic coming from the interconnection network for filtering the message content [13,32]. Authenticating the benign roaming partners would be another possible strategy if the operators can run a public-key infrastructure.

Table 1. Common subpaths

# of nodes	Count	Path
3	6	(Exploiting roaming agreements, GTP-based techniques, Bypass firewall)
	5	(Exploiting roaming agreements, DIAMETER-based techniques, Bypass firewall)
	5	(Internal resource search, Exploiting roaming agreements, SS7-based techniques)
	5	(Exploiting roaming agreements, SS7-based techniques, Blacklist evasion)
	5	(Exploiting roaming agreements, SS7-based techniques, Bypass firewall)
	4	(Target intelligence gathering-R, Access from Radio Access Network, UE knocking)
	4	(Access from Radio Access Network, UE knocking, Pre-AKA techniques)
	4	(UE knocking, Pre-AKA techniques, UE protection evasion)
	4	(Exploiting roaming agreements, DIAMETER-based techniques, Blacklist evasion)
	4	(Internal resource search, Exploiting roaming agreements, GTP-based techniques)
	4	(Operator network mapping, SIP-based techniques, Exploit misconfigurations and implementation errors)
	4	(Access from Radio Access Network, Operator network mapping, Pre-AKA techniques)
4	5	(Internal resource search, Exploiting roaming agreements, SS7-based techniques, Blacklist evasion)
	5	(Internal resource search, Exploiting roaming agreements, SS7-based techniques, Bypass firewall)
	4	(Internal resource search, Exploiting roaming agreements, GTP-based techniques, Bypass firewall)
	3	(Target intelligence gathering-R, Access from Radio Access Network, UE knocking, Pre-AKA techniques)
	3	(Internal resource search, Exploiting roaming agreements, DIAMETER-based techniques, Bypass firewall)
	3	(Access from the public Internet, Command and control channels, UE knocking, IP-based techniques)
	3	(Infected UE hardware or software, Operator network mapping, SIP-based techniques, Exploit misconfigurations and implementation errors)
	3	(Infected UE hardware or software, Operator network mapping, SIP-based techniques, UE protection evasion)
5	2	(Target intelligence gathering-R, Access from Radio Access Network, UE knocking, Pre-AKA techniques, UE protection evasion)
	2	(Access from Radio Access Network, UE knocking, Pre-AKA techniques, UE protection evasion, Location tracking)
	2	(Access from Radio Access Network, UE knocking, Pre-AKA techniques, UE protection evasion, Identity-related attacks)
	2	(Target intelligence gathering-R, Access from partner mobile network, CN-protocol scanning, Exploiting roaming agreements, DIAMETER-based techniques)
	2	(Access from partner mobile network, CN-protocol scanning, Exploiting roaming agreements, DIAMETER-based techniques, Blacklist evasion)
	2	(Access from partner mobile network, CN-protocol scanning, Exploiting roaming agreements, DIAMETER-based techniques, Bypass firewall)
	2	(Access from the public Internet, Command and control channels, UE knocking, IP-based techniques, Redirection)
	2	(Access from the public Internet, Infected UE hardware or software, Operator network mapping, SIP-based techniques, Exploit misconfigurations and implementation errors)
	2	(Access from the public Internet, Infected UE hardware or software, Operator network mapping, SIP-based techniques, UE protection evasion)
	2	(Target intelligence gathering-R, Access from the public Internet, Command and control channels, UE knocking, IP-based techniques)
	2	(Access from the public Internet, Command and control channels, UE knocking, IP-based techniques, Exploit misconfigurations and implementation errors)

4.2 Loss of Connectivity

Figure 4 shows the loss of average connectivity after removing edges to and from a particular technique node. As shown in the figure, operator network mapping and internal resource research, the two most commonly used discovery techniques, have a significantly higher percentage in loss of connectivity than the rest. Our prior network analysis experience confirms that operator network mapping and internal resource techniques are commonly observed. These techniques help the attackers learn information about the target node, such as IP address and open port. The attacker then effectively uses them in the later stages of an attack, such as lateral movement techniques.

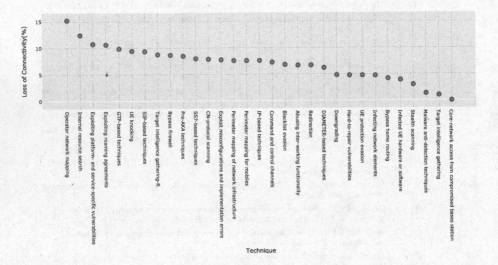

Fig. 4. Loss of connectivity after removing edges to and from individual technique

On the other end, malware and anti-detection techniques, target intelligence gathering in the discovery phase, and core-network access from the compromised base station are the ones with the most negligible loss of connectivity. This result is also consistent with the impression we got from our reviewing and attack modeling process since not many publicly available attacks that gain access to core networks through compromised based stations or perform malware anti-detection techniques were found, and target intelligence sharing is primarily already used in the reconnaissance phase.

Strategy 3: An operator can use the loss of connectivity result to prioritize the defense against those techniques that are more important to attackers. In Fig. 4, the most important technique would be "operator network mapping". So, the operator has to deploy defense mechanisms that hinder the attackers from mapping their network, or at worst case, alerts them if any network-wide mapping activity is observed. It could also imply that the operators audit their network regularly, for example, to close any ports that are left open.

4.3 Unique Paths

Figure 5 shows the result from the unique paths calculation. From the initial access dimension, we found that attacks from UE, radio access networks, inside the operator network, and public Internet have more diverse paths to reach the target impacts. The result is predictable as we did not find many attacks involving compromised insiders and human errors, access from operators' IP network infrastructure, and SIM-based compromise.

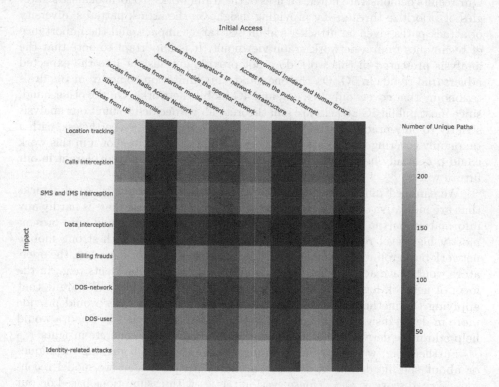

Fig. 5. Number of unique paths from initial access to impact

From the impact dimension, there are more unique paths to reach location tracking, SMS and IMS interception, billing frauds, DOS-user, and identify-related attacks. We can interpret that these impacts are relatively easy to achieve than call or data interception since call interception is only possible in lower generation (e.g., 2G) where the communication is not required to be encrypted.

> **Strategy 4:** From the result of the unique path, the operator can prior-itize their defense effort in two ways. One is to evaluate from the attack-ers' point of view, based on the potential threat actors' capability to gain initial access and their final target impacts. Another is to analyze the operator's own system to identify the weakest points in the network that an attacker might gain access to and the most impacted assets. Once focused on specific initial access or impact combination, the operator can investigate each unique path and strengthen their defense.

5 Discussion

Our results demonstrate potential uses of the framework—to form defense strate-gies or prioritize threats—by providing insight on the attack patterns, diversity of attack paths given an attacker's ability or target impact, and the importance of techniques from a network graph viewpoint. It is important to note that the analysis presented in this work does not provide any insight into the expected adversarial trends in 5G. On the one hand, this limitation comes from Bhadra's taxonomy that covers only 2G, 3G, and 4G mobile networks. On the other hand, since most public 5G attacks are still theoretical, we decided to limit our analysis strictly to only practical attacks while creating our sample. Nevertheless, with a taxonomy covering the 5G attack surface, similar analysis as shown in this work could potentially help uncover new attack patterns. We aim to explore it in our future work.

We sampled publicly available literature to collect various types of attacks that are indicative of an operator's network premises because there is hardly any information on the attacks observed in the wild. Hence, we could only present mostly high-level results that may seem trivial to readers with strong mobile network backgrounds. Nevertheless, while analyzing real-world attacks, the oper-ators would have access to intrinsic details of the security incidents (e.g., in the form of network logs and configuration settings of their nodes). We argue that applying the methodology presented in our work in such cases would provide more in-depth insights. Similarly, adding more sub-techniques to Bhadra would help add more details while modeling, offering potentially concrete insights.

Furthermore, we had to make assumptions either about missing techniques or about specific details of attack procedures. In particular, we model recon-naissance, discovery, and defense evasion tactics with assumptions based on our domain expertise due to the lack of descriptions about the actual procedure in the sources we referred to. Our sources from the attack collections are mostly experiments conducted in academic lab setup or high-level reports on observed attacks in the wild. We missed knowing how exactly an attacker would perform reconnaissance, discovery, and defense evasion in either case. Therefore, we admit that some of our results may be skewed. For instance, even though operator network mapping and internal resource search are the two highest in terms of connectivity loss, they may not be representative of real-world scenarios.

The lack of real-world attack data of the mobile communication networks is a major barrier for academic research. Although sometimes the attacks and lessons learned from defending them are discussed in 3GPP and GSMA meetings, operators rarely share any specific data about attack incidents, even among themselves. One of the reasons for the hesitance to openly discuss security issues could be that operators seem to believe that any such discussions would affect their business and reputation. Nevertheless, we argue that sharing information about security incidents and learning from each other's failures could be beneficial. In this direction, Bhadra would provide a suitable abstraction for sharing threat- or attack-related incidents. We urge that the operators utilize such abstractions, apply a similar analysis as shown in this work, and release it in the public domain to inculcate future research efforts.

6   Conclusion

Our work demonstrated that a conceptual framework like Bhadra establishes a common taxonomy to describe adversarial behaviors and provides valuable insights when combined with analysis methodologies to find relations between different attacks. In particular, our work provides high-level insights into the adversarial trends in mobile communication systems. Using Bhadra, we model 60 attacks that are carefully chosen as a representative sample of different kinds of attacks on the mobile network. We analyze the modeled attacks using graph analysis techniques to understand the importance of the techniques to attackers, the diversity of attack paths an attacker can choose, and the common attack patterns. We also discuss how these insights on different adversarial trends can help the operators prioritize defense strategies. We demonstrated the potential of Bhadra for analyzing the security posture of an operator's network and explored how Bhadra can help simplify the complexity of mobile network security for security communication (such as threat intelligence sharing). Given the initial results and the potential use of the analysis presented in this work, we hope future research efforts can extend a similar study on a large scale and include more diverse attacks (e.g., 5G). Also, we hope our work initiates wider adoption of Bhadra and more collaboration on threat intelligence sharing.

Acknowledgement. The authors would like to thank Professor Tuomas Aura for providing constructive feedback and Nokia Bell Labs for funding the research work.

Appendix

Table 2. Attacks collected from different sources for modeling

Title	Attack name (as per the source)
Billing Attacks on SIP-Based VoIP System [47]	– SIP-based VoIP Billing Attack
Survey of network security systems to counter SIP-based denial-of-service attacks [8]	– SIP message payload tempering – SIP message flooding – SIP message flow Tempering
Mobile data charging: new attacks and countermeasures [27]	– Toll-free data access attack – Stealth Spam Attack in UDP-based Services - VoIP – Stealth Spam Attack with Malicious Link Connection
SIM cards are prone to remote hacking [22]	– Remote SIM hacking
Unveiling the hidden dangers of public IP addresses in 4G/LTE cellular data networks [23]	– Data Quota Drain – Battery Drain
Gaining control of cellular traffic accounting by spurious TCP retransmission [11]	– TCP retransmission attacks - Usage Inflation – TCP retransmission attacks - Free riding
On Her Majesty's Secret Service: GRX & A Spy Agency [34]	– GTP Data Session Hijacking
Analysis and mitigation of recent attacks on mobile communication backend [29]	– Location disclosure using call setup messages
LTE and IMSI catcher myths [3]	– Simple IMSI Catcher
Unblocking stolen mobile devices using SS7-MAP vulnerabilities: Exploiting the relationship between IMEI and IMSI for EIR access [31]	– Unblocking stolen mobile devices using SS7-MAP
Breaking and fixing volte: Exploiting hidden data channels and mis-implementations [20]	– VoLTE Mis-implementation: Permission model mismatch – VoLTE Mis-implementation: Direct Communication in P-GW
Massive Hack of 70 Million Prisoner Phone Calls Indicates Violations of Attorney-Client Privilege [19]	– Illegitimate Surveillance
User location tracking attacks for LTE networks using the interworking functionality [15]	– IMSI catcher with interworking functions – Location disclosure using CAMEL messages
New security threats caused by IMS-based SMS service in 4G LTE networks [42]	– IMS-based SMS - Silent SMS abuse – IMS-based SMS - client DoS – IMS-based SMS - SMS spoofing – IMS-based SMS - SMS spamming towards IMS
Subscriber profile extraction and modification via diameter interconnection [13]	– Extraction and Modification of Subscriber Profile
Diameter Security: An Auditor's Viewpoint [24]	– DoS on subscriber via S6a messages – Location tracking via Sh User-Data-Request
Threats to packet core security of 4G networks [40]	– EPC Tunnel Endpoint Identifier Thief – GTP-based IMSI catcher – GTP-based billing evasion - Create session Request – Exploit Charging Gateway Function – Connection Hijacking with GTP messages – GTP-based DoS attack on subscribers – GTP-based DoS attack on the operator's equipment – Control packets inside a user tunnel: GTP-in-GTP
SMS and one-time-password interception in LTE networks [14]	– Diameter-based SMS Interception
GUTI Reallocation Demystified: Cellular Location Tracking with Changing Temporary Identifier [16]	– Location Tracking Attack on VoLTE User – Smart Tracking Attack
How Criminals Recruit Telecom Employees to Help Them Hijack SIM Cards [10]	– SIM Swap Attack
LTEInspector: A systematic approach for adversarial testing of 4G LTE [17]	– 4G LTE Paging Channel Hijacking – 4G LTE Authentication Relay Attack
Touching the untouchables: Dynamic security analysis of the LTE control plane [21]	– BTS resource depletion attack – Blind DoS attack
Understanding How IMSI- Catchers Exploit Cell Networks [25]	– IMSI Catcher - Communication Interception – Basic Location Area Test – Smart Paging Test – Active GPS location tracking – TAU Reject - Communication Interception – TAU Reject - DoS
Breaking LTE on layer two [35]	– LTE User Data Manipulation Attack – Passive Layer 2 Attack - Identity Mapping Attack
MESSAGETAP: Whofis Reading Your Text Messages? [33]	– MessageTap
LTE security disabled: misconfiguration in commercial networks [5]	– Impersonation Attack based on Misconfiguration
LTE Phone Number Catcher: A Practical Attack against Mobile Privacy [45]	– LTE Phone Number Catcher
Hidden Agendas: bypassing GSMA recommendations on SS7 networks [28]	– SS7 - Use ACN for illegitimate component – SS7 - Modify user profile with InsertSubscriberData Message – SS7 - Operation Cod Tag Misuse
Simjacker - Next Generation Spying Over Mobile [37]	– SimJacker
IMP4GT: IMPersonation Attacks in 4G NeTworks [36]	– IMPersonation Attacks in 4G Networks

References

1. Al-Shaer, R., Spring, J.M., Christou, E.: Learning the associations of MITRE ATT&CK adversarial techniques. In: 2020 IEEE Conference on Communications and Network Security (CNS), pp. 1–9. IEEE (2020)
2. Beineke, L.W., Oellermann, O.R., Pippert, R.E.: The average connectivity of a graph. Discret. Math. **252**(1–3), 31–45 (2002)
3. Borgaonkar, R., Shaik, A., Asokan, N., Niemi, V., Seifert, J.-P.: LTE and IMSI catcher myths. BlackHat Europe (2015)
4. Chen, H.-Y.: Domain-specific threat modeling for mobile communication systems. Master's thesis, Department of Computer Science and Engineering, Aalto University School of Science and Technology, Espoo, Finland (2021)
5. Chlosta, M., Rupprecht, D., Holz, T., Pöpper, C.: LTE security disabled: misconfiguration in commercial networks. In: Proceedings of the 12th Conference on Security and Privacy in Wireless and Mobile Networks, pp. 261–266. ACM (2019)
6. The MITRE Corporation. The MITRE ATT&CK. https://attack.mitre.org/
7. Duque-Anton, M., Bruyaux, F., Semal, P.: Measuring the survivability of a network: connectivity and rest-connectivity. Eur. Trans. Telecommun. **11**(2), 149–159 (2000)
8. Ehlert, S., Geneiatakis, D., Magedanz, T.: Survey of network security systems to counter SIP-based denial-of-service attacks. Comput. Secur. **29**(2), 225–243 (2010)
9. Forsberg, D., Horn, G., Moeller, W.-D., Niemi, V.: LTE Security. Wiley, Chichester (2012)
10. Franceschi-Bicchierai, L.: How criminals recruit telecom employees to help them hijack SIM cards (2018). https://www.vice.com/en/article/3ky5a5/criminals-recruit-telecom-employees-sim-swapping-port-out-scam. Accessed 25 Apr 2021
11. Go, Y., Jeong, E., Won, J., Kim, Y., Kune, D.F., Park, K.: Gaining control of cellular traffic accounting by spurious TCP retransmission. In: NDSS. Internet Society (2014)
12. Hagberg, A., Swart, P., Chult, D.S.: Exploring network structure, dynamics, and function using NetworkX. Technical report, Los Alamos National Lab. (LANL), Los Alamos, NM (United States) (2008)
13. Holtmanns, S., Miche, Y., Oliver, I.: Subscriber profile extraction and modification via diameter interconnection. In: Yan, Z., Molva, R., Mazurczyk, W., Kantola, R. (eds.) NSS 2017. LNCS, vol. 10394, pp. 585–594. Springer, Cham (2017). https://doi.org/10.1007/978-3-319-64701-2_45
14. Holtmanns, S., Oliver, I.: SMS and one-time-password interception in LTE networks. In: 2017 IEEE International Conference on Communications (ICC), pp. 1–6. IEEE (2017)
15. Holtmanns, S., Rao, S.P., Oliver, I.: User location tracking attacks for LTE networks using the interworking functionality. In: 2016 IFIP Networking Conference (IFIP Networking) and Workshops, pp. 315–322. IEEE (2016)
16. Hong, B., Bae, S., Kim, Y.: GUTI reallocation demystified: cellular location tracking with changing temporary identifier. In: NDSS. Internet Society (2018)
17. Hussain, S., Chowdhury, O., Mehnaz, S., Bertino, E.: LTEInspector: a systematic approach for adversarial testing of 4G LTE. In: NDSS. Internet Society (2018)
18. Idika, N., Bhargava, B.: Extending attack graph-based security metrics and aggregating their application. IEEE Trans. Dependable Secure Comput. **9**(1), 75–85 (2010)

19. The Intercept: Massive hack of 70 million prisoner phone calls indicates violations of attorney-client privilege (2015). https://theintercept.com/2015/11/11/securus-hack-prison-phone-company-exposes-thousands-of-calls-lawyers-and-clients/. Accessed 25 Apr 2021

20. Kim, H., et al.: Breaking and fixing VoLTE: exploiting hidden data channels and mis-implementations. In: Proceedings of the 22nd ACM SIGSAC Conference on Computer and Communications Security, pp. 328–339 (2015)

21. Kim, H., Lee, J., Lee, E., Kim, Y.: Touching the untouchables: dynamic security analysis of the LTE control plane. In: 2019 IEEE Symposium on Security and Privacy (SP), pp. 1153–1168. IEEE (2019)

22. Security Research Labs: SIM cards are prone to remote hacking. https://srlabs.de/bites/rooting-sim-cards/. Accessed 17 June 2021

23. Leong, W.K., Kulkarni, A., Xu, Y., Leong, B.: Unveiling the hidden dangers of public IP addresses in 4G/LTE cellular data networks. In: Proceedings of the 15th Workshop on Mobile Computing Systems and Applications, pp. 1–6 (2014)

24. Mashukov, S.: Diameter security: an auditor's viewpoint. J. ICT Stand. 5(1), 53–68 (2017)

25. Nasser, Y.: Gotta Catch 'Em All: Understanding How IMSI-Catchers Exploit Cell Networks. White paper, Electronic Frontier Foundation (2019). https://www.eff.org/files/2019/07/09/whitepaper_imsicatchers_eff_0.pdf

26. NetworkX: Network Analysis in Python. A generator that produces lists of simple paths (2019). https://networkx.org/documentation/stable/reference/algorithms/generated/networkx.algorithms.simple_paths.all_simple_edge_paths.html. Accessed 25 Sept 2021

27. Peng, C., Li, C., Tu, G., Lu, So., Zhang, L.: Mobile data charging: new attacks and countermeasures. In: Proceedings of the 2012 ACM Conference on Computer and Communications Security, pp. 195–204 (2012)

28. Puzankov, K.: Hidden agendas: bypassing GSMA recommendations on SS7 networks. In: Hack in the Box Conference (2019)

29. Rao, S.P.: Analysis and mitigation of recent attacks on mobile communication backend. Master's thesis, Department of Computer Science and Engineering, Aalto University School of Science and Technology, Espoo, Finland (2015)

30. Rao, S.P., Holtmanns, S., Aura, T.: Threat modeling framework for mobile communication systems. arXiv preprint arXiv:2005.05110 (2020)

31. Rao, S.P., Holtmanns, S., Oliver, I., Aura, T.: Unblocking stolen mobile devices using SS7-MAP vulnerabilities: exploiting the relationship between IMEI and IMSI for EIR access. In: 2015 IEEE Trustcom/BigDataSE/ISPA, vol. 1, pp. 1171–1176. IEEE (2015)

32. Rao, S.P., Kotte, B.T., Holtmanns, S.: Privacy in LTE networks. In: Proceedings of the 9th EAI International Conference on Mobile Multimedia Communications, pp. 176–183 (2016)

33. Leong, D.P.R., Dean, T.: MESSAGETAP: Who's Reading Your Text Messages? (2019). https://www.fireeye.com/blog/threat-research/2019/10/messagetap-who-is-reading-your-text-messages.html. Accessed 25 Apr 2021

34. Corelan Cybersecurity Research: On Her Majesty's Secret Service: GRX & A Spy Agency. https://www.corelan.be/index.php/2014/05/30/hitb2014ams-day-2-on-her-majestys-secret-service-grx-a-spy-agency/. Accessed 25 Apr 2021

35. Rupprecht, D., Kohls, K., Holz, T., Pöpper, C.: Breaking LTE on layer two. In: 2019 IEEE Symposium on Security and Privacy (SP), pp. 1121–1136. IEEE (2019)

36. Rupprecht, D., Kohls, K., Holz, T., Pöpper, C.: IMP4GT: impersonation attacks in 4G networks. In: Symposium on Network and Distributed System Security (NDSS). ISOC (2020)
37. AdaptiveMobile Security: New Simjacker vulnerability exploited by surveillance companies for espionage operation (2019). https://simjacker.com/. https://www.adaptivemobile.com/blog/simjacker-next-generation-spying-over-mobile. Accessed 25 Apr 2021
38. Sedgewick, R.: Algorithms in C, Part 5: Graph Algorithms. Pearson Education, Boston (2001)
39. Shostack, A.: Experiences threat modeling at microsoft. MODSEC@ MoDELS (2008)
40. Positive Technologies: Threats to Packet Core Security of 4G Network. White paper, GSMA (2017)
41. Positive Technologies: Threat vector: GTP (2020). https://positive-tech.com/storage/articles/gtp-2020/gtp-2020-eng.pdf. Accessed 24 May 2021
42. Tu, G.-H., Li, C.-Y., Peng, C., Li, Y., Lu, S.: New security threats caused by IMS-based SMS service in 4G LTE networks. In: Proceedings of the 2016 ACM SIGSAC Conference on Computer and Communications Security, pp. 1118–1130 (2016)
43. Welch, B.: Exploiting the weaknesses of SS7. Netw. Secur. **2017**(1), 17–19 (2017)
44. Xiong, W., Legrand, E., Åberg, O., Lagerström, R.: Cyber security threat modeling based on the Mitre enterprise ATT&ACK matrix. Softw. Syst. Model., 1–21 (2021)
45. Yu, C., Chen, S., Cai, Z.: LTE phone number catcher: a practical attack against mobile privacy. Secur. Commun. Netw. **2019** (2019)
46. Zeng, J., Shuang, W., Chen, Y., Zeng, R., Chengrong, W.: Survey of attack graph analysis methods from the perspective of data and knowledge processing. Secur. Commun. Netw. **2019** (2019)
47. Zhang, R., Wang, X., Yang, X., Jiang, X.: Billing attacks on SIP-based VoIP systems. WOOT **7**, 1–8 (2007)

Trust

Trusted Sockets Layer: A TLS 1.3 Based Trusted Channel Protocol

Arto Niemi$^{(\boxtimes)}$ ⓘ, Vasile Adrian Bogdan Pop, and Jan-Erik Ekberg

Huawei Technologies Oy (Finland) Co. Ltd., Itämerenkatu 9, Helsinki, Finland
{arto.niemi,bogdan.pop,jan.erik.ekberg}@huawei.com

Abstract. Trusted channels are important when communication requires end-point integrity assurance in addition to secure channel guarantees. To facilitate adoption, trusted channel protocols are often designed as extensions to the widely-used TLS protocol by augmenting it with mutual attestation. We discuss the security requirements for such protocols, and provide a survey of prior art. Then, we present a new TLS 1.3 based trusted channel protocol that can be conveniently implemented via callback function interfaces of existing TLS libraries. Distinguishing itself from earlier proposals, our protocol uses the latest and most secure TLS version, requires no additional round-trips for end-point attestation, and has stronger channel bindings between TLS handshake and attestation to prevent relay and collusion attacks.

Keywords: Trusted channel · Trusted computing · Remote attestation · TLS

1 Introduction

A *secure channel* can be defined as a bidirectional communication medium that authenticates its end-points and provides a message transmission facility with confidentiality, integrity and freshness guarantees. End-points can establish a secure channel by executing a *secure channel protocol*. One such protocol is *Transport Layer Security* (TLS), defined in RFC 8446. It is the most widely-used [15] security protocol in the Internet, where it is typically layered on top of TCP, providing a transparent secure channel for the transmission of application layer messages, such as HTTP, FTP or SMTP payloads [21].

A secure channel protects data *in-transit*, but provides no protection against compromised end-points. In the words of Gene Stafford, *"using encryption on the Internet is the equivalent of arranging an armored car to deliver credit card information from someone living in a cardboard box to someone living on a park bench"* [12]. This lack of end-point integrity guarantees is unacceptable in many applications, including, for example, digital rights management, mobile wallets or Covid-19 tracking applications. For such use cases, a critical requirement is that the end-point software must be *trustworthy*, i.e. trusted to follow a certain security policy when handling the data.

© Springer Nature Switzerland AG 2021
N. Tuveri et al. (Eds.): NordSec 2021, LNCS 13115, pp. 175–191, 2021.
https://doi.org/10.1007/978-3-030-91625-1_10

Informally, a software component can be deemed trustworthy when it is guaranteed to perform the expected operations and nothing more. The guarantee is typically established using a cryptographic proof, delivered via *remote attestation*—a process in which a receiving component produces, for the sender, a verifiable statement that vouches for its trustworthiness. Vice versa, for the receiver, getting assurance that the sending entity is well-behaved and not, for example, susceptible to injection of malicious data or code, is equally important. A communication channel that provides *mutual attestation* in addition to secure channel guarantees is called a *trusted channel* [12].

While it possible to design a trusted channel protocol from scratch, it is easier and safer to integrate attestation into a well-established secure channel protocol such as TLS. A large number of proposals for this have been presented in prior work. However, all these solutions suffer from at least one of the following disadvantages: they mandate drastic changes to the TLS protocol or its implementation, work only with a specific kind of hardware, such as *Trusted Platform Modules* (TPMs), use insufficient channel bindings, or integrate only with an obsolete TLS version, such as TLS 1.2. Especially, the lack of strong channel bindings can be considered a major flaw, as this leaves the door open for relay and collusion attacks, where the operator of a compromised end-point extracts an attestation from a valid end-point, and then presents it as its own.

In this paper, we first study and analyze previous proposals for integration of TLS and attestation. Then, we present a new, convenient and well-argumented design for a TLS 1.3 based trusted channel protocol. Attestations are generated during the handshake to allow for strong channel binding and to avoid having to run an extra attestation protocol on top of TLS. Our solution can be implemented as a TLS extension, without requiring changes to the protocol spec and can be taken into use in a TLS application with minimal code changes. Thus, our solution upholds the TLS promise of transparent, easy-to-use security. We conclude that our protocol seems ideal for migration of mobile agents between secure enclaves.

2   Background

2.1   Transport Layer Security

Transport Layer Security (TLS) combines authenticated key exchange with authenticated encryption to create a secure channel between two communication end-points (client and server). TLS must be layered on top of a reliable transport mechanism, like TCP. It is intended to provide a transparent secure channel service for applications, as indicated by its earlier name, *Secure Sockets Layer* (SSL). For example, the OpenSSL implementation provides the `SSL_write` and `SSL_read` APIs that have similar semantics to standard `write` and `read` system calls that are used with Unix sockets.

TLS consists of two main sub-protocols. Authenticated key exchange (AKE), parameter negotiation and key confirmation are provided by the *handshake protocol*, while authenticated encryption and replay protection is provided by the *record protocol*. The end result of the handshake protocol are two sets of symmetric application data protection keys (one for each direction), with the guarantee that only an end-point that successfully participated in the AKE can compute the keys.

TLS has a long, checkered history of attacks and reactive fixes. Some, but not all, of the attacks can be mitigated within the same protocol version by disabling certain features or by sending additional extension messages. However, it is always more secure to switch to a newer version that has built-in protections for the attacks. Indeed, in March 2021, the IETF formally deprecated TLS versions 1.0 and 1.1 due to lingering vulnerabilities [18]. Even version 1.2 is not secure by default. It supports insecure cryptography such as the CBC mode of encryption, which is vulnerable to padding attacks against the MAC-then-Encrypt construction (e.g. Lucky Thirteen [1]) or RSA key transport, which is not forward secure and is vulnerable to attacks against RSA PKCS #1.5 padding (e.g. the Bleichenbacher attacks such as ROBOT [9]). Furthermore, TLS 1.2 supports insecure protocol features such as renegotiation [20] or compression [19, pp. 158–162], and transmits authentication messages in plaintext. The latter represents a privacy risk, as these messages typically bind a public key value to an identifier such as a DNS name or device serial number. Only the latest 1.3 version [23] can be regarded as secure by default. In TLS 1.3, most of the handshake is encrypted, only secure cryptographic primitives are allowed, and the protocol flow has been optimized for better latency.

2.2 Trusted Computing

Trusted computing[1] is an umbrella term that refers to technologies for establishing trust in computer systems [3]. All trusted computing solutions depend on a *trusted computing base (TCB)*—the part of the system that is unconditionally trusted without proof, and whose failure would compromise the security of the system as a whole [3,17]. The TCB usually consists of both software and hardware components. These components work together to create one or more *secure execution environments (SEEs)* [26], in which it is possible to execute programs under certain isolation guarantees. Especially, an SEE protects the code and memory of the program from the operating system and from applications running outside the SEE. Other key features typically provided by SEEs are secure storage for secrets and the ability to convince remote verifiers. There are three kinds of SEEs deployed in practice: external security elements such as hardware security modules (HSMs), embedded ones such as Trusted Platform Modules (TPMs) [25] and SIM cards, and processor secure environments such as Intel SGX or ARM TrustZone [3].

---

[1] In the cloud context, the term *confidential computing* is sometimes used instead of trusted computing.

2.3 Attestation

In trusted computing, *attestation* refers to a process in which a *target environment*, or a *prover*, with the help of a TCB-backed *attesting environment*, produces a proof regarding some of its locally observable properties, and presents the proof to a *verifier* [25,27]. The properties that are covered by the proof are called *attestation claims* and the proof itself is called *attestation evidence*. The attestating environment vouches for the attestation claims by signing them with its secret key. To validate the attestation evidence, the verifier checks the signature, and then the attestation claims. If the signature is valid, and the attestation claims match the verifier's *attestation policy*, the verifier accepts the attestation evidence. To ensure that the attestation evidence is fresh, the verifier typically initiates the attestation process by sending an *attestation challenge* to the prover. An attestation evidence is then considered valid only when the same challenge is included in the attestation claims.

The attesting environment must be in the position to verify the properties of the target environment that will be listed in the attestation evidence. This can be accomplished with a process called *measuring*, which typically involves hashing, for example, the target environment's code. Analogously, the verifier must be in a position to compare the attestation claims against some expected, known-good values.

Attestation evidences are typically transmitted in the form of X.509 certificates. These are digitally signed documents that list the properties of the target environment, such as the hashes of the application binary and the operating system kernel. The attesting environment indicates that it vouches for these properties by signing the certificate with its secret key. Such certificates are called *attestation certificates*, to differentiate them from standard public-key certificates used e.g. in TLS end-point authentication. Note that an attestation certificate may, and in practice usually does, contain a public key.

The desired end-effect of attestation is that the verifier program receives a valid proof that a prover application is trustworthy. This requires the prover application to provide evidence that it is running in a trustworthy SEE. The SEE, in turn, needs to prove that it is secured by a trustworthy TCB. The TCB component that produces evidence about the rest of the TCB and the SEE is called a *root-of-trust*. The root-of-trust needs to be trusted by the verifier. One way to establish the trust is to pre-provision authentic copies of the root-of-trust's public keys to potential verifiers.

2.4 Channel Binding

A secure channel protocol must authenticate its end-points to ensure that no man-in-the-middle (MITM) attacker gets access to the channel's payload protection keys. Successful end-point authentication is not enough, however: the protocol must also ensure that the entity that gets access to the payload protection keys is the same entity that was authenticated [4,16]. Similarly, when combining two security protocols—such as a remote attestation and a secure channel protocol—it must be guaranteed that only the end-point of the first protocol can get access to the session keys of the second protocol. The process of establishing that no MITM exists between the two end-points that have authenticated in one protocol (called the *inner protocol*), but are using a secure channel provided by another, *outer protocol*, is called *channel binding*. The standard technique for channel binding is to compute a unique identifier for the outer protocol, and bind it to the run of the inner protocol. The unique identifier is called, following the terminology of [30], *channel bindings*.

Channel binding can be accomplished either by including the channel bindings as an extra input in the derivation of the secure channel keys, or by mandating the participants of the first protocol to verify that they have independently computed matching channel bindings for the secure channel. We call the former approach *implicit channel binding* and the latter *explicit channel binding*. Implicit channel binding is used e.g. in TLS 1.3, to bind the end-point authentication of the handshake protocol to the record protocol session by including the handshake transcript, which covers the authentication messages (Certificate and CertificateVerify) in the derivation of the record protection keys (Section 7.1 of [23]). Explicit channel binding is useful when converting a secure channel to a trusted channel protocol, by requiring the end-points to successfully participate in a separate remote attestation protocol as a precondition for establishing the secure channel.

RFC 5056 defines two types of channel bindings: *unique channel bindings* that identify the secure channel uniquely in time, and *end-point channel bindings* that identify the authenticated channel end-points, without identifying the channel uniquely in time [30]. For TLS 1.2 and below, RFC 5929 [2] specifies the *tls-unique* unique channel bindings. The *tls-unique* is a byte sequence consisting of the first Finished message sent in the TLS connection. TLS Finished messages contain a MAC of the previously exchanged messages, including authentication messages. However, tls-unique is not defined for TLS 1.3 [23, Appendix C.5.]) and it is vulnerable to the triple handshake attack, violating the promise that tls-unique uniquely identifies the TLS connection [8]. The TLS 1.3 specification [23, Section 7.5.] recommends instead to use the key material export mechanism (TLS-Exporter) [22] to derive channel bindings. TLS-Exporter is a mechanism for deriving new, handshake-specific secret key material from a label and a base secret. The base secret can be either the *early exporter master secret* (affected by the ClientHello message and possible PSK value) or the *exporter master secret* (affected by the handshake messages from ClientHello to server Finished) and the ECDHE shared secret. TLS libraries typically provide an API for deriving the exporter values, making it easy to use TLS-Exporter for derivation of channel bindings.

3   Survey: Combining TLS and Attestation

3.1   Design Considerations

The designer of the trusted channel protocol faces two critical questions: *when* to generate the attestation evidence and *how* to link the attestation to the TLS session. Attestation can be generated either before, during or after the TLS handshake. We call these approaches *pre-handshake*, *intra-handshake* and *post-handshake* attestation. Of these, *post-handshake* is the simplest to implement, but requires a full round-trip to perform attestation over the negotiated TLS record layer connection. The pre-handshake approach makes it hard to bind the attestation evidence to a specific handshake, risking replay and relay attacks. The intra-handshake approaches seems the most promising from a security and efficiency point-of-view. In this section, we describe a few selected examples of each approach from the literature.

Without channel binding between attestation and the TLS connection a *relay attack* is possible, as discussed for the first time by Goldman et al. [13]. In such an attack, a compromised end-point receiving an attestation challenge over a TLS connection can open a separate TLS connection to forward the challenge to a valid end-point. Then, the compromised end-point can present the attestation evidence returned by the valid end-point as its own to attest successfully over the first TLS connection. To prevent relay attacks, Goldman et al. [13] proposed to include the TLS end-point authentication certificate among the attestation claims. This binds the attestation to the long-term TLS end-point identity of the prover. However, this approach has drawbacks, discussed in subsequent work, such as [12]. First, it does not bind the attestation to the current TLS connection, leaving the door open for replay attacks. Second, the solution requires the prover to have a distinct TLS end-point identity (such as a DNS name) and CA-signed TLS end-point certificate. Third, if the attacker controls both a compromised and a valid end-point, he can perform a *collusion attack* by extracting the TLS end-point keypair from the valid end-point and using it in the compromised end-point—this makes attestation evidence of the valid end-point look valid even when it is actually presented by the compromised end-point. Clearly, channel binding between TLS end-point identity and attestation is insufficient for trusted channel establishment.

3.2   Proposals with Pre-handshake Attestation

Knauth et al. [14] present a trusted channel protocol between two enclaves. They embed SGX attestation evidence into a TLS end-point authentication certificate. The prover enclave creates a new TLS end-point authentication keypair, called RA-TLS, when the enclave is launched. A hash of the public key is included in the attestation claims. The quoting enclave then signs the claims to produce the attestation evidence. Next, the enclave requests a TLS authentication certificate for RA-TLS, embedding the attestation evidence in a custom X.509 extension. The certificate can be either CA-signed or self-signed with SGX as the trust root.

The certificate is re-generated periodically. to keep the attestation fresh. When establishing a TLS connection with the verifier, the prover sends the certificate in the standard TLS Certificate handshake message. The attestation extension can be verified in the certificate validation callback offered by most TLS libraries. This makes the solution especially convenient for verifiers. However, the attestation evidence is not bound to a specific handshake, and the attestation certificate may be used in multiple handshakes, risking replay and collusion attacks.

The pre-handshake approach is also used by Walsh et al. [29], whose aim is to replace PKI-based authentication with attestation-based authentication for microservices. In contrast to [13], Walsh et al. include the public key of the ephemeral (EC)DH keypair, used in the key exchange portion of the TLS handshake, in the attestation claims. This decreases the risk of replay attacks, provided that the (EC)DH public key is used for only one connection, although the paper proposes to generate a new key pair only when connecting to a peer for the first, and to reuse the key after that, as an optimization. Collusion attacks may still be possible, especially if the ECDH keypair is cached, as the attestation is bound only to the ECDH key, but not to the handshake itself. The claims are exchanged over the established TLS connection, meaning that an extra round-trip is needed for mutual attestation.

3.3 Proposals with Intra-handshake Attestation

An example of the intra-handshake approach is the work of Gasmi et al. [12]. The authors propose a deeply modified TLS 1.0 handshake that relies on RSA key transport, where the RSA decryption key is bound to a specific end-point configuration (attestation claims) and is fully confined to the TCB, which in this case is the TPM module. Only the TCB can compute the record protection keys and allows them to be used only when the end-point configuration is unchanged. The solution is rather complex, and requires major modifications to the TLS protocol and its implementation. For example, because the handshake messages are sent unencrypted in TLS 1.0, an additional exchange of public attestation evidence encryption keys is performed using ClientHello and ServerHello extensions. In addition, the solution offers no forward security due to the use of RSA key transport, and is tightly bound with TPMs, making it hard to reuse with other kinds of SEE, such as enclaves.

The proposal of Yu et al. [31] also supports intra-handshake attestation, although the authors are not explicit about whether attestation evidence should be generated before or during the handshake. The main issue in their proposal is that they do not seem to include a handshake-specific challenge, or even a nonce, in the attestation claims. Thus, their protocol is vulnerable to simple relay attacks. Although Yu et al. claim that their protocol is compliant with the TLS 1.1 specification, they send attestation evidences as extra messages during the handshake, while TLS only allows extra messages if they have been registered with IANA, which is not the case here. Second, sending attestation evidences during the handshake in TLS 1.2 and below means that they are sent in plaintext, possibly leaking privacy-sensitive data to eavesdroppers.

3.4   Proposals with Post-handshake Attestation

The benefit of post-handshake attestation is that it requires no changes to the TLS protocol or its implementation. The designers of two protocols used in practice, the *Posture Transport Protocol over TLS* (PT-TLS) [24] and *Industrial Data Space Communication Protocol* (IDSCP) [28] have chosen this approach. In PT-TLS, the TLS connection is established first, and the posture (a form of attestation evidence) is transmitted as application data over the connection. To prevent relay and collusion attacks, PT-TLS proposes to include the tls-unique channel bindings in the attestation claims. However, as noted in Sect. 2.1, this only works for TLS 1.2 and is vulnerable to the triple handshake attack. IDSCP is similar, but uses a hash of verifier's TLS authentication certificate and a nonce, transmitted over the TLS connection prior to attestation, as the channel bindings. This results in the same problem as in [13], namely, that attestation is bound only to the end-point identity, and not to the secure channel instance. A collusion attack against IDSCP was presented by Wagner et al. [28]. In their attack, a compromised end-point first establishes a TLS connection with the verifier who, at this point, cannot detect that the other end-point is compromised. The compromised end-point stores the verifier's TLS authentication certificate from the handshake and receives the verifier's nonce over the established TLS connection. Finally, it sends the verifier's authentication certificate and the nonce as attestation challenges to a valid end-point on the same device. The returned attestation thus has the right channel bindings, and will be deemed valid by the verifier, even though it was generated for an end-point that is not a participant in the current TLS session. Both PT-TLS and IDSCP require two round-trips over the TLS connection to perform the mutual attestation.

An example of an academic protocol that uses post-handshake attestation is the proposal of Aziz et al. [6]. After the initial TLS connections, the endpoints derive fresh AIK (attestation signing) keys and certificates. A "unique identifier" from the prover's TLS authentication certificate and a nonce from its hello message are included in the AIK certificate as channel bindings. During the remote attestation phase, both parties exchange additional nonces, that are to be included in the attestation claims. The claim are signed using the AIK key. One possible weakness this approach is that the channel bindings for the AIK key are both over-the-wire in plaintext. When combined with a successful insider attack that extracts the long-term TLS private key of a valid end-point, a relay attack becomes possible. Another interesting feature in their proposal is the reuse of the TLS record protection key as a MAC key to protect the remote attestation messages. Reusing a key for two different purposes violates the key separation principle, which is considered important for security, see e.g. [7, p. 33]. For this reason, most TLS libraries do not provide an API for extracting the record protection key, making the proposed solution somewhat inconvenient to use. Finally, like [12], the authors present their protocol as a TPM-specific trusted channel solution.

3.5   Summary and Conclusions

	Goldman	Knauth	Walsh	Gasmi	PT-TLS	IDSCP	Aziz
TLS version	1.0	1.2	1.2	1.0	1.2	1.2	1.0
Changes TLS spec.	No	No	No	Yes	No	No	No
Attestation generation	Pre-HS	Pre-HS	Post-HS	Intra-HS	Post-HS	Post-HS	Post-HS
Channel bindings	Auth. public key	Auth. public key	(EC)DH public key	DH public key	tls-unique	Auth. cert	Auth. cert, hello nonce
Attestation privacy	No	No	Yes	Yes	Yes	Yes	Yes
Extra RTTs for attestation	0	0	1	0	2	2	1.5
Targeted TCB hardware	TPM	SGX	TPM	TPM	All	TPM	TPM
Relay or collusion attacks	Yes	Yes	See text	No	Yes	Yes	Yes
Key separation	Yes	Yes	Yes	Yes	Yes	Yes	No

Fig. 1. Comparison of the surveyed trusted channel protocols from [6, 12–14, 24, 28, 29].

The results of our survey are summarized in Fig. 1. From our study, we deduce the following lessons for the design of a TLS-based trusted channel protocol:

- To prevent relay and collusion attacks, the attestation claims should contain channel bindings of the TLS handshake that is used to establish the trusted channel. It is not enough to tie attestation to a long-term end-point identity keypair. The pre-handshake approach is hard to use securely, since it is not possible to include a unique channel bindings in the attestation claims before the handshake has started.
- To minimize the round-trips, it is best to generate and present the attestation evidences during the TLS handshake, i.e. to use the intra-handshake approach.
- The tls-unique channel bindings should not be used, as tls-unique is only defined for TLS 1.2 and below and is vulnerable to attacks.

4   Trusted Sockets Layer Protocol

4.1   Requirements

Our goal is to establish a trusted channel between two end-points on different host devices. The end-points are supported by TCB-backed modules. These modules (attesting environments) must be able to measure the end-points (provers), generate attestation evidences and to verify each other's attestation evidences. The last requirement can be fulfilled with e.g. a *public key infrastructure* (PKI), where each attesting environment has a public key certificate signed by a common *certification authority* (CA). The attesting environment then uses the corresponding private key to sign attestation claims.

We have the following security requirements:

- **SR1 (Secure channel guarantees).** Confidentiality, integrity and freshness of the exchanged application data and authentication of the channel end-points.
- **SR2 (End-point trustworthiness).** The secure channel end-points must exchange and verify attestation evidences. Based on the attestation claims, each end-point can decide whether the other end-point fulfills its security policy requirements. No TLS connection shall be established without successful attestation.
- **SR3 (Channel binding).** Each attestation evidence must be valid only in a specific TLS connection, and only if it has been generated for the sending end-point in the connection, in order to prevent relay and collusion attacks.
- **SR4 (Privacy).** The attestation claims and the end-point identities must not be revealed to unauthorized third parties.
- **SR5 (Forward secrecy).** Disclosure of long-term keys should not lead to compromise of previous protocol runs.

4.2 Threat Model

We assume the attacker has similar capabilities as in the Dolev-Yao model [11]. He can, for example, read or modify transmitted data, replay old messages or relay messages to another end-point. Furthermore, we assume that the attacker may have both compromised and uncompromised end-points at hand, and may have administrator level access to valid end-points. This means the attacker can extract long-term secrets, such as TLS authentication keypairs of that end-point without modifying its code or state and thus without being detectable via attestation. Such an attack is called *insider attack* by Wagner et al. [28]. Critically, however, we assume that the attacker cannot extract or use keying material of a live handshake or session from an uncompromised end-point. This kind of attack could be prevented by running the TLS end-point in a secure enclave, as in [5]. However, this requires hardware support for enclaves, such as Intel SGX, and reduces performance. We do not take this approach here, but instead allow the TLS software to run as normal untrusted code, and execute only attestation generation and verification within an SEE or in the TCB.

The goal of the attacker is to get access to confidential data or to cause transmitted data to be processed against the security policy of the sender, by compromising the recipient's platform. We assume that attesting environment is either an SEE or part of the platform's TCB. Thus, while a compromised end-point may be under the control of the attacker, attestation evidences generated for the compromised end-point will be rejected by all uncompromised end-points.

Furthermore, we assume that the endpoints have a secure channel with their local attestation modules.

4.3 Design

We call our protocol Trusted Sockets Layer (TSL) to highlight the some of its critical features. No modifications are needed to the TLS protocol specification: all extra functionality can be accomplished using protocol extension messages and implemented with callbacks provided by the TLS library.

The main features of our trusted channel protocol design are:

- As the underlying secure channel protocol, we use TLS 1.3. This avoids the multitude of security vulnerabilities associated with earlier TLS versions, provides privacy protection for the attestation, because handshake messages after ServerHello are encrypted in TLS 1.3.
- We use the intra-handshake attestation approach, i.e. attestation evidences are generated and exchanged during the handshake. This optimizes the protocol execution time as no additional round-trips are needed for attestation, and turns TLS 1.3 into a single, convenient trusted channel protocol without requiring an extra attestation protocol on top.
- All functionality we add on top of standard TLS 1.3, i.e. the generation and verification of attestation evidences, is performed in the TLS library callbacks. This allow us to conform to the TLS specification and use existing TLS implementations without modifications.
- Channel bindings are derived using TLS-Exporter when possible and included in the attestation claims. We use explicit channel binding, where both ends are required to verify that they have computed and attested the same channel bindings.

The next section describes our protocol in more detail.

4.4 Protocol Flow

The flow of our protocol is shown in Fig. 2. The figure shows the differences of our protocol compared to standard mutually authenticated TLS 1.3.

TLS 1.3 Configuration. We require that an end-point must generate a new ECDH key pair for every handshake attempt. Caching of ECDH key pairs is not allowed. It is forbidden to send early 0RTT data, as this will not be protected by attestation. Also, session resumption is not allowed; each handshake must be a full one with mutual attestation. This is because in our threat model, the attacker may have access to long-term secrets of an uncompromised (from the attestation point-of-view) platform, including session tickets.

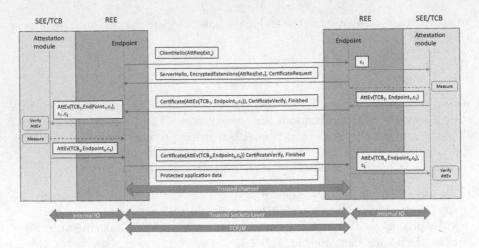

Fig. 2. TLS 1.3 handshake with mutual authentication and attestation

Parameter Negotiation. The first difference compared to standard TLS 1.3 is the attestation request extension (AttReqExt in Fig. 2), sent by the client and the server in the ClientHello and EncryptedExtensions messages, respectively. This extension serves two purposes: it is a demand for the remote end-point to attest itself and it indicates the verifier's attestation policy. The latter enables the prover to choose the attestation claims so that they may fulfill the verifier's policy. The policy may also indicate e.g. the roots-of-trust whose signatures the verifier is willing to accept. The extensions are obligatory in our protocol. If either extension is missing, the receiver must terminate the handshake with a fatal alert.

Generation of Attestation Evidence. End-points are required to generate attestation certificates during the handshake. The certificates must contain a public key (PK_{TLS}) and the attestation claims, one of which must be a handshake-specific challenge (c_S or c_T in Fig. 2). The other claims depend on the attestation policy and the specific TCB hardware. Typically, both claims about the endpoint and the TCB are included in the attestation evidences (AttEv in Fig. 2). The challenge c_S, to be included in the client's certificate, must be generated using TLS-Exporter, with the exporter master secret as the base secret. For c_T, there are two alternatives: the challenge can be either the SHA-256 hash of the ClientHello handshake message or derived with TLS-Exporter, but now with the early exporter master secret as the base secret. These two alternatives are equivalent security-wise, as both depend on the ClientHello hash, but which challenge is easier to compute depends on the TLS library implementation. To generate the attestation evidence, the end-point passes the challenge, and optionally the verifier's attestation policy, to the attestation module. The evidence is then inserted into a X.509 public-key certificate within a custom

X.509 extension. The certificate must be freshly signed. The certificate is transmitted in the standard Certificate handshake message. Extra certificates, e.g. a certificate chain leading up to an attestation root-of-trust may be included as usual. For end-point authentication, it is often possible to rely entirely on attestation. However, if the end-point also has a distinct network-level identity, such as a DNS name, CA-signed certificate may also be needed. In the latter case, two certificate chains need to be sent, but the TLS authentication public key PK_{TLS} should be the same in both leaf certificates, to confirm that both the attestation and the CA-signed certificate were created for the same end-point. Even when end-point authentication relies on attestation, we still require the attestation certificate to contain a public key PK_{TLS} in order to comply with the protocol specification. The private counterpart of PK_{TLS} must be used to sign the CertificateVerify message.

Verification of Attestation Evidence. After receiving a Certificate message, the end-point must invoke a trusted verification module to validate the certificate. To verify the challenge in the attestation claims, the end-point must independently compute a reference challenge (c'_S or c'_T), which should be passed as a parameter to the verification module. The attestation module must at least verify the signature of the certificate and that the included challenge matches the reference value. If case of validation failure, the end-point must immediately abort the handshake and send a fatal alert message. Thus, the handshake results either in a fatal alert or in the establishment of a trusted channel. It should be noted that the generation and verification of attestation evidence is always dependent on the underlying TCB hardware. We leave the binding of our protocol with specific TCB hardware for future work.

4.5   Implementation

Our protocol has been designed so that the extra steps compared to standard TLS 1.3 can be implemented entirely with callback functions offered by widely-used TLS libraries. For sending and processing custom client and server parameter negotiation extensions such as AttReqExt in Fig. 2, most TLS libraries provide standard APIs. The attestation evidences and attestation certificates can be conveniently generated in the certificate selection callbacks offered by most TLS libraries. The challenges are easy to compute as well, as most TLS libraries provide an API for TLS-Exporter, as well as a mechanism for computing the ClientHello hash. All TLS libraries provide certificate validation callbacks, that can be used to perform custom validation steps. These callbacks can be used to send the attestation evidence to the attestation module for verification.

Proof-of-Concept. We first implemented our protocol using our proprietary, size-optimized, stand-alone TLS 1.3 library. The code footprint of our library can be as low as 20 KB for some configurations, and a fully-featured build for x86 results in a code size of around 60 KB. In addition, there are no dynamic memory allocations within the library. This makes the library ideal for constrained environments, including secure enclaves or TrustZone-style trusted applications. Augmenting the library with mutual attestation only required the addition of two custom callback functions for certificate selection and validation to the existing client and server applications. We are currently working towards an open source release of our TLS library, including the TSL proof-of-concept code.

To evaluate the effort of implementing our protocol with a well-known TLS library, we wrote a second proof-of-concept using OpenSSL. Here, the attestation request extensions can be set and processed using the `SSL_CTX_add_custom_ext` API. It was not possible to use the `SSL_CTX_set_cert_cb` API to generate the attestation evidence, as the callback is called too early, before the TLS-Exporter base secret is available. Instead, we used the `SSL_CTX_set_msg_callback` API, which provides much more flexibility. The message callback can be used to compute the challenges and to generate the attestation evidence and certificate. Given that OpenSSL does not provide the possibility to compute the early exporter master secret without using early data, the TLS-Exporter is used only for the challenge c_S that is included in the client's attestation evidence. As the server's challenge (c_T), we used the ClientHello hash. The implementation of the message callback is mostly the same on both end-points, the only difference lies in the specific hanshake state where the challenges are computed or where the certificate is set. The validation of the attestations is done by comparing the received challenge against the self-computed challenge in the message callback. In OpenSSL, the additional custom validation code of the X509 certificates can be set using the `SSL_set_verify` API.

4.6 Security Analysis

The security requirements of Sect. 4.1 are fulfilled by our protocol as follows:

- **SR1 (Secure channel guarantees).** Our protocol augments the TLS 1.3 handshake in two ways. First, we use the TLS 1.3 protocol extension mechanism (Section 4.2. of [23]) to send and process the attestation requests. Second, attestation evidences are added into X.509 public-key certificates within a custom X.509 extension. This extension provides extra inputs to certificate verification, but does not otherwise change the validation process. More specifically, we add an extra step (verification of attestation evidence) to the certification path validation algorithm of RFC 5280 [10], as allowed by Section 6.2. of the RFC 5280.
- **SR2 (End-point trustworthiness).** Since we perform mutual attestation as part of the handshake and require the verifier to terminate the handshake with a fatal alert when it fails to verify the received attestation, no secure channel can be established without mutual trustworthiness guarantees.
- **SR3 (Channel binding).** We claim that the challenges included in the attestation claims strongly bind each attestation evidence to the current handshake. First, we consider server-side relay and collusion attacks. Assume

that the attacker controls a compromised server-side end-point (S_1) and an uncompromised one (S_2). A ClientHello (CH) message is sent by target client (C) to S_1. In TLS, the CH message includes a unique, unpredictable nonce (client_random). Thus, the server's attestation evidence, including the CH-dependent challenge $(c_T$ in Fig. 2) among its claims, is valid only in a handshake that includes this specific CH message. Now, S_1 may relay the CH to S_2, which sends back attestation evidence in the Certificate message. However, this message is encrypted with handshake keys. Decryption would require the attacker to get access to the private ECDHE key of either C or S_2, but this is not possible: according to our threat model, the attacker may have administrator-level access to S_2, and be able to extract the end-point's long-term secrets, but is unable to extract the handshake-specific secrets such as the handshake keys or S_2's ECDH private key. The attacker may try to switch the ECDHE public key in CH with its own, but this affects the value of the challenge c_T included by S_2 in the attestation evidence so that it will not match the reference challenge c'_T computed by C. Thus, it not possible for the attacker to get access to a server-side attestation evidence that will be deemed valid by C. Next, we consider the client-side. The challenge c_S is influenced by the handshake messages up to and including server Finished, but also by the handshake secrets. This makes the challenge not only specific to a single handshake (as in the case of the server challenge), but also confidential, i.e. visible only to the end-points of the handshake, making relay and collusion attacks even harder against server-side verifiers. Replay attacks are prevented on both sides because the challenges are affected by handshake-specific values chosen or otherwise influenced by the verifier.

- **SR4 (Privacy).** Privacy of the attestation evidences and the TLS end-point identities against eavesdroppers is provided by standard TLS 1.3 handshake message encryption. A compromised client can still receive the server's certificate message by initiating a handshake with the server. This is caused by a chicken-and-egg problem, also present in the TLS 1.3 protocol: one end-point must authenticate and attest itself before the other. Privacy of the client side is stronger, because the client will only send its certificate after it has successfully authenticated and attested the server. For attestation privacy, this asymmetry is a feature of the intra-handshake attestation generation approach. The benefits of the intra-handshake approach still outweigh the disadvantage, especially since a similar asymmetry exists in the security requirements of many use cases. For example, in credential injection, it is typically more important to avoid injecting a secret to a compromised (server-side) device than to ensure that a credential comes from an uncompromised (client-side) source.

- **SR5 (Forward secrecy.)** Since TLS 1.3 only offers forward-secure cipher-suites, and re-using an ECDHE key pair for multiple handshakes is not allowed, the only long-term secret that the attacker may try to compromise is the TLS end-point authentication private key. But this is not useful (i.e. cannot be used to establish a trusted channel) without a valid attestation, and the TCB's attestation signing key is secure by definition.

5   Conclusions and Further Work

In this paper, we have presented a TLS 1.3 based trusted channel protocol called Trusted Sockets Layer (TSL). We have shown how our protocol fulfills the security requirements of a trusted channel, is secure against relay and insider attacks, and can be easily implemented with callback functions, without modifying TLS library code. We believe our protocol has wide applicability in domains where trusted communication is required. This includes, for example, key injection, digital rights management, IOT device-to-device communication, collection of privacy-sensitive data, etc. In future work, we plan instantiate our protocol with TPM-based attestation, and to use it to migrate mobile agents between secure enclaves.

References

1. AlFardan, N.J., Paterson, K.G.: Lucky thirteen: breaking the TLS and DTLS record protocols. In: Proceedings of the IEEE Symposium on Security and Privacy, pp. 526–540, May 2013
2. Altman, J., Williams, N., Zhu, L.: Channel bindings for TLS. RFC 5929, July 2010
3. Asokan, N., et al.: Mobile trusted computing. Proc. IEEE **102**, 1189–1206 (2014)
4. Asokan, N., Niemi, V., Nyberg, K.: Man-in-the-middle in tunnelled authentication protocols. In: Christianson, B., Crispo, B., Malcolm, J.A., Roe, M. (eds.) Security Protocols 2003. LNCS, vol. 3364, pp. 28–41. Springer, Heidelberg (2005). https://doi.org/10.1007/11542322_6
5. Aubling, P.L., et al.: TaLoS: secure and transparent TLS termination inside SGX enclaves. Technical report, Department of Computing (2017)
6. Aziz, N., Udzir, N., Mahmod, R.: Extending TLS with mutual attestation for platform integrity assurance. J. Commun. **9**, 63–72 (2014)
7. Barker, E.: NIST Special Publication 800–57: Recommendations for Key Management: Part I - General, May 2020. https://nvlpubs.nist.gov/nistpubs/SpecialPublications/NIST.SP.800-57pt1r5.pdf
8. Bhargavan, K., Lavaud, A.D., Fournet, C., Pironti, A., Strub, P.Y.: Triple handshakes and cookie cutters: breaking and fixing authentication over TLS. In: Proceedings of the 2014 IEEE Symposium on Security and Privacy. IEEE, March 2014
9. Böck, H., Somorovsky, J., Young, C.: Return of Bleichenbacher's oracle threat (ROBOT). In: Proceedings of the 27th USENIX Security Symposium, August 2018
10. Cooper, D., Santesson, S., Farrell, S., Boeyen, S., Housley, R., Polk, W.: Internet X.509 public key infrastructure certificate and certificate revocation list (CRL) profile. RFC 5280, May 2008
11. Dolev, D., Yao, A.C.: On the security of public key protocols. IEEE Trans. Inf. Theory **29**, 198–208 (1983)
12. Gasmi, Y., Sadeghi, A.R., Stewin, P., Unger, M., Asokan, N.: Beyond secure channels. In: Proceedings of the 2007 ACM Workshop on Scalable Trusted Computing, pp. 30–40. ACM Press, New York, January 2007
13. Goldman, K., Perez, R., Sailer, R.: Linking remote attestation to secure tunnel endpoints. Technical report, IBM Research Division (2006)
14. Knauth, T., Steiner, M., Chakrabarti, S., Lei, L., Xing, C., Vij, M.: Integrating remote attestation with Transport Layer Security. Technical report, Intel Labs (2018)

15. Kotzias, P., Razaghpanah, A., Amann, J., Paterson, K.G., Rodriguez, N.V., Caballero, J.: Coming of age: a longitudal study of TLS deployment. In: 2018 Internet Measurement Conference. ACM (2018)
16. Manulis, M., Stebila, D., Kiefer, F., Denham, N.: Secure modular password authentication for the web using channel bindings. Int. J. Inf. Secur. **15**(6), 597–620 (2016). https://doi.org/10.1007/s10207-016-0348-7
17. Martin, A.: A ten-page introduction to trusted computing. Technical report, Oxford University Computing Laboratory (2008)
18. Moriarty, K., Farrell, S.: Deprecating TLS 1.0 and TLS 1.1. RFC 8996, March 2021
19. Oppliger, R.: SSL and TLS: Theory and Practice, 2nd edn. Artech House, Norwood (2016)
20. Ray, M., Dispensa, S.: Renegotiating TLS. Technical report, PhoneFactor, Inc. (2009)
21. Rescorla, E.: SSL and TLS - Designing and Building Secure Systems. Addison-Wesley, Boston (2001)
22. Rescorla, E.: Keying material exporters for Transport Layer Security (TLS). RFC 5705, March 2010
23. Rescorla, E.: The Transport Layer Security (TLS) Protocol version 1.3. RFC 8446, August 2018
24. Sangster, P., Cam-Winget, N., Salowey, J.A.: A posture transport protocol over TLS (PT-TLS). RFC 6876, February 2013
25. Segall, A.: Trusted Platform Modules: Why, When and How to Use Them. Institution of Engineering and Technology, London, United Kingdom (2017)
26. Szefer, J.: Principles of Secure Processor Architecture Design. Morgan & Claypool Publishers, San Rafael (2019)
27. Trusted Computing Group: DICE Attestation Architecture, March 2021. Rev. 0.23
28. Wagner, P.G., Birnstill, P., Beyerer, J.: Establishing secure communication channels using remote attestation with TPM 2.0. In: Markantonakis, K., Petrocchi, M. (eds.) STM 2020. LNCS, vol. 12386, pp. 73–89. Springer, Cham (2020). https://doi.org/10.1007/978-3-030-59817-4_5
29. Walsh, K., Manferdelli, J.: Mechanisms for mutual attested microservice communication. In: UCC 2017 Companion: Companion Proceedings of the 10th International Conference on Utility and Cloud Computing, pp. 59 64. ACM, December 2017
30. Williams, N.: On the use of channel bindings to secure channels. RFC 5056, November 2007
31. Yu, Y., Wang, H., Liu, B., Yin, G.: A trusted remote attestation model based on trusted computing. In: Proceedings of the 12th IEEE International Conference on Trust, Security and Privacy in Computing and Communications, pp. 1504–1509. IEEE (2013)

Preliminary Security Analysis, Formalisation, and Verification of OpenTitan Secure Boot Code

Bjarke Hilmer Møller[1], Jacob Gosch Søndergaard[1], Kristoffer Skagbæk Jensen[1], Magnus Winkel Pedersen[1], Tobias Worm Bøgedal[1], Anton Christensen[1]([✉]) [iD], Danny Bøgsted Poulsen[1] [iD], Kim Guldstrand Larsen[1] [iD], René Rydhof Hansen[1] [iD], Thomas Rosted Jensen[2], Heino Juvoll Madsen[2], and Henrik Uhrenfeldt[2]

[1] Department of Computer Science, Aalborg University, Aalborg, Denmark
bjarke.h.moeller@gmail.com, jacob.gosch97@gmail.com,
kristoffer.sj111@gmail.com, magnus.w.p@inktopixels.com,
tobias.boegedal@gmail.com, {achri,dannybpoulsen,kgl,rrh}@cs.aau.dk
[2] Huawei, Copenhagen, Denmark
{thomas.rosted.jensen,heino.madsen,henrik.uhrenfeldt}@huawei.com

Abstract. We perform a preliminary security analysis of the initial boot stage for the OpenTitan silicon root of trust, including formalisation and verification of relevant security goals using both bounded model checking and (unbounded) model checking. We further report on a potential vulnerability in the platform and show how it can be reproduced using formal modelling and argue that co-verification would be able to detect such vulnerabilities for high assurance projects.

Keywords: Security · Co-verification · Formal methods · Hardware modelling

1 Introduction

Protecting sensitive operations and cryptographic keys of a system against attackers that have physical access to the system is a fundamental and difficult challenge in security engineering. One commonly proposed solution is to rely on specialised hardware, e.g., a security token/key, a Hardware Security Module (HSM) or secure storage. However, that leaves the challenge of designing and implementing such secure hardware to be sufficiently robust against attacks, itself a non-trivial task where even the smallest mistakes may be exploited by an attacker [4,19,22].

Due to the critical nature and challenging threat model of security hardware in general, co-verification using formal methods has been proposed in the literature to ensure a high degree of security and assurance for such systems [3,5]. Here, co-verification is the simultaneous verification of both the software (firmware) and the hardware of an application. While co-verification facilitates deep analysis for a specific system or system specification, it frequently requires specialised tools, training, and methods [3,5,6,20].

© Springer Nature Switzerland AG 2021
N. Tuveri et al. (Eds.): NordSec 2021, LNCS 13115, pp. 192–211, 2021.
https://doi.org/10.1007/978-3-030-91625-1_11

In this paper we perform a preliminary security analysis of the OpenTitan[1] silicon Root-of-Trust (RoT) and investigate how two off-the-shelf modelling and verification tools, CBMC and UPPAAL, can be applied not only to formal (co-)verification of security properties but also as tools for formally modelling, exploring, and documenting a system under design. We have chosen to use these two tools, employing widely differing technology, based on our experience that they complement each other well and thus cover different aspects well. The OpenTitan boot ROM is a hardware RoT since it is immutable and it is intrinsically/inherently trusted as the foundation of the chain of trust[2]. Therefore, finding vulnerabilities and proving correctness and security before tape-out is crucial for avoiding costly new hardware revisions or chip respins and maintaining brand reputation. OpenTitan is inspired and motivated by the *Titan Security Key*[3], Google's secure hardware keys, and is sponsored by a consortium of partners from industry, including Google, and academia.

We further report on a potential vulnerability in a cryptographic signing module, called the HMAC (see next section for more details), that may leave the entire platform compromised. We show how the vulnerability can be reproduced and could be detected using CBMC and UPPAAL, demonstrating the usefulness of formal modelling and co-verification even during the design stage, not least for security critical systems that involve both hardware and software.

Contributions. In summary the contributions of this paper are *(1)* the first (to our knowledge) security analysis of the OpenTitan platform; *(2)* steps toward formal methods based co-verification of security properties (using off-the-shelf tools); and *(3)* the discovery of a potential security vulnerability in the OpenTitan platform.

Related Work. Although co-verification is not a novel idea it has primarily been simulation- and testing-based [1]. As noted independently in [9,12] there is only little published work on applying formal methods for co-verification.

In addition to UPPAAL and CBMC based approaches [7,8], the so-called Instruction Level Abstraction (ILA) of [5,20] includes semi-automatic modelling, heavily based on SMT solving, and mostly automatic proofs of equivalence, e.g., between specification and implementation. Finally, CoCo is a novel highly specialised tool for co-verification of masked programs in cryptographic modules [3].

2   OpenTitan

OpenTitan is a reference design for a silicon Root of Trust, which can be defined as "a system element that provides services, including verification of system, software & data integrity and confidentiality, and data (software and information)

---

[1] https://opentitan.org/.

[2] Here chain of trust is taken to mean establishing, through cryptographic certificates, that only certified and allowed software is executed on the platform.

[3] https://cloud.google.com/titan-security-key.

integrity attestation between other trusted devices in a system or network" [2]. In other words, a silicon RoT provides a way to move trust boundaries and security mechanisms down to the silicon level. Furthermore, a RoT must provide the means to maintain and verify the security and integrity of the onboard boot code and firmware, as well as cryptographic material and any additional application specific code. In the following we give a necessarily brief, high-level overview of the OpenTitan components that are relevant to our purposes. We refer to the OpenTitan website for further details.

OpenTitan is first and foremost concerned with the design of the hardware components and additionally suggests how Original Equipment Manufacturers (OEMs) can design a set of secure boot stages that provide only OEM selected features to the loaded kernel and userspace layers. In Fig. 1 we see that OEMs, OpenTitan calls these *creators*, have the responsibility of the first boot stage that is stored in ROM, i.e., the code that runs first during boot. This ROM stage loads the subsequent boot stage that is either a larger, less security critical, updatable and rollback protected *ROM extension stage* ('ROM_EXT' in the OpenTitan terminology), or a product *owner*'s initial kernel bootloader. In OpenTitan a ROM extension is firmware provided by OEM's that is executed at boot time, e.g., in order to initialise OEM specific hardware or configurations. Either way the ROM must make sure the system is in an uncompromised state and verify that the subsequent stage is unmodified and cryptographically signed by a valid key.

2.1 Hardware Components

This paper will deal exclusively with the initial ROM stage and the on-chip peripherals required to load the boot code for the second stage of the overall boot process. The only exception is the potential attack in Sect. 4 which may involve an attacker entering at a later stage. The hardware components of primary significance here are:

Flash Controller: The Flash Controller defines a common open source interface for software to interact with different closed source flash implementations. The flash controller is used to load the later boot stages.

Key Manager: The Key Manager manages secret keys and controls what software and hardware components get access to them. Before the Key Manager exposes a key to either software or hardware, it first performs a signed hashing operation on the key. This way the secret keys are never given directly to any component. Furthermore, the Key Manager derives keys as the system progresses in booting. Depending on the current boot stage, the input for this derivation differs. As an example, the first key (the so called CreatorRootKey) is derived by combining other key material, e.g., a seed, with information about the specific hardware configuration [15,16].

Life Cycle Controller: This component manages configuration information regarding a chip's current stage in its life cycle, e.g., manufacturing, development, deployment.

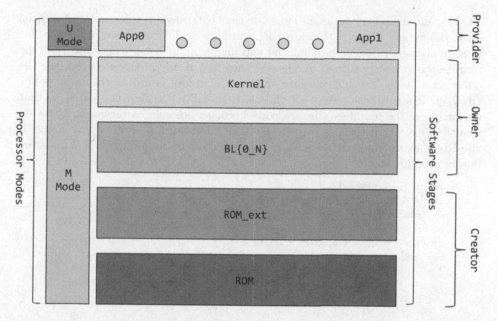

Fig. 1. Diagram showing a proposed boot stack on OpenTitan (source [17]). In the diagram "U mode" refers to user mode, "M Mode" to machine mode, and "BL{0_N}" to bootloader(s), e.g., for booting an operating system or an application.

PMP: The Physical Memory Protection (PMP) is a RISC-V feature that allows for handling access rights to specific memory regions. The main benefit of using PMP to handle memory access rights is that once memory regions are locked with PMP, they cannot be unlocked by software or hardware until the system is reset. For OpenTitan the PMP is used to ensure that memory cannot be executed until it is verified (among other things).

OTBN: The OpenTitan Big Number Accelerator (OTBN) is a co-processor specifically used for cryptographic operations such as those used for RSA.

HMAC: The Hash-based Message Authentication Code (HMAC) module is used to check the validity of signed messages. It does so by generating (secret) key based authentication codes that can then be verified. The key to use is a parameter chosen at runtime by the HMAC client.

Since the OpenTitan project does not have a complete version of the boot ROM code at the time of writing, we have created our own version based on the available documentation [21]. This code is used as basis for our verification throughout this paper. The top level function 'mask_rom_boot()' of the boot code is shown in Listing 1.1 and proceeds as follows: First, the boot policy found in flash is read. This boot policy contains information about which manifests[4] the

---

[4] A boot manifest is an "on-disk" data structure containing the image code for the next boot stage along with important metadata, e.g., version, timestamp, and signature.

ROM stage should try to load. The code then extracts this information from the boot policy and iterates through the manifests and checks their validity. This mainly consists in checking that the specified signing key is valid and that the manifest is correctly signed by the specified key. If any of these checks fail, the code goes on to (try to) validate the next manifest found in the boot policy (if any). If a manifest passes all checks, then a PMP region is created so that execution of the manifest's image code becomes possible. Afterwards, the code transfers execution to the corresponding ROM extension code's entry point. If the ROM extension code returns or if no manifest is validated, then the system enters a failure state.

```
1   void mask_rom_boot(){
2    policy_t boot_policy = read_boot_policy();
3    rom_exts_manifests_t manifests = rom_ext_manifests(boot_policy);
4
5    for (int i = 0; i < manifests.size; i++) {
6     rom_ext_manifest_t current_rom_ext_manifest =
7       manifests.rom_exts_mfs[i];
8     pub_key_t rom_ext_pub_key = read_pub_key(current_rom_ext_manifest);
9     if (!check_rom_ext_manifest(current_rom_ext_manifest) ||
10      !check_pub_key_valid(rom_ext_pub_key) ||
11      !verify_rom_ext_signature(rom_ext_pub_key,current_rom_ext_manifest))
12        continue;
13     pmp_unlock_rom_ext();
14     if (!final_jump_to_rom_ext(current_rom_ext_manifest))
15       boot_failed_rom_ext_terminated(boot_policy,current_rom_ext_manifest);
16    }
17    boot_failed(boot_policy);
18   }
```

Listing 1.1. mask_ROM pseudocode

3 Security Analysis

In the following, we discuss a preliminary security analysis of the OpenTitan platform. Preliminary because, as already noted, OpenTitan is a project that is still in development. However, due to the inherent complexity and high assurance requirements of the OpenTitan platform, or indeed any security critical platform, we argue that important and necessary insights can be gained by performing security analyses at the early design stage and continually throughout the project lifetime. Furthermore, we argue (and illustrate in later sections) that early stage security analyses can benefit from a formal approach by showing how a potential flaw in the OpenTitan HMAC module can be exploited. In addition to documenting and disambiguating designs, formal models may also be used to verify and prove formal properties of a system thus enabling very high levels of assurance.

We focus here on a subset of the full security analysis, and refer to [11] for the analysis in its entirety. The subset analysis considered here is concerned with the 'overarching security objective of establishing *the system's ability to securely transfer execution from the initial boot stage (mask_ROM) to a verified boot ROM extension (ROM_EXT)*. Here we consider an *attacker model* in which the attacker is interested in subverting the OpenTitan boot process in order to execute (malicious) code on the platform. We further assume that an attacker has access to the platform to be able to *flash arbitrary code/data to the ROM_EXT*. However, we do not take *glitching* or other sophisticated physical attacks into account. The attacker cannot alter the mask_ROM code or anything else stored in ROM. Next we define the security policies and goals needed to establish the overall security target mentioned above.

3.1   Security Policies and Goals

The security analysis proceeds by first defining the high-level *security policies* (**P1** through **P4** below) that are needed to support the overarching security objective of the system. The policies are derived from a close reading of the OpenTitan documentation including explicit (and implicit) security objectives. Each of the policies are broken down into one or more *security goals* (denoted **G** below) mapping security policies unto the corresponding security mechanisms of the platform. The goals are thus more specific and amenable to verification. Finally, the goals are further broken down into *security properties* relating goals to concrete elements of the system description and the corresponding tool-dependent model of the system, e.g., what is needed to perform a signature validation. Since the specific formulation of properties depends on the (tool-specific) model, we do not further describe properties here, but refer to the later tool-specific sections where they will be exemplified.

The policies and goals considered are as follows[5]:

P1: The mask_ROM must only execute code that securely transfers execution to a verified ROM_EXT or terminates.
If the boot process does not validate the authenticity and integrity of code before executing it, it is easy for an attacker to execute malicious code by flashing it to the ROM_EXT. Therefore the mask_ROM stage must ensure that ROM_EXT has not been tampered with before transferring control.
  G1: The cryptographic signature of the *ROM_EXT* image must be verified by *mask_ROM* before it is executed, to ensure authenticity and integrity of the image.
P2: Boot stages must only succeed in validating the following boot stage if the environment that the boot was initiated from is secure.
The Key Manager component in OpenTitan derives several cryptographic keys throughout the booting process of the system. If these keys become public then an attacker could sign their own messages to fool the system into

---

[5] Security goals are not numbered sequentially, instead they retain the numbering from the full security analysis [10,11,21]; some goals have been rephrased to fit better with the flow of the paper.

accepting malicious messages. The first key derived by the Key Manager, that is used throughout the rest of the key derivation scheme, uses *Health State Measurements* as part of the input for its creation; these include the device life cycle state, state of debug mode, and a hash of the boot ROM [15]. This is necessary, since an environment that is compromised by an attacker could affect the key derivation in an adverse manner and thereby potentially be able to guess or reconstruct secret keys held by the Key Manager.

G5: *mask_ROM* must validate *ROM_EXT* using a unique key that is "baked" into the silicon. If the environment, e.g., the health state as mentioned above, is not as expected the validation must not succeed.

P3: Cryptographic material and other secrets must not be leaked.
The OpenTitan authenticity and integrity checks of ROM_EXT and any subsequent software stages are dependent on the secrecy of the keys used for signing. If a cryptographic key is compromised then the attacker could forge a valid signature for malicious boot code and pass the authenticity and integrity checks.

G8: Only authorised applications have access to cryptographic keys.

G9: Secret information stored in memory must be cleared or scrambled after the termination of the respective boot stage.

P4: The privilege hierarchy must be enforced, i.e., access rights must be configured correctly.
OpenTitan uses RISC-V PMP regions to restrict or grant access to memory regions. Configuration of the PMP must follow the order specified in the OpenTitan documentation. If OpenTitan code could disregard preceding configuration of PMP regions then the memory would be susceptible to attacks that read secrets, jumps to execute previous boot stage code, and overwrite memory.

G10, G11, G12: The PMP configuration must ensure that only software with write/read/execute access to some memory section may modify/read/execute it.

In the following sections, we first discuss a potential vulnerability in the implementation of the HMAC module; followed by sections describing how the OpenTitan secure boot can be modelled in CBMC and UPPAAL and how these models can be used to examine and verify (some of) the security goals above.

4   Potential Vulnerability in HMAC Wipe

While the models discussed in the following sections are designed to fit the OpenTitan documentation as faithfully as possible, we discovered an inconsistency between the specification of the HMAC module and its implementation[6]. The module has a *wipe* feature whereby the documentation states that when a value is written to the wipe register "The internal variables will be reset to

---

[6] We have raised the issue with the OpenTitan developers, tracking it at: https://github.com/lowRISC/opentitan/issues/8506.

```
121  always_ff @(posedge clk_i or negedge rst_ni) begin
122    if (!rst_ni) begin
123      secret_key <= '0;
124    end else if (wipe_secret) begin
125      secret_key <= secret_key ^ {8{wipe_v}};
126    end else if
127      ...
128    end
129  end
```

Listing 1.2. Wipe function implementation in Verilog [14]

the written value" [13]. Wiping of internal hardware registers is a security measure that can be requested by a client of the HMAC module (other modules have similar functionality) in order to erase potentially sensitive cryptographic information. Wiping is implemented at the hardware level as a register update. However, looking at the implementation, reproduced in Listing 1.2, we see that instead of overwriting the secret_key directly with the wipe value, the secret_key is assigned the value of itself XOR'ed with eight copies of the wipe value.

By modelling the implementation rather than the specification, we found a potential attack that may compromise the security of cryptographic keys used for signing with HMAC: The attack relies on using a guessed or known wipe value to perform a second wipe, i.e., another XOR, of a secret key in the HMAC module and thereby *reversing* the effect of the first wipe action. This allows an attacker to reinstate and freely use a secret key in the HMAC module. This would allow an attacker to sign arbitrary messages and undermine the trust base of the entire system.

If the attacker does not have prior knowledge of the wipe value, it can be brute-forced with relative ease since wipe values are only 32 bits long. Thus instead of 2^{255} guesses on average to guess a secret signing key an attack can be mounted with only 2^{31} guesses on average. Note that the attack only enables an attacker to sign arbitrary messages with the HMAC module, it does not provide the attacker with the actual key (in cleartext). Below, we describe the brute-force attack in more detail. In Sect. 5.1 and 6.1 we model the wipe implementation, using CBMC and UPPAAL respectively, and show how such formal models enable a developer to find the "double wipe" attack. Both models show the system is vulnerable and as such, in adherence to security goal **G9**, we must treat the wipe value with the same level of security as the secret keys and take care to remove it from memory.

Systematic Discovery. Based on the experience and work reported on in this paper, we conjecture that any serious attempt at verifying that the HMAC module implementation follows the specification would discover the vulnerability discussed here. However, a more abstract approach to verification, assuming the specification to be correct or verifying only the software parts, would likely not discover the vulnerability. This emphasises the potential and importance of co-verification.

4.1   Brute Forcing Wipe Values

If we can verify that a message has been signed with a valid key, then simply iterating through and calling wipe for every possible 32-bit wipe value should eventually yield the HMAC module in a state where the attacker can sign messages. For every value that yields no result, we must reset the state by wiping with the same value again.

```
1    for i in [0..(2^32 - 1)]:
2        hmac.wipe(i)
3        if verify(hmac.sign(msg)):
4            return i
5        else:
6            hmac.wipe(i)
```

In modelling the attack in CBMC and UPPAAL we did not model the attacker this way, instead leaving the tools to find the right strategy by letting it choose any arbitrary sequence of actions on the HMAC API.

5   Formalisation and Verification in CBMC

In the following, we discuss the development of a formal model of parts of the OpenTitan platform boot process suitable for verification using the CBMC tool. Since CBMC is a tool primarily developed to verify properties of C programs, models and properties must be formulated directly in the C programming language, albeit with specialised macros for specifying properties to be verified. This approach is well-suited to co-verification, where C programs simulating or modelling hardware are often developed as a testing harness or runtime environment for developing the concomitant firmware, typically also using C. We finish this section by showing how CBMC can be used to verify one of the security properties needed to show that the OpenTitan boot process is in compliance with the security goals discussed in Sect. 3.

Since OpenTitan is still in development, it was necessary to write code modelling not only the relevant hardware, but also for the boot process itself. This code is based on OpenTitan pseudocode and documentation [18]. Since the documentation is also work in progress and not always up to date, we have had to make certain assumptions regarding the implementation to be able to model a functional system, e.g., exactly which cryptographic keys are used to sign the ROM_EXT. In this particular case we chose to model the signature key as a separate key stored in mask_ROM.

CBMC is a *Bounded Model Checker* for C code [7]. Bounded model checking represents a program and a set of constraints formalising properties to check as a SAT-problem which can then be solved by a SAT/SMT solver. This is very similar to the way symbolic execution works, but quite different from "classic" model checking, e.g., using UPPAAL as discussed in Sect. 6. This approach enables a form of verification that is better suited for taking (some) data flow into account, compared with traditional model checking. Furthermore, it allows a relatively precise analysis of the code, albeit only for a bounded number of loop iterations: CBMC combines loop unrolling with a loop bound property to check that loops have been unrolled "enough".

A further concern is to avoid running out of memory during model checking, or indeed most forms of automated verification. One traditional way of managing memory consumption, is by working on abstract data or data of reduced size, e.g., assuming limited size on input. This is exemplified in our OpenTitan model by the ROM_EXT model: the size of ROM_EXT is limited to 10 bytes: big enough to model the relevant fields and properties but also small enough to keep the state space in check. While this is a common approach both in bounded and in classic model checking, it does mean that the verification results in principle come with the major caveat that they are only guaranteed for a subset of data values. However, for properties that are mainly control flow dependent or structural, such as many of the properties discussed here, the impact is minimal or non-existent.

5.1 Wipe Attack in CBMC

In order to recreate the wipe attack using CBMC, we first modelled the Verilog implementation (of the wipe function) as C code (the input language of CBMC). We next modelled an (abstract) attacker guessing the HMAC wipe value and non-deterministically calling the HMAC module in order to determine if the wipe of a key can be reversed, leaving the HMAC module open for abuse. Both of these models are straightforward and we thus elide them here.

Running CBMC on these models showed that, indeed, if the wipe value is known to an attacker, it is possible to recreate the original secret key used for HMAC computation and thus enabling an attacker to impersonating the key's owner and signing messages and code with the owner's key.

5.2 Modelling and Verification of Security Goals

In the following we show how to specify and verify a single security property in more detail, as discussed in Sect. 3, and refer to [21] for the full list of security properties. The property discussed here (Property 6) is fundamental to one of the main security goals (**G1**) that captures the essential secure boot security requirement to ensure that only verified code is executed. The property specifies where execution should continue after validation:

Property 6: If all validation steps have succeeded, then transfer execution to ROM_EXT by starting execution at the entry point of the ROM_EXT image code. If execution returns, execute the fail_ROM_EXT_returned function provided by the boot policy.

```
1   void __PROOF_HARNESS() {
2     policy_t boot_policy = FLASH_CTRL_read_boot_policy();
3     manifests_t manifests = FLASH_CTRL_manifests(boot_policy);
4     ...
5     __CPROVER_assume(boot_policy.fail == &__func_fail);
6     __CPROVER_assume(
7       boot_policy.fail_rom_ext_terminated == &__func_fail_rom_ext);
8     ...
9     for (int i = 0; i < manifests.size; i++) {
10      ...
11      if(__validated_manifests[i]) {
12        ...
13        __CPROVER_postcondition(__rom_ext_called[i],
14        "PROPERTY 6: rom_ext VALIDATED => rom ext code inititated");
15        ...
16      }
17      else{ //invalidated
18        ...
19        __CPROVER_postcondition(!__rom_ext_fail_func[i],
20        "PROPERTY 6: invalid rom_ext => rom_ext term not called");
21        ...
22   }
```

Listing 1.3. CBMC Proof Harness

For convenience we have included the full list of properties needed to verify **G1** in Appendix 1.

Listing 1.3 shows an excerpted version of the '__PROOF_HARNESS' function which is the main driver of our CBMC verification responsible for setting up the *verification environment* and base assumptions[7]. The function is written in C with CBMC specific annotations (prefixed with '__'); these annotations are translated directly to constraints that must be satisfied in the SAT/SMT model of the code generated by CBMC. The __PROOF_HARNESS non-deterministically creates and initialises (using CBMC assumptions) all the objects needed for verification (lines 2–7). The main verification is performed at lines 13 and 19 where we assert that if a ROM_EXT manifest is validated then the ROM_EXT image code is executed otherwise the ROM_EXT fail_function is executed (implying that the image code is not executed).

We will not go into further detail with the CBMC code here, merely refer to [21] for full details.

---

[7] The full source code is available at: https://github.com/Tutter/OpenTitan-Formal-Verification.

5.3   Results of CBMC Verification

Using CBMC the property discussed above, Property 6, can be verified. In addition we have used a similar approach to verify all the properties related to security goal **G1** (see Appendix 1 for a full list) and thus conclude that the full goal has been verified for (our model of) the OpenTitan platform.

Using a similar approach we have modelled and *partially* verified security goals **G10/G11/G12** all related to the PMP configuration (see Sect. 3 for details). These goals have only been partially verified, since our current CBMC model does not include a sufficiently detailed model of the PMP module to fully verify these goals. This was mainly caused by lack of time and we conjecture that it would be straightforward to extend our model to include the PMP module and, by extension, to verify these goals. In the same vein goals **G8** and **G9** have not been attempted since these require more detailed models of memory and relevant peripherals.

6   Formalisation and Verification in UPPAAL

Model checking, as used here, is the process of creating a model of a system, in the form of a timed automaton, and verifying that the model satisfies a specification or a property defined in terms of logic formulae, often called *query*. These queries are written in a subset of *Timed Computation Tree Logic* (TCTL) [8]. Given these the model checker executes the queries against the model and outputs either that the model satisfies the specification or a counterexample if it does not.

UPPAAL is a model checker that uses *timed automata* as the foundation of its modelling formalism [8]. Like other automata, timed automata are defined in terms of states and state transitions, but extend these fundamentals with the notion of time, represented by so-called *clocks* that are used to specify timing aspects of a model, e.g., how long a timed automaton can stay in a given state or how long time a transition takes. For the purposes of this paper, we will not delve further into the timing aspects. The UPPAAL model checker further supports a rich C-like language for specifying and enhancing models, simplifying advanced model building.

Using UPPAAL we have modelled the initial boot stage of OpenTitan. This is done by reading through the available OpenTitan documentation in detail and creating models based on that information. Concretely, the C code for the boot stage is modelled by a straightforward translation of the code's control flow graph into a timed automaton. The boot stage code is then used as a starting point for determining what hardware to model: only those modules that are needed to execute the boot stage (and the modules they transitively depend on) need to be modelled. Consider for example the Flash Controller which is used to access flash memory but flash memory operations have to go through the PMP module. Because of this we need to model all these hardware components to correctly model flash memory.

The resulting model captures a sequential flow through the code and the relevant hardware components. The automaton created for the mask_ROM boot code itself can be seen in Fig. 2. The code fetches the ROM_EXT manifests from a boot policy (solid green box) and goes through the checks needed to validate the identifier (blue dashed box), public key (red dotted box), and image signature (black dashed and dotted box). If a manifest passes these three checks it is considered valid. Lastly, execution is transferred to the ROM_EXT if a valid manifest has been found as seen in the pink dashed and double dotted box. The automaton uses channel synchronization (a UPPAAL feature allowing automata to synchronize with other automata on signals sent over channels) to invoke the functions used throughout mask_ROM. Similarly, it waits for similar synchronization messages from these functions which signify return statements. The full UPPAAL model can be found in [10][8].

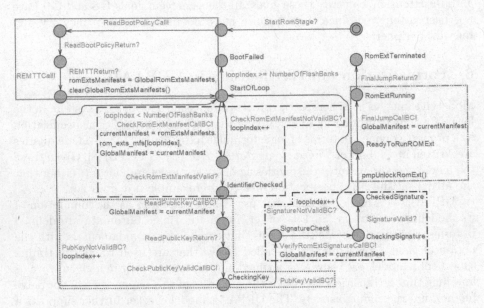

Fig. 2. The model created for the boot code in UPPAAL.

In order to manage the large input domains of some of the OpenTitan components, e.g., cryptographic keys and manifests, we model (some) specific data types in an abstract way. This is similar to the approach taken for CBMC (Sect. 5). It is for example infeasible to directly model and check the RSA-3072 image signature of each manifest along with the rest of the initial boot stage because UPPAAL would have to enumerate all possible signatures. Concretely, we represent an image signature as either 1 (correct) or 2 (incorrect). This level of abstraction is sufficient to model how the system should behave given a correct or incorrect signature but avoids the overhead of a full implementation of the

---

[8] The source files in full are available at: https://github.com/Tutter/OpenTitan-Formal-Verification.

RSA algorithm. This approach is sufficient to verify properties that are mainly concerned with the control flow through the system, e.g., that proper checks are performed before executing code.

Figure 3 shows an example of how the data abstraction affects the modelling of hardware. For the hardware models, we wish to represent the state transitions they perform but not the details of how these transitions are performed. When the OTBN is called it starts collecting the necessary data to perform signature validation from RAM. It then collects the manifest signature, the digest (created by the HMAC module in a previous step), and the manifest public key. Once these items have been fetched, they are used by the function 'checkSignature()' which evaluates to a bool. This bool is true if the items have the expected values and false otherwise. Using this function as a guard on the transitions away from the CheckingSignature location, the OTBN either synchronizes over the channel RSAValid (if the signature is valid) or RSANotValid (if the signature is not valid) and goes back to the Idle location.

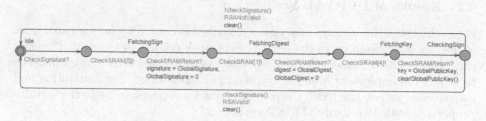

Fig. 3. The model created for the OTBN module in UPPAAL.

6.1 Wipe Attack in UPPAAL

To recreate and model the wipe vulnerability in UPPAAL (see Sect. 4): we have implemented a version of the HMAC module which models the implementation rather than the specification. Furthermore, we have modelled that the ROM_EXT is malicious and is trying to exploit the vulnerability to reuse a previously used secret key. With these changes to the model, we have formulated the following query in UPPAAL:

```
E<> exists(i : int[0, NumberOfFlashBanks - 1]) RomExt(i).Success
```

This query is executed to verify that there exists a path, i.e., a sequence of state transitions, in the model such that for an integer i that is in the range of the number of flash banks currently in the system, RomExt(i) is eventually in the Success location. The Success location in this case indicates that the ROM_EXT has been able to reuse a secret key to create a valid authentication code. This query succeeds, showing that an attacker can use the protocol to reuse a secret key by brute force guessing wipe values. Figure 4 shows the ROM_EXT model.

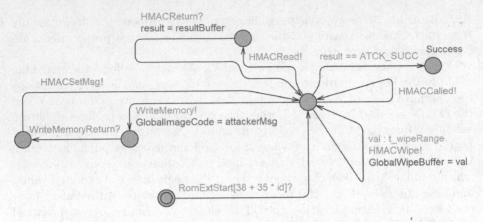

Fig. 4. The ROM_EXT model created to test the wipe vulnerability in UPPAAL.

6.2 Results of UPPAAL Verification

For each goal of the security analysis as described in Sect. 3 we have created a set of queries corresponding to the security properties related to the goal. The only exception is **G5** of the security analysis since, as mentioned earlier, it is infeasible to model full implementations of cryptographic operations. For illustration and convenience we have included the full set of queries corresponding to the security properties needed to verify **G1** in Appendix 2.

As an example, consider the query below, specifying what it means for a manifest to have a correct signature: The query states that it must always hold for all paths (indicated by the A[]) that if the ROMStage model is in a state where the signature has been checked, denoted CheckedSignature, then the current manifest must have correct values, since otherwise the initial boot stage is incorrectly validating the signature of untrusted ROM_EXT manifests. However, this query alone is not enough to validate **G1** since, e.g., it does not verify that the image code contained in correctly signed manifests are eventually executed. This is why we have several queries to verify **G1**.

```
A[] ROMStage.CheckedSignature                          imply
(ROMStage.currentManifest.identifer == 1               &&
ROMStage.currentManifest.publicKey.modulus == 1        &&
ROMStage.currentManifest.publicKey.exponent == 1       &&
ROMStage.currentManifest.signature == 1)
```

When using UPPAAL to evaluate all the queries related to **G1**, (see Appendix 2) on the model, they all pass. This means that the model satisfies **G1**. Using this strategy for proving whether the model satisfies the different goals or not we have been able to fully verify **G1**, **G9**, **G10**, **G11**, and **G12**. Furthermore, we have been able to partially verify **G8**; it is considered partially verified because the model does not capture enough detail to fully verify that only intended receivers are able to access keys. We can only state that keys used during the initial boot stage are not stored in SRAM.

7   Summary Results and Evaluation

In the following we give a brief summary of the results obtained by modelling and verifying the OpenTitan boot process. Table 1 summarises our formal findings.

First and foremost, we uncovered a potential security flaw in the wipe functionality of the OpenTitan HMAC module and showed how both UPPAAL and CBMC are able to uncover this flaw. Second, but equally important, the primary security goal, **G1**, has been verified with both UPPAAL and CBMC; goals **G10**, **G11**, and **G12** have been fully verified in UPPAAL and partially verified in CBMC due to lacking a model of the OpenTitan PMP module. Furthermore, goal **G8** has been partially verified and **G9** fully verified in UPPAAL, but neither has been attempted in CBMC and are therefore left for future work. We believe that, in part, this is because UPPAAL lends itself very well to modelling at this level of abstraction. In contrast, our CBMC models tended to include more details, arguably enabling more precise modelling and verification. Finally, goal **G5** has not been verified by either tool, mainly because it requires verification of implementations of cryptographic algorithms, something that requires more specialised tools.

Table 1. Comparison of CBMC and UPPAAL verification.

	G1	G5	G8	G9	G10/G11/G12	Time
CBMC	✓				(✓)	16 m 34 s
UPPAAL	✓		(✓)	✓	✓	2 h 30 m 50 s

Even within the limited scope of this project, we have in relatively short time been able to model parts of a complex system and verify a number of essential security properties, and hence security goals, of a security critical hardware/-software co-design.

8   Conclusion

We have shown how formal models, in CBMC and UPPAAL, of the OpenTitan boot process can be used to document a system that is being designed as well as perform early verification of important security properties. This has allowed us to find a security flaw in the wipe functionality of the HMAC module for cryptographic signing, potentially subverting the authenticity and trust base of the entire platform.

Appendix 1   Security Properties

Here we list the full set of security properties, formulated for the CBMC analysis, related to security goals **G1**, **G10**, **G11**, and **G12**. For a full list of security policies, goals, and their related security properties we refer to [21].

1.1   Goal G1

Property 1: The ROM_EXT manifest for a ROM_EXT must be signed with a RSA-3072 signature. If a ROM_EXT manifest for a ROM_EXT is unsigned (i.e., the signature is a sequence of zeros) the ROM_EXT is considered invalid to boot from.

Property 2: The public RSA-3072 key used for the signature contained in the ROM_EXT manifest must be valid in order to be valid to boot from.

Property 3: The HMAC hash must be calculated by either a SHA2-256, SHA3-256, SHA3-384, or SHA3-512 hash function.

Property 4: The computed HMAC hash message must be calculated from $(system\_state\_value \parallel device\_usage\_value \parallel signed\_area(ROM\_EXT))$.

Property 5: The signature in the ROM_EXT manifest must be validated using the RSASSA-PKCS1-V1_5-VERIFY function with inputs: public RSA-3072 key, the appended message $(system\_state\_value \parallel device\_usage\_value \parallel signed\_area(ROM\_EXT))$, and RSA-3072 signature. If the function returns false the ROM_EXT is invalid to boot from.

Property 6: If all validation steps have succeeded, then transfer execution to ROM_EXT by starting execution at the entry point of the ROM_EXT image code. If execution returns, execute the fail_ROM_EXT_returned function provided by the boot policy.

Property 7: If at any point a ROM_EXT is invalidated, the ROM_EXT is considered unsafe to boot from and the mask_ROM must proceed to validate the next ROM_EXT.

Property 8: If validation fails for all the ROM_EXTs, mask_ROM must execute the fail function provided by the boot policy.

1.2   Goal G10/G11/G12

Property 9: The entire flash must be covered by a PMP region at the initialization of mask_ROM. The PMP region must be locked and restricted to read-only access.

Property 10: If a ROM_EXT is validated, then mask_ROM must create a PMP region covering the ROM_EXT memory that is locked and allows for read and execution access.

Appendix 2   UPPAAL Queries for G1

Table 2 shows all the queries made for the verification of **G1**. They are excerpts from [10].

Table 2. Queries made for checking if the UPPAAL model satisfies **G1**.

Name	Query
Checking Manifest Identifier	`A[] ROMStage. IdentifierChecked imply` `ROMStage.currentManifest.identifier == 1`
Checking Valid Manifest Identifier	`A[] (CheckRomExtManifest.manifest.identifier == 1)` `== CheckRomExtManifest.checkRomExtManifest()`

Checking Public Key	`A[] ROMStage.CheckingSignature imply`
	`(ROMStage.currentManifest.identifer == 1 &&`
	`ROMStage.currentManifest.publicKey.modulus == 1 &&`
	`ROMStage.currentManifest.publicKey.exponent == 1)`

Checking Signature	`A[] ROMStage.CheckedSignature imply`
	`(ROMStage.currentManifest.identifier == 1 &&`
	`ROMStage.currentManifest.publicKey.modulus == 1 &&`
	`ROMStage.currentManifest.publicKey.exponent == 1 &&`
	`ROMStage.currentManifest.signature == 1)`

PMP Execute	`A[] ROMStage.ReadyToRunROMExt`
	`imply (PmpRegions[0].execute &&`
	`PmpRegions[0].startAddress <=`
	`ROMStage.currentManifest.entryPoint &&`
	`PmpRegions[0].endAddress >=`
	`ROMStage.currentManifest.entryPoint + 4)`

Valid Key ID	`A[] (CheckPubKeyValid.currentPubKeyId == 1) ==` `CheckPubKeyValid.checkPublicKey()`

Valid Key Leads to Valid Key ID	`(CheckPubKeyValid.publicKey.exponent == 1 &&`
	`CheckPubKeyValid.publicKey.modulus == 1) -->`
	`CheckPubKeyValid.currentPubKeyId == 1`

Valid Signature	`A[] (OTBN.signature == 1 &&`
	`OTBN.digest == 3 &&`
	`OTBN.key.modulus == 1 &&`
	`OTBN.key.exponent == 1)`
	`== OTBN.checkSignature()`

Valid Manifest Leads to Rom Ext Running	`EqualManifestContents(validManifest,`
	`ROMStage.currentManifest) -->`
	`(FinalJumpToRomExt.ROMExtRunning &&`
	`EqualManifestContents(validManifest,`
	`ROMStage.currentManifest))`

Invalid Manifest Leads to Failure	`!EqualManifestContents(validManifest,`
	`ROMStage.currentManifest) --> (ROMStage.StartOfLoop`
	`|| ROMStage.BootFailed)`

Invalid Key Leads to Invalid Key ID	`(CheckPubKeyValid.publicKey.exponent != 1 ||`
	`CheckPubKeyValid.publicKey.modulus != 1) -->`
	`CheckPubKeyValid.currentPubKeyId == 0`

References

1. Andrews, J.R.: Co-verification of Hardware and Software for ARM SoC Design. Elsevier (2005)
2. Casper, W.D., Papa, S.M.: Root of trust. In: Encyclopedia of Cryptography and Security, 2nd edn. pp. 1057–1060. Springer, New York (2011). https://doi.org/10.1007/978-1-4419-5906-5_789
3. Gigerl, B., Hadzic, V., Primas, R., Mangard, S., Bloem, R.: COCO: co-design and co-verification of masked software implementations on CPUs. In: Proceedings of the 30th USENIX Security Symposium (USENIX Security 2021), pp. 1469–1468, August 2021. https://www.usenix.org/conference/usenixsecurity21/presentation/gigerl
4. Google: Advisory: Security issue with Bluetooth Low Energy (BLE) Titan security keys. Google Security Blog, May 2019. https://security.googleblog.com/2019/05/titan-keys-update.html. Accessed 21 Aug 2021
5. Huang, B., Ray, S., Gupta, A., Fung, J.M., Malik, S.: Formal security verification of concurrent firmware in SoCs using instruction-level abstraction for hardware. In: Proceedings of the 55th Annual Design Automation Conference (DAC 2018), pp. 91:1–91:6 (2018). https://doi.org/10.1145/3195970.3196055
6. Huang, B., Zhang, H., Subramanyan, P., Vizel, Y., Gupta, A., Malik, S.: Instruction-level abstraction (ILA): a uniform specification for system-on-chip (SoC) verification. CoRR abs/1801.01114 (2018). http://arxiv.org/abs/1801.01114
7. Kroening, D., Tautschnig, M.: CBMC – C bounded model checker. In: Ábrahám, E., Havelund, K. (eds.) TACAS 2014. LNCS, vol. 8413, pp. 389–391. Springer, Heidelberg (2014). https://doi.org/10.1007/978-3-642-54862-8_26
8. Larsen, K., Pettersson, W., Yi, W.: Uppaal in a nutshell. Int. J. Softw. Tools Technol. Transf. **1**, 134–152 (1997)
9. Mukherjee, R., Joshi, S., O'Leary, J., Kroening, D., Melham, T.: Hardware/software co-verification using path-based symbolic execution. arXiv CoRR abs/2001.01324 (2020). http://arxiv.org/abs/2001.01324
10. Møller, B., Pedersen, M., Bøgedal, T.: Formally Verifying Security Properties for OpenTitan Boot Code with Uppaal. Master's thesis, Aalborg University (2021). https://projekter.aau.dk/projekter/files/422795285/P10_24_.pdf
11. Møller, B.H., Søndergaard, J.G., Jensen, K.S., Pedersen, M.W., Bøgedal, T.W.: Evaluation of Tools for Formal Verification of Open-Titan Boot Code. Project report, Aalborg University (2020). https://github.com/Tutter/OpenTitan-Formal-Verification/blob/d830c/P9-EvaluationOfToolsForFormalVerificationOfOpenTitan.pdf
12. Nunes, I.D.O., Eldefrawy, K., Rattanavipanon, N., Steiner, M., Tsudik, G.: VRASED: a verified hardware/software co-design for remote attestation. In: 28th USENIX Security Symposium (USENIX Security 2019). pp. 1429–1446 (2019). https://www.usenix.org/conference/usenixsecurity19/presentation/de-oliveira-nunes
13. OpenTitan: HMAC HWIP technical specification. https://docs.opentitan.org/hw/ip/hmac/doc. Accessed 26 Aug 2021
14. OpenTitan: hmac.sv. https://github.com/lowRISC/opentitan/blob/dcdadc72072/hw/ip/hmac/rtl/hmac.sv#L121. Accessed 26 Aug 2021
15. OpenTitan: Identities and root keys. https://docs.opentitan.org/doc/security/specs/identities_and_root_keys/. Accessed 19 Aug 2021

16. OpenTitan: Key manager HWIP technical specification. https://docs.opentitan.org/hw/ip/keymgr/doc/. Accessed 25 Aug 2021
17. OpenTitan: OpenTitan logical security model. https://docs.opentitan.org/doc/security/logical_security_model/. Accessed 17 Aug 2021
18. OpenTitan: Opentitan secure boot. https://docs.opentitan.org/doc/security/specs/secure_boot/. Accessed 19 Aug 2021
19. Roche, T., Lomné, V., Mutschler, C., Imbert, L.: A side journey to Titan. In: Proceedings of the 30th USENIX Security Symposium (USENIX Security 2021), pp. 231–248, August 2021. https://www.usenix.org/conference/usenixsecurity21/presentation/roche
20. Subramanyan, P., Vizel, Y., Ray, S., Malik, S.: Template-based synthesis of instruction-level abstractions for SoC verification. In: Proceedings of Formal Methods in Computer-Aided Design (FMCAD 2015), pp. 160–167 (2015)
21. Søndergaard, J., Jensen, K.: Formally Verifying the Correctness and Safety of OpenTitan Boot Code using CBMC. Master's thesis, Aalborg Univeristy (2021). https://projekter.aau.dk/projekter/files/422795280/P10_23_.pdf
22. Yubico: Security advisories, security advisories relating to Yubi key. Yubico web page. https://www.yubico.com/support/security-advisories/. Accessed 21 Aug 2021

Author Index

Printed in the United States
by Baker & Taylor Publisher Services

Printed in the United States
by Baker & Taylor Publisher Services